ALL AT SEA

ALL AT SEA

Twenty Years at the Helm of Tall Ships

Dominick Jones

To Henry & Janet
who introduced us
to Daniel & bargain wines.

Dominick.

McFarland & Company, Inc., Publishers
Jefferson, North Carolina, and London

LIBRARY OF CONGRESS CATALOGUING-IN-PUBLICATION DATA

Jones, Dominick, 1930– author.
All at sea : twenty years at the
helm of tall ships \ Dominick Jones.
p. cm.
Includes glossary and index.

ISBN 978-0-7864-7580-3

softcover : acid free paper ∞

1. Jones, Dominick, 1930– —Travel. 2. Sailors—Biography.
3. Sailboat living. 4. Offshore sailing. 5. Coastwise navigation.
6. Sailing barges—Maintenance and repair. 7. Schooners—
Maintenance and repair. I. Title.
GV812.5.J66A3 2013 797.1092—dc23 [B] 2013018392

BRITISH LIBRARY CATALOGUING DATA ARE AVAILABLE

On the cover: A new bowsprit built, this time in steel using old
Coast Guard tapered lamp standards (photograph courtesy William Cussans)

Manufactured in the United States of America

*McFarland & Company, Inc., Publishers
Box 611, Jefferson, North Carolina 28640
www.mcfarlandpub.com*

To Cecilia without whose vigorous leadership
this story would never have happened.

Table of Contents

Acknowledgments

This story starts more than 45 years ago, a long stretch for anyone's memory.

Fortunately, I was originally trained as a scientist, and learned how to observe and how to record. When I left school, my first and only salaried job was as a journalist in Reuters news agency. There I learned the importance of sourcing, and of separating fact from comment. The result is that I am an assiduous recorder of what goes on in my life.

So, when we bought our first large sailing vessel, I started a narrative log from the first day, that is, 30 May 1966. It recorded the names of those who attended William's fifth birthday on board the Thames barge *Gipping*. This log continues in narrative form, written after the event intended to be read as a story, until January 1977, but by that time it had become redundant because in 1970 I started a contemporaneous style of log in which the entries were restricted to bare observations, dated and timed, inserted in the log at the time of the observation.

These logs were kept in a Students Sectional Book measuring $10\frac{1}{4}" \times 8"$ with a semi-stiff cover, ruled with graph paper on the left and lines on the right. They have survived in remarkably good condition.

I refer to them as the rough log. A typical entry might be a dated and timed observation such as "whale spouting astern." In rare instances, there may be more complex observations such as "two very heavy rolls on the way over did considerable damage" or even some tentative conclusion such as "noon fix seems to show we experienced a Gulf Stream current setting 083T at 4 knots," and on the squared paper of the left hand page might be calculations to show how I reached that conclusion. There might also be an occasional drawing, for example, of a repair I made on my screw cutting lathe to an air pressure cylinder valve. In brief, the rough log was intended to be practical and reliable rather than literary.

Because I navigated almost uniquely on a calculator, there are very few supporting marks on the many charts which I have kept, all the navigational triangles being sketched on the left-hand page of the rough log book.

There are five such logbooks starting on the 2 July 1970 (when I took delivery of *Gray*, a Baltic trader) and finishing on 9 August 1987 (when I went ashore for the last time). They make the dullest possible reading, but without them, the narrative log, a social record and some accounts, I would have been completely unable to write this book. I kept all my charts—upwards of 200 of them. The Edinburgh Channels, and the light vessels in the Thames Estuary were very important to us, but the former is no longer marked and the latter have been withdrawn, although both are marked on my charts. I even have one based on the meridian of Paris (which competed with Greenwich as the prime meridian of the world from Louis XIV to the First World War).

To begin with I recorded permanent information about *Gray* at the end of each logbook (for example, an attempt to find out the volume of the fuel tanks). But my mania for recording evidently outgrew this system, so there is a sixth logbook in which I recorded statistics about *Gray*. The rough log was kept by the steering position and anyone was supposed to make navigationally relevant entries. In practice, most of the entries are mine.

I was interested to see the other day that during part of the time that we were in France, I kept the rough log in French, presumably partly to be able to produce it if there were any untoward incident in France, and partly because I was becoming more familiar with French technical terms than with English ones.

It is hard to say with any certainty when I started writing the present book but it was probably before 1990 when I was living alone. Judging by publishers' letters dated in 2001 onwards, I had finished enough of the book to think that it might be capable of being published. At that time it ended with our arrival in Mediterranean France. I am extremely grateful for the professional care that Thomas spent editing this version.

From time to time during the next 10 years the subject would come up and I would lend the manuscript to a friend. The reaction from two of them (Dinah Barlow and Henry Vaillant) was surprisingly similar. They offered their comments several years apart, neither being aware that the other had read the manuscript. Neither liked the uncomfortable way in which I had attempted to tell both a personal and a technical story. To my surprise, when Rosalind Michahelles read the manuscript she said she was interested more in the technical narrative than in the personal one. Since we have lived together for 20 years, she has done an immense amount of painstaking reading of the manuscript and so she should know what she is talking about. Her point of view was the more interesting because she holds degrees in literature and the humanities but can barely use a screwdriver.

Nothing much happened to the book until about 2011 when Rosalind's daughter married Louis Munroe whose godfather is the president of McFarland. Robbie Franklin quickly tasted the book, said there were possibilities, and very soon I had clear guidance. McFarland is a scholarly publisher, and so one instruction was to remove all dialogue since it could not possibly be accurate after a lapse of so many years. Their other instruction was to expand the technical side. I complied with both instructions (throwing heaps of lovely dialogue away), but the reward was that I felt able to bring the book up to the end of my ownership of *Gray.*

At a very late stage, Nick Kilmer, himself a prolifically published author, offered to read the manuscript, and pinpointed quite a number of holes which it was not too late to fill. The factual preface is due to him.

It will be evident from the book that there are other important actors, principally Cecilia Cussans, and to whom this book is dedicated. She bought the Thames barge without reference to me; I would not have bought the Baltic trader without her support; and throughout she was essentially the charismatic leader while I remained the talented technician.

Preface — Some Facts

My full name is Dominick Jones. Seeking (with success) to avoid my involvement in a bureaucratic career, my parents omitted to give me a middle name, although the nickname Tucker stuck for my first 20 years. I was in my mid-thirties in 1966 when this book begins.

My father was Sir Roderick Jones KBE, born in 1877. He went to South Africa in his mid-teens, spent 20 years there, reporting from both sides of the Boer War. He read the rebellious President Kruger a chapter of the Bible in Dutch and introduced me to his friend former Prime Minister Jan Smuts when I was in my teens. He was managing director of Reuters from 1915 to 1941. I am not alone in knowing very little about his background.

My mother's family was military with an engineering bent. She was Enid Bagnold CBE, who wrote the novel *National Velvet* and the play *The Chalk Garden*, among other works. *National Velvet* subsequently became a film starring Elizabeth Taylor. My mother's father, Colonel Arthur Bagnold CB CMG, and her brother, Brigadier Ralph Bagnold FRS OBE, were both in the army in the Royal Engineers.

I was educated at Eton and Oxford, doing my military service with the Grenadier Guards. My first and only salaried job was with Reuters News Agency. Later in life, I trained in the British government–run School of Navigation, and later still I gained my MBA and an advanced certificate in business administration at Babson College in the United States.

I married Joanna Catherine Grant of Monymusk, daughter of Sir Arthur Grant Bt and the then Lady Tweedsmuir (after Sir Arthur was killed in the Second World War, she had married a Buchan, and subsequently became Baroness Tweedsmuir in her own right). Our son Romily is also an engineer and website designer.

Cecilia Cussans, whom you will meet in this book, already had five children by a previous marriage: Emma, Thomas, Victoria, Lucy and William. We lived together for 21 years.

The *Gipping*, a Thames sailing barge, built in 1889, was 64¾ gross register tons, 80 × 18½ × 4 feet, with a Ford Scripps V8 33 hp marine petrol engine. Fuel bunkers about 15 Imperial gallons. Fresh water 400 Imperial gallons.

The *Gray*, a Baltic trader, built in 1920, was 99 gross register tons, 87 (with bowsprit 137) × 22 × 8 feet with a 1951 Burmeister & Wain 134 hp diesel engine. Fuel bunkers about 4,000 liters. Fresh water 5,000 liters.

A register ton is a measure of volume. The *Gray* was advertised as 160 tons deadweight, a measure of weight carried, which means her displacement could have been 200 tons (about 450,000 pounds).

Introduction

I was in my mid-thirties when I met Cecilia. I was divorced from my wife, Joanna, by whom we had had a son, Romily. I was living with him alone in London. Cecilia had five children by a previous marriage. I was working in Reuters News Agency. I was a not very successful journalist who became a more successful administrator. But, I suppose my heart wasn't in it. Cecilia didn't have to apply much pressure to suggest that there might be better things in life than trying to invent policies for staff worldwide.

We both had houses in London, mine freehold in Newton Road, not far from the Portobello Road, and her rather larger house in Maida Vale, a leasehold with an awkward fifteen years or so to run. That meant that any improvements we might make to her house would be lost at the end of the lease. So, I moved in with Cecilia and her children while my house was enlarged to take us all. Her youngest, William, was four years old. When Cecilia decided we had to have a boat for the summer vacations, she bought a Thames sailing barge. William had his fifth birthday on board.

In due course, we moved half the furniture from Maida Vale to Newton Road. Thieves moved it out during the night. We moved the other half into an empty house the next day. The resulting large insurance claim bought me a very expensive gold Cartier watch. And a lot of jewels for Cecilia.

When one of the younger children fell overboard from the barge, I waited for her to surface so I could ask if she was the one who could swim. I couldn't tell them apart, not because they were so similar but because it was early days. I don't much like children. Also, I was wearing the new Cartier watch which I preferred to an act of unnecessary heroism if it were a swimming child.

It was.

Being flat bottomed, barges tend to stay pretty upright. The children were too young, or too numerous, to be interested in the sailing, so they kept on with their shore preoccupations. One of them was The Beatles. They only had one disc. After a bit I began to protest that I knew both sides by heart. Their answer was to play elsewhere. I was left on deck with the record player, which they had forgotten to turn off, while they went below to play draughts (checkers) or chess or cards. I turned the record player off and began to live again in my own world.

I was tired and my eyes smarted. The tide had been very early, and it had taken us several hours to get down to the mouth of the river. I hadn't at that early stage learned that I wasn't very good at steering for long periods. Cecilia later took on that role, but at the time she didn't have much to spare from making nine cups of tea or milk, followed by nine plates of bacon and eggs, followed by 18 slices of bread, butter and honey. Imagining her world, I felt but the ninth mouth to feed after the au pair girl.

By the time the river widened into an estuary full of sand banks, the children seemed to have quieted down, they were out of sight below somewhere, and the record player was off. Cecilia had a free moment. We had to tack. We were pleased with ourselves for doing it efficiently, in fact, for being able to do it all.

Then it all started up again. Cries of rage from below resolved into a fight over the card game or the chess game or the draughts (checkers). William appeared on deck, streaming angry tears. He said he had been winning and accused me of tipping the table at his time of success so that everything fell on the floor.

We went on out between the sand banks, a nice little brisk wind. We would be running on the way back to the mouth of the river. We had worked out we could beat out into the estuary for a few hours, and then run back and anchor for lunch in the shelter of a bank at the river mouth. It would be easier to cook, and I could sit down to lunch, too.

In light weather, when you turn round to run, after going into the wind, the apparent wind drops considerably. The ship rolls a little more, but the sound level reduces to a pleasant hiss, interrupted by a few relieving belches as a tiny swell lifts the stern and passes under.

Gazing contentedly up at the mainsail I noticed the main brail had parted.

On a spritsail barge, instead of lowering the sail to the deck, you lift it up to its throat, cradled by the brail, a sort of harness designed to spill the wind out of the sail, which stays aloft from the beginning to the end of the season, whatever the weather. When sailing, the brail is of course slack, but it gets chafed through eventually and has to be replaced.

Without it, we would sail on forever.

The shore, so distant a moment before, seemed almost upon us the second after I noticed the parted brail. I had no idea what to do, except that I had to get up there somehow. Working it out, with Cecilia at the wheel, I needed teams of children, directed by the au pair girl, who understood little English and was clearly enduring, rather than enjoying, the sailing, far from part of her job description in any case.

The children suddenly began to take me seriously. I felt flattered. I showed them how to wrap the foresail halyard round the winch barrel, and to make sure they kept some weight on the tail so the coils of rope wouldn't just fall off, letting me down with a bump on deck 30 feet below. They were very serious, sorted things out amongst themselves, and got me up to the throat of the mainsail. I was nearly finished with the repair, getting less terrified of the height and the rolling motion, seeing that the land, despite my earlier fears, was still a way off. I began to make out some of the words from down below: It's my turn... No it's not... Stop pushing... A fight had broken out about who was to tail the winch.

They let go to continue the dispute.

I grabbed the fall of the rope as it started upwards. When aloft, I never again relied on those on deck.

1

Buying the barge

But that was the second summer. It all started thuswise.

Eighteen months before I finally moved in with my little suitcase and just one son, I saw Cecilia off for the summer vacation somewhere. In France, I think. She had her own five children, and mine, making six. I had to earn my living, so I didn't go with them. I don't think I was even invited. Besides, there would never have been room in the Volkswagen van. When I met her on Waterloo Bridge on the way back...

...Why Waterloo Bridge? I can't remember. Was I in another car, and going to escort her?

...She didn't have to tell me that six was just one, if not two, over the limit. I can remember the van — it was a side load, a feature that became important later on. Children were embroidered over the side door opening. She was in the front seat, upright like a truck driver, but much smaller, of course.

After I moved in with Cecilia, we decided to go on a sort of honeymoon, skiing. We took turns driving the Volkswagen across France.

For me, skiing was one of those dedicated things in which you stand in line at the bottom of the lift, get to the top frozen, shoot down and then stand in line again, ultimately rather relieved that the end of the day has taken away the guilt of stopping, of playing chicken. Like a Pekinese dog, Cecilia thought she was equal to anything. She wasn't. She acquired a little bump on her bottom, and that finished her off on the first day. It also meant I drove solo on the way back, filling in for her.

On the north side of the Massif Central, we went over a hump-back bridge through a medieval town. It hurt her bottom. The next town, the next hump-back bridge, she announced that we had to have a boat. The Volkswagen wasn't big enough.

A couple of weeks later, we went to see a Dutch botter somewhere on the East Coast of England. I knew nothing about sailing boats. I had fished for lobster from a nine-foot dinghy in my late teens, but that was about it. However, even I could

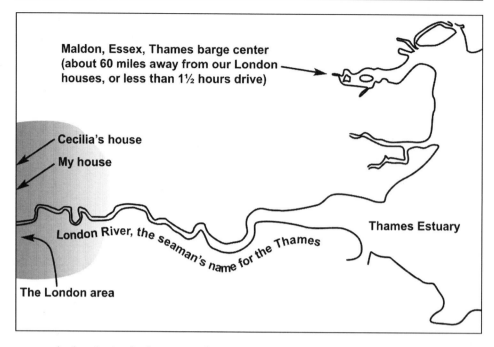

count the bunks in the botter to discover there was no way to fit in the eight of us plus, possibly, an au pair girl — nine little coffin spaces to find. Even so, at 40 feet or so the botter was vaster than anything I could imagine.

Back at work, the more senior I became, the less admired by my colleagues, the more original and inaccessible (to them) my work became... And the smaller my office. It became so small that my secretary and I no longer gazed at each other across our desks, but at the wall with our backs to each other, unable to afford the full passage space between the desks. After she had answered a call one day, she turned round to face my back to inform me that, rather than go home that night, I was to go to Liverpool Street train station, meet Cecilia's cousin, and take the train down to Maldon to look over the boat she had bought.

Bought? She had bought? I still didn't know Cecilia very well, but my surprise was tinged with a little admiration.

At the time, I was much fatter than I am now. The middle section of my three-piece suit stuck out unless I weighted it down with a heavy gold chain. I had a rolled umbrella, a bowler hat, and polished shoes. I took this lot down with me to Maldon, Essex — paunch, gold Albert and all.

It wasn't very easy to make out what was boat and what was not. The tide was low, and several large sailing vessels were lying at a slight angle on the mud. When I could begin to make things out in the twilight, I saw they were all vast (at least 80 feet it turned out). There were so many stalks working their way towards the sky that I couldn't tell what belonged to what, what was mast and what rigging.

The cousin seemed to be quite used to all this, but I was not. For a start, I was

I wish I could find a better picture to portray the essence of barging in the mid sixties than this one does. Because of the tides, the sandbanks and the estuaries, the barges very often sailed in company. This one shows several barges taking the last of the flood back up the Blackwater to their berths in Maldon. Note the heavy coils of natural fiber mooring warps on the coachroof. They would later be replaced by plastic. The steering position was always open. The commercial barge skippers must have been a hardy lot. It was bad luck to shave on the day you sailed until after you had reached your destination — to assume your safe arrival by shaving beforehand might tempt Fate to prove you wrong (attributed to David Kelly).

brought up to the idea that people issued from the sides of houses, not the tops. The owner emerged vertically from the deck. I mean the former owner, whom I now asked how I sailed it. It was quite easy, he said, I should hire a skipper.

On my salary?

However, all this was academic. The ship was bought, and it was at least twice the size of the botter — already too large for me to handle but too small to house us. I learned we had bought — I mean, Cecilia had bought — a Thames barge. Fairly soon, I also learned that available skippers came suspiciously cheap.

Thames barges are handy and beautiful to sail. There's nothing fancy: they have a huge mainsail set on a sprit which runs diagonally across the sail, free of it on one tack, rubbing against it on the other, above it a topsail set on a headstick, a decent sized foresail, a dainty little mizzen, set outboard to help the rudder turn the ship, mostly no bowsprit, and a very pretty painted stern. Ours spent half the day filling up with water, afloat, and the other half draining it out again, beached on the mud. In those days, I thought nothing of this torrent of water ebbing and flowing inside the vessel. If too much flowed in, we simply found a piece of mud to sit on, took out the plug at the back, and there we were all dry again. We got to be connoisseurs of mud banks, partly to dry out, and partly to have a little rest on the way from one place to another. Water coming through the bottom wasn't much trouble. The rain coming through the deck was much more tiresome: I didn't like sleeping in oilskins.

The barges had been cargo ships until the thirties when the Depression laid them out of work. They moored to buoys and to each other so thickly in the Thames it was hard for working craft to find a way past. They never became economical again. In the sixties, it was becoming fashionable for people like us to buy them up cheaply, convert the insides for accommodation, re-rig and sail them. Ours, the *Gipping* (known locally as the *Dripping*), had already been converted. But we were late on the scene, and the best barges had already changed hands.

On the East Coast, life was wholly governed by tides and sandbanks. Later, I discovered this was exceptional if you look at it globally. By the end of my time at sea, we drove off at any time which suited us, went out of the harbor, turned left, sailed around a bit, turned right and came back in. But in those days there was no option but to start and end the weekend at high water. We tided down the river, sailed around a bit, and then tided back up, aiming to reach the berth just before the turn of the tide.

To get to our berth, we would ram the opposite bank of the river, the Black-water, letting the last of the flood take the stern upstream. We would thus have turned round ready to sail off our berth the next weekend. The better barge skippers sailed off the bank across the stream into the berth. We never attained that rever-enced class. We had a small unreliable petrol (gasoline) engine, which we used for these berthing maneuvers but otherwise we really did sail, when we weren't just floating one way or the other with the tide.

This obligation to the tide had its merits. Sometimes, it is true, we would have to be down in Maldon by midnight to start in the very earliest hours of the morning. There might be a moon which would make it easier to see the way. But a midnight tide also meant that we had to be back by another midday, too early to drive back to London forthwith. Thus we had the afternoon to do further nautical things, like bending on sails or caulking decks. And, of course, everyone else was doing the same thing on the other barges, with maybe time for a drink in the pub before going back to London. Each weekend was different.

I was very happy with the structure of life on the barges as it stood, and I had no desire to innovate. At the time, Maldon had half a dozen barges in commission, and we knew that there were others elsewhere on the East Coast. They were all being converted from cargo to passenger use, but the accent was on making the conversion as traditional as possible. Someone had written a labor of love about the details of the rigging of the Thames barges, and this now became our bible. It laid down exactly how a brail, for example, should be rigged. Never mind that this was something way up the mast out of sight and didn't always work very well in grabbing the belly of the sail in a wind. It had to be reproduced just as the book described with worming, parceling and serving round the natural-fiber rope which would probably only last a season anyway. Skimp on the worming (laying yarns into the strands of the rope not only to give it a rounder appearance but to spread the chafe a little) and one of the locals would notice the resulting unevenness.

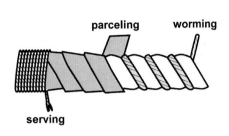

To begin with therefore I scarcely dared to touch the barge, which I regarded as held in trust for the barge community as a whole and not merely owned by Cecilia. Not in the sense that she could do what she wanted with it. Like football fans, we rooted for Maldon as the home of the best-kept barges.

In many ways, this support group was a great comfort. I never had to worry how to do anything. I just asked Barry. He worked for the boatyard, maybe owned it even then — he certainly did later on. Barry lived alone on his smack. Although he seldom sailed it, he was somehow vaguely of no fixed abode. Communicating with him by telephone from London was, of course, not the way things were done. You had to find Barry, a sort of contact-sport activity since he was mostly in transit from one barge to another. That is, I remember him most in profile, walking past us, seldom end on. His nose was quite distinctive. From time to time, he would wash his socks, which he then pegged to the rigging. It was useful to know this, as wash days, when he was not available, were random and could occur at weekends, the only time when we ourselves were available. He had asthma for which he carried a small apparatus that he had to whip out from an inside pocket from time to time in order to be able to continue talking with me.

But Barry Pearce was far from eccentric. He was a young man of considerable charm and ability who kept an eye on us. Once, after I managed to collide with some eel traps as we left our berth, starting in the early morning on a moonless night, I knew I had done some damage, but the tide swept us along. Barry was on the quay when we returned the next day.

Did we have a nice sail, he wanted to know. Barry was usually too busy to ask this sort of question. Did we get as far as Bradwell, he asked? Have a calm night? Barry would have known perfectly well what sort of a night we had had since Bradwell was only a short hop down the river, and in any case he would have heard from other barges if anything had been difficult down there.

Then he wanted to know about his knees.

Barry had undertaken the previous winter to rebuild the huge oaken struc-tures, called knees, which held up the windlass barrel, and which in effect tied the ship to the ground when we anchored. They had been under construction for so long that they were called Barry's knees, as in: Seen Barry? Yes, he's on his knees.

I said they were a superb job, and meant it. The conversation drifted along awhile.

"I had to give the kiss of life to six eels," Barry remarked. "Nearly done for, they were."

Barry had lulled me into a sense of security, but now I rushed to confess all my wrong doing, pray for forgiveness, expunge the stain on my character.

He didn't want to kiss any more eels back to life, he said.

That was the extent of the reprimand, but reprimand it surely was. It was only what you would expect from Nanny in this highly structured and supportive world, where nothing could go amiss, but Nanny knows—and puts it to rights.

But all that was learned slowly, much of it after we had been broken in by our skipper. His real name was Frank Farrington, but we always called him Pilot.

I think I had been expecting him to be a clone of Tommy Baker, the skipper who was right at the very pinnacle of our tiny parochial ladder. I had been directed to Tommy as a possible source of skippers looking for employment. He was a very small, spare man whose undersized white dungarees were still too big for him. I suppose my lord-of-the-manor manner must have grated, for very soon there I was, once again the inefficient cub reporter, taking notes from Tommy at way above dictation speed, scrambling after the information he scattered like hot pennies strewn to the poor. Tommy was a master of intimidation. He took us sailing twice while we were looking for a skipper. His methods were quite simple: anything Cecilia did was marvelous; I was given studiedly calm instruction, directed more to the children than to me, with innuendo asides to Cecilia. I never subsequently felt I had the right to dress up to him although our paths crossed repeatedly during the next few years.

Therefore, when Pilot walked on board for the third outing (Tommy had taken us out for the first two), I was quite prepared to be intimidated once more. Pilot's silence surrounded him with authority. He wanted to know where we were going, adding "Sir." Expecting him to give the orders, I hesitated.

Up the river was not navigable. Down the river was the only choice.

Both Pilot and, by this time, the children knew what to do to get us moving. I glanced down at my feet, hoping I had not accidentally come wearing patent-leather shoes. We were thus, wordlessly, in the middle of the river pointing down-stream.

Pilot, steering with one hand, beckoned me to sit next to him on the coachroof.

We were sailing gently down the river, half our speed from the wind, the other half from the ebbing tide, the whole hardly amounting to an old man's leisurely amble. Silence. For a long while. It was the Blackwater, and it would take us nearly a tide (that is, some six hours) to get to the mouth.

Cecilia wasn't much about. She had children to look after. Pilot told me to get out the chart. I had one, not because I had worked out in advance that that was one of the things you have to have at sea—like a road map or air in the tires—but because someone on the quayside had handed me theirs.

It didn't seem all that complicated. The British Admiralty had chosen excellent colors and an elegant typeface, easy to read and informative. Symbols looked like what they were supposed to represent. I could see that important marks, like buoys, were emphasized by magenta flashes. Later I learned the magenta meant they had lights, and you still had to mind the buoys if they had no magenta—only, of course, they were hard to see at night.

Pilot told me to keep my eyes open for a light vessel dead ahead. It would probably be hull down right now, but would come into view in a bit. We would round it and start back home, he said.

Then, silence. I could see nothing ahead.

Cecilia came briefly on deck. Had she seen a light vessel, I whispered to her? I didn't want Pilot to hear because I feared some sarcastic crack about being tied to my mother's apron strings, something Tommy Baker would have said. Pilot was gazing contentedly ahead. He hadn't heard.

Anyway, neither Cecilia nor I could see anything which resembled a light vessel, but we could see a substantial buoy where we supposed Pilot thought there should be a light vessel.

We steered on for a while. The river had opened out, and there was plenty of sea room, although it remained quite sheltered. A speedboat came by with a huge wake. The barge rocked a little.

Pilot fell off the coachroof.

He was a heavy man. He was instantly awake and struggled to his feet. He had just dozed off on this lovely day, he said. I had difficulty understanding. He went back to steering, and then a few moments later asked me to take the wheel for a moment while he went below.

He seemed to stumble a little. But back he came quite quickly. Been for a pee, I had no doubt. Except that every other male hung onto the rigging and peed overboard. No matter.

He settled back to steer, but not for long as he said it was about time for us to turn round and go home. He told us what to do, and, with no bother at all, we were sailing back the way we had come.

I was puzzled by the light vessel which we hadn't rounded after all. We hadn't even rounded the buoy. Was this a change of plan? Or, had I noticed the wrong symbol on the chart? When I pressed Pilot to explain, to give me a lesson, so to speak, he promised to do so, but said he couldn't just then.

It was so exciting and wonderful being on this gently moving platform, the fields gliding past, the cows getting nearer, even the tufts of grass clearer as we approached Maldon that I forgot to pursue the little matter of the light vessel. Even if I had remembered, learning to read a chart would have seemed bathos compared to watching the mud slip by the stemhead as we turned to ram the opposite bank, just like the big boys.

So the little weekend outings progressed through the summer. Pilot's silence was not that of authority. He and his wife were childless. He was charmingly unsure of himself with our own children — no assumed command, no raised voice — timidly appearing to want to be with them with the same sensual physical urge that Englishmen have for their puppy dogs.

We were nearing the time for the children's vacations in August. Pilot seemed willing to come, but a little anxious that he might be in the way, not stressing the point we all tacitly knew: no holiday without Pilot. The weekend before we were due to start (six children, one of their friends, the two of us, an au pair girl, a Tibetan Apso and Pilot), Mrs. Pilot came to visit. Would she come, too? No, she would love to, but it was a man's world. Not so, we said, half of us were women. Well, nevertheless, she wouldn't come, and it became touchingly apparent why. He had been talking and thinking of nothing else himself. He would be back on the river as master of a sailing barge. For 40 years he had only been the boy, up and down the Thames, back and forth over the same ground, and only in motor barges. Now he would have a command. She did not want him to have the humiliation of being reminded to do this and that, to take his injections on time, for instance. He could do that all for himself without her help, she said affectionately.

"Injections?" Cecilia perked up. For his diabetes, Mrs. Pilot said.

Next day at the doctor's office, Cecilia and I felt foolish. Not only had we failed to ask him anything about his background — the first shock had been to find that his experience was on motor, not sailing, barges — but we had also failed to make a routine check on health. Pilot was old enough for such personal questions to be appropriate. We did some reverse engineering. The doctor explained that the eyes get affected — no wonder his refusal to read the chart — but we could be his eyes. We described the scene with his wife, her matter-of-factness, the implication he had only just retired. The doctor said it sounded as though the diabetes was well established in which case it would be likely he had it under control, and we need not worry.

Canceling the vacation at this late stage seemed pusillanimous, besides being a huge problem for the children. The summer had gone pretty well to date. Everyone was learning a bit. Pilot didn't appear to need help. We could probably support him in minor ways if necessary. Besides, we were only planning to go up and down the East Coast rivers, seldom more than a few miles from land.

There were two contenders to be capital of the barging world: Maldon, on the Blackwater, where we had started; and Pin Mill, on the river Orwell. At the mouth of the Blackwater, there was a large area sheltered by sands. This is where we had been sailing. It's called the Wallet, and is sheltered by the Buxey and the Gunfleet sands for a matter of some 15 miles or so parallel to the coast. To get to Pin Mill, we would have to sail the length of the Wallet, and then risk the open sea (how thrilling!) for another ten miles to get to Harwich (rhymes with carriage), the major commercial port at the confluence of the Orwell and the Stour. Pin Mill was a few miles up the Orwell, not so far as Maldon from the sea.

The Wallet runs northeast. We had learned that the prevailing summer wind was southwest. In all likelihood, we would be blown easily up the Wallet to Harwich. We might have difficulty returning to reality against the wind, but all that was a long way off.

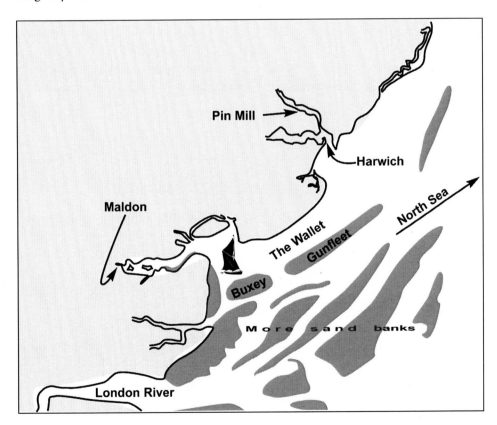

The two principal contenders to be barging capital of the world were Maldon and Pin Mill (about 40 nautical miles apart), although barges lay all over the East Coast. From Maldon up through the Wallet to Harwich and Pin Mill was our nursery where we learned to sail, protected by the outlying sands (like the Buxey and the Gunfleet) from rough weather. The sandbanks are navigational obstacles and are shown in grey. Big ship channels lie northeast to southwest, but there was a couple of ways through them northwest/southeast involving narrow channels and fast tidal streams.

And that was just how it happened. When we arrived in Harwich that evening, we couldn't make it up the Orwell against the ebb and so we anchored across from the commercial port at a place called Shotley, where there was a naval training establishment, HMS *Ganges*.

We felt like lions.

I would have stayed on board — I never like going ashore — but the dog needed to have a pee, and the eldest Emma, 13, and Victoria, 8, and their friend wanted to land. Pilot offered to mend a tear in the mainsail while we were absent. This meant he would have to go up the mast a little way in the bosun's chair. I offered to heave him up, but he said no, it was only a little way and he could manage by himself. We wandered around on shore for a bit, came back, went below, looked up through the hatch, and there was Pilot, on his back, about six feet off the deck, strapped into the bosun's chair, flailing like an overturned insect.

I had very little idea how to get up and down a mast — that was to come later — so it was hard to get Pilot down on deck. Besides, he was not in the least cooperative, and became more and more belligerent as we got him into the saloon. Cecilia tried to get some sweet tea into him, but he was too quarrelsome and sick to swallow it. Besides, we hadn't checked with the doctor that this was universally the right thing to do. Perhaps it would kill him, we thought, so his struggles against the tea might have been for a good reason.

He began to slip into a coma. I decided to go ashore for help. It was getting dark. If he recovered while I was gone, Cecilia said she would put out the stern light. That way, we would avoid making something which might be relatively minor into a major excitement.

I tied up at the jetty and climbed up the hill to run into two sailors loving it up with their girlfriends.

I said we needed help. There had been an accident on board, and someone was in a coma. They didn't seem to understand. One of the sailors mimicked my accent. I could see they were not taking me seriously. I said one of the crew needed to go to hospital. Could they help?

The boys snapped out of their love-making mode, and very soon quite a large group of sailors in off-duty clothes was gathering at the jetty head. This was just the kind of ostentation I wanted to avoid. I ran down the steps to have a look and there was that damn stern light showing. He'd recovered. This was all a fuss about nothing.

I ran up and began to say it was all right after all. A very unpleasant looking heavy-set man, a petty officer I thought, sidled over to me, wanted to know what all the fuss had been about, why I had dug them all out of the pubs on a Saturday night. I explained that it looked pretty bad when I left but that I didn't want to hang around to see if he recovered as it would take a while to get ashore. So, I had arranged with my wife (as I described her) to call off the rescue operation if needed by exhibiting the stern light, which she had obviously done.

What had been wrong, the petty officer asked.

Diabetic coma, I said. But it must be all right by now.

The petty officer looked at me, and after a pause marched down to the jetty beckoning the others. He shoved me so roughly into their work boat that I fell onto the bottom boards. The others piled in after him.

His mate had had diabetes, he explained, as we chugged off to the barge.

Pilot had recovered, then relapsed. The seamen manhandled him into their boat, but there was nowhere for him to sit without danger of falling overboard. So we got a deck chair, put it on the engine room coachroof, and then surrounded it with men. Pilot got more and more agitated, tried to get out of the chair to throw himself overboard. At his last attempt he pretty much succeeded but by that time we were alongside. He was put on a stretcher. They passed a leather strap round him and the stretcher. And then another one.

First we went to the naval hospital, but there was no equipment for testing diabetes which is, after all, not the sort of thing you get from battle wounds. So we drove on to Ipswich hospital. Pilot vomited on me.

I was made to go outside while they wired him up at the hospital. The ambulance driver said he would wait for me. About half an hour later I was called in to see Pilot. He was looking pretty tired, but otherwise absolutely normal. He reminded me of one of those paper pellets you put in water, to blossom forthwith into paper flowers. It was miraculous.

He had overdosed himself, he said, in order to take the additional exercise. But he had gone too far, and he knew he couldn't be sure of getting it right. He wouldn't come back, he said. I could see tears trickling down his cheeks. I grasped his forearm and was gone.

It was all rather a relief really. We had had a good summer, but the barge was a crazy idea for keeps and Pilot's illness seemed to put the lid on it. We could probably have just as much fun taking the children to some local hotel, sell the barge, or just let it sink — it hadn't cost much.

When I got back, I told Cecilia that Pilot had recovered, was probably safe, but couldn't come along with us. I assumed we would just get to bed, and then figure out in the morning how to spend the rest of the children's vacation.

She agreed but said we would have to be up early to catch the last of the flood up to Pin Mill.

That's how I learned to sail.

As a matter of fact, we had little option. It began to blow during the night into the harbor where we lay. We ran for it up the river, starting before dawn on the early part of the flood, flat meadows on either side, divided from us by the mud flats which eventually we began to love. Just imagine: five miles of virgin countryside displayed to you twice a day for your personal enjoyment, complete with sandhoppers, lugworms, sea anemones, and that bunch of noisy entrepreneurs, the seagulls.

It was our first visit to Pin Mill, the other barging center. Pin Mill, a cluster of a few houses, and its pub, the Butt & Oyster, was undoubtedly prettier than Maldon, but it didn't have the marine facilities. This defect was nearly made up for by the Webb family, father and two sons, all shipwrights. They said: What for do you need a workshop on land for barges that float? They had the blocks and Maldon didn't. Come to them for underwater repairs, they said. Reuben's voice carried six fields. That was the father, a very different approach from Barry.

At this stage in my relationship with large objects, it hadn't yet occurred to me to ask searching questions about how they work. For instance, I owned a fairly large house in London, but I didn't know how the sewers worked. In my experience, such things could be put off until needed when a specialist could be found who would put matters to rights. I had been even less inquisitive about how you get to the underside of the barge, or of any other vessel for that matter. So, not only did I not know what blocks where, but I also had no idea what sort of repairs might be needed underneath the flat bottomed barge. Besides, when someone pointed out the blocks (balks of timber the width of the barge laid around half tide so you could float on, dry out, do your repair work and then float off) it was hard to see how any serious work could be done lying horizontally in a crawl space in the mud.

Pin Mill had something else Maldon lacked: a hard, a concrete road surface about 50 feet wide and nearly 600 feet long which sloped gently down over a length of a few minutes' walk from above the high-water mark to (nearly) the low-water mark, which must have been a drop of about 10 feet. On either side was mud, not the best quality mud—I eventually became an expert on mud—but nice and soft and sittable-in for our rotting barges. The idea was to enable anyone afloat to come ashore at any state of the tide.

It didn't always work like that because it was usually necessary to get into a dinghy to reach the hard, and then the dinghy tended, depending on the tide and how long you were in the pub, to get left high and dry or float in water too deep to wade. There was nowhere but the pub to go, after all. Also, the end of the hard stopped short of low-water springs, which could mean a very muddy trip from dinghy to pub. Someone had mudshoes, rather like snowshoes. They didn't catch on.

• The moon goes from full to full in just over a month; when it is more than half full, it is called gibbous; waxing when it is getting bigger towards full moon, and waning when it gets smaller; it passes overhead (called meridian passage) about 50 minutes later each day pulling a wave of water round the world and causing high tide somewhere near where the moon is overhead, and a balancing wave on the opposite side of the world. Thus, there are two high tides every day. But, some high tides are higher than others; these higher tides are called springs (at full moon and new moon when the sun and moon are lined up—called syzygy—and in the tide tables, called High Water Full & Change), while the lower high tides are called neaps (when the sun and moon are at right angles to each other—called quadrature);

the interval between neaps and springs is around a week; during the week when the high tides are getting bigger, they are said to be coming on; from springs to neaps they are said to be taking off. Sometimes, successive high waters are of very different heights, caused by high declination of the moon which changes from summer to winter once a month unlike the sun which changes only once a year. Although the moon is whizzing north and south of the equator once a month throughout its cycle, the declinations of full

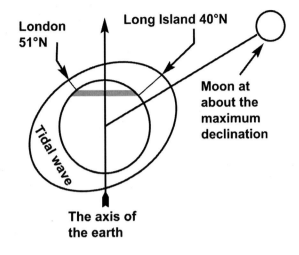

moon change only once a year, being at maximum southerly declination around June and maximum northerly declination around the shortest northerly day. Thus, in midsummer, successive spring tides can be of such different heights that eggs laid in the sand at the highest spring tide just as the tides start taking off may not be washed by water for another month since the springs at quadrature are usually less than the springs at syzygy. I find it interesting that the sometimes sensational Harvest Moon is more or less on the equator, or the same as the sun. At sea, you can watch a fiery red sunset (more dust at the end of the summer), then switch round and watch a baleful moon rising on the opposite side.

If you live on the water, you get very used to this rhythm because everything seems flat and uninteresting during neaps, but much more exciting during springs, particularly as, wherever I sailed, high water springs took place in the middle of the day, when the sea breeze (if there is one) is starting to rattle everything around. The corresponding extreme low waters reveal unknown areas of mud, sand and rock during the mysterious gloamings at the ends of the day. They say more old men die when a falling tide is taking off before daybreak; more births take place during the waning than during the waxing moon, with the maximum just after full moon; unwanted bleeding is worst when the moon is gibbous. Old wives tales, I think, but I always bow to the new moon nine times, turn clockwise three times (never widdershins—that's the way witches take off on their broomsticks) to make sure I don't have a lousy month. Just in case.

So a visit to the land, which meant a visit to the Butt & Oyster, became the subject of calculation, argument and opinion as to what was the state of the tide, and, more particularly, at what state of the tide we would be likely to want to come back, and how to keep the dinghy from banging on the concrete or being stranded on the mud.

Since the problems were never formidable, they were always solved, but with just sufficient communal endeavor to make us deserve the pub instead of merely using it.

This first summer of 1966 was one of the most romantic of my life. I started knowing almost nothing about sailing, so every escape from danger seemed such a huge success that I never thought to wonder why we had been in danger in the first place. That was to change as I grew more expert, but right then I knew it was bliss. I hugged myself in the car all the way back to London Sunday after Sunday at the thought of what we had done over the weekend.

And then, Cecilia.

It was not just that I was in love with her. There was indeed deep sexual attraction, but that wouldn't have lasted long if Cecilia hadn't been what she was. She was at the same time lover and mother. I had grown to sexual maturity with that repudiating phrase "you only want me for my body" ringing in my ears. When Cecilia told me "I would be insulted if you didn't want my body" it blew away all the cobwebs of that phrase. This practical and loving stoutness was her through and through. There was nothing she couldn't manage, do, or achieve if she wanted to. So while I knew I had the skill, I felt that it was she who was unleashing it, that without her it would have remained hidden in the backroom as one of little Dominick's hobbies he did in there. Indeed, this book would never have been written but for her, because I would never have done what I did without her. She took the lead, but I was perfectly happy about this, saw in it nothing but pleasure and advantage for me, had total confidence in her.

And while not a child lover, or ever adept at conversing with children on their terms not mine, the noisy cheerful bunch she brought along with her were delightful even in their rages, tears and accidents. They completed a world around me which I found totally sufficient.

We spent three summers sailing, but the log I kept as a handwritten narrative began to reveal the realities. *Gipping* was really very rotten, and becoming more and more unseaworthy.

During the second year's sailing we decided to cross the Channel. It was the first time for many years that *Gipping* had not spent twice a day on the mud having a rest and emptying the bilge water. On our way back, the wind dropped and the petrol engine would not start. Way off, there was a large buoy. Maybe the wind would get up again. I took a compass bearing of the buoy. It didn't change. I realized that inevitably, in a calculable time not long distant from now, the tide would bear us down to strike the buoy.

I knew what was wrong with the engine — some spring on the throttle had broken off. I also knew the number of steps required to effect a repair. But I didn't know how long each step would take and, in particular, whether the sum of those steps would exceed the time taken to reach the buoy. It was all calculable, predestined one might say, but I just didn't have some of the pieces of information, and wouldn't have until it was too late. So I couldn't form an alternative plan. I couldn't say to myself: "As a result of all these steps, the engine will be working at 11:07, but we will strike the buoy at 11:06, so we would be better employed launching a dinghy

Gipping *lying alongside a wharf in a quiet harbor in the middle of a town somewhere on the East Coast of England (attributed to Milo Grubisic).*

and towing *Gipping* clear." And every moment considering the problem was deducted from the time allowed me to solve the problem. The best I could do was to start one end of the process, and work through to the other, knowing that a slip — a screw dropped in the bilges, for instance — would negate the entire process. Nor could I watch the buoy to see how I was doing. I just had to make sure my hands didn't shake. But they did. Over the years, this sweaty tunnel of anxiety got familiar.

In the middle of all this, the au pair girl came by to ask me what to do about her slippers which were floating around in her cabin.

That we missed the buoy was immaterial: the controlled fear, oozing out like toothpaste, was not.

The third summer was far from happy, at any rate for Cecilia and me, although the children by this time had several small sailing boats, and probably enjoyed themselves at least as much as if they had been sailing on *Gipping*.

Over Easter, on our first visit to the barge, we had just heaved the mast and sails up into a sailing position (they had been stored on deck during the winter). I asked Cecilia to stop painting for a moment and help me uncoil the stay fall from the windlass barrel which was freewheeling in reverse with the pall off. Cecilia caught her rubber gloved hand in the gear mesh. The windlass jumped on its loose bearings and sprang back. For fear of leaving the finger behind in the glove we drove to the hospital her only slightly nicked yellow glove still on her hand.

I had to leave her at the hospital to get back and feed the children. Cecilia had been half way through making their supper when the accident had occurred. I served the children the half-completed fish pie to complaints I had forgotten to put in the hard-boiled eggs.

The finger began to darken. Emma, now nearly 15, took over the children. One of the nurses quoted the consultant as saying that if it turned black the next day, he would have to amputate. I lurked for the consultant and then barred his way. In those days there were strict rules governing doctor/family relationships. Blood relations or spouses were acceptable, but interest in a patient from someone else of the opposite sex was considered to be prurient at best.

Thinking of treatment I had had for frostbite (all ten fingertips had been frozen to a sharp line dividing them from the rest of the red hand), I asked if it were a question of circulation. He and his posse stopped briefly. Who was I, the consultant asked. Not lover, I thought. So, I said I was looking after her children. There was a nerve and an artery left, the consultant said. Fishing for what he was going to do about it, I presumed he must be trying to boost what little circulation was left.

He said there was no hyperbaric oxygen unit in the hospital, if that was what I meant. I confirmed it was. There was a machine in London, he thought, but he would take no responsibility for the case if she were removed from his care. Then the posse moved on.

A young doctor peeled off and dragged me to the telephones. He said he would find the machine while I found an ambulance. There was no time to lose, he said. It should have been done two days before.

These telephones were diagonally across a hallway in the basement. Even in summer, the hospital ran its own heating, and the pipes were in the booth I occupied. I began to pour with sweat so badly I couldn't see to find the telephone numbers or make notes. Both booths had glass doors. I could see him steaming up in his. We fell out of our booths. He said he had found a machine at the London Hospital; they were waiting for us, he said.

Waiting for what? Cecilia was by this time drunk on National Health Service brandy. The finger was hurting. Owing to her impending treacherous departure the hospital had cut off up-to-date care. I had been unable to find an ambulance. So what? A finger doesn't need a whole ambulance, and so we drove up to London in our Volkswagen van.

The staff in intensive care had been waiting for her. Immediately, Cecilia was given a book to read, bound to a stretcher, and slid into what looked like a diver's decompression chamber, a body length plastic cylinder. It was transparent. A nurse swung the circular hatch shut and bolted it. Had it been me inside, I would have immediately developed an itch in the nose; Cecilia waved to me calmly and began reading the book. At this depth into the medical hierarchy, the prohibitions surrounding lovers ceased to exist. The nurse treated me like an ordinary human being with specialist knowledge as interested as her in seeing whether the machine would work. She explained that they had had fingers before, but from frostbite, the last case being an Everest climber. But usually, they used the machine for gangrene and carbon monoxide poisoning.

The nurse looked surprised when I said I didn't know what the machine could do. Hadn't I known before asking for it, she wanted to know? No, I said and explained that all I knew was that there was a choice between doing nothing (and amputating) or doing something (I knew not what). I had merely chosen the latter.

The nurse turned to the cylinder in which Cecilia lay. She explained that the first thing to do was to sweep out all the air by pumping in pure oxygen at one end and letting the air out at the other. Just increasing the air pressure might help, she said, but increasing the oxygen pressure would help even more. So, after a while she would cut off the air exit and continue pumping in oxygen. The pressure inside the cylinder would rise and this would mean that the little blood getting to Cecilia's finger would carry more oxygen and hopefully save the finger while the healing process went on. But there were dangers in giving oxygen in such a dramatic way, and dangers in increasing the pressure. So she would limit herself to a bar or so tonight (doubling the atmospheric pressure), and see how she did. They could go as high as three bar, she said. Hyperbaric referred to the pressure, so hyperbaric oxygen was super pressure oxygen.

In those days, it was a somewhat experimental technique. In Cecilia's case it was coupled with keeping her whole body at fever heat to dilate the blood vessels. Electric fires, hot-water bottles. Her room was like a sauna. She was covered in thermometers. The next day a nurse told me she had gotten the armpit temperature up to 104 degrees. She seemed pleased. As I saw that both armpits had thermometers, I asked what the other one read. Not so good, she said, only 39 degrees.

They were evidently running out of British thermometers.

At the rate of six hours per day immobilized in that glass coffin unable to scratch or move, Cecilia accumulated 28 hours of hyperbaric oxygen, sometimes inside the bomb for up to six hours at a stretch. She spent eight days in hospital. She still has her finger today. You probably wouldn't even notice. It has its deficiencies, but it's there. She was back on board at Whitsun, six weeks after the accident.

It wasn't a good start to the sailing year. *Gipping* was in such bad shape that it was not until August that we could actually leave the quayside and go sailing. For the first time, I undertook structural work on *Gipping* myself because I realized that help from shore was going to be too slow. I put a chain through the quarter from side to side to prevent *Gipping* bursting asunder in the midst. Automatically, I therefore added myself to the objects of Cecilia's pressure to get things done.

At the end of the summer holiday we spent the weekend on the blocks in Pin Mill, but I seem not to have realized the implication of my observation at the time that the butts and chines move. I now wonder how we stayed afloat at all.

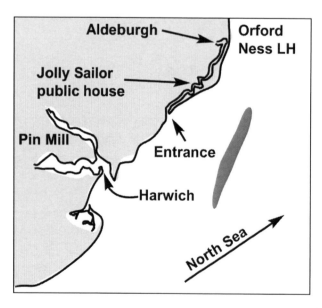

The Jolly Sailor public house was not far from Aldeburgh, the site of an annual music festival and about 20 nautical miles by sea from Pin Mill.

There was, however, one glorious day when we sailed into the narrow river which leads up to Orford a little way north of Harwich. We had slopped around outside trying to find the entrance. We were disappointed, we couldn't see it, we were about to go home, and then the slit showed up. The tide was pouring in. We poured in, too. The banks raced past, close enough to touch, but not quite, and we were there on a beautiful summer's day, achievement in our bellies and fun before us. We played hide and seek with the children round some monument. We spread ourselves on some seafood lunch. We went back to the barge languourous but not too exhausted. We had to take the last of the tide out. Once on board, my spectacles were missing. I went back alone in the twilight to the Jolly Sailor pub. Freshly mown hay assailed me. Two steps down, and tumble into the pub. One of the three old men looked up, the others went on playing checkers. The low ceiling beams compressed the smell of mild ale. My hurry to find my spectacles and catch the tide dropped to the floor like a tight belt in the caressing lethargy I found inside. I came back to the barge a man who has taken a sacrament.

I remembered that day two years later when we again gazed at the little slit in the coast through which we slithered.

By 1969, the fourth year of *Gipping*, we never sailed at all. We spent the summer on an endless round of repairs, not so much to prevent the barge from sinking — it spent the day on the mud — but to keep us dry in the rain. In fact, pumping out 700 gallons of seawater a day — I mean good heavy English gallons, not those light-weight American things — seemed to be something which came with the territory (6 American gallons can be extracted from 5 English gallons).

2

And now a Baltic trader

The high point of our *Gipping* lives — the year we crossed the Channel in 1967 — was also the year I moved back into my London house — with Cecilia and her family. For two years, I had been living as a guest in Cecilia's enormous establishment, enormous because it now had six children, two au pairs, and the two of us, making it necessary to squeeze in ten bodies. I had been living for six years before that — the last 18 months myself, my son, Romily, and an au pair, but no wife — in a house which was so little disturbed by our presence that even the motes of dust stood to attention for us. My wife was sick. There was little time for anything else.

Cecilia's house in Maida Vale, large though it was, hemmed us in. It had a lovely garden and it was double fronted. My house had neither of these advantages. However, Cecilia's was on a main road and was a leasehold, so I had spent the previous two years making my house in Newton Road large enough for the entire new family.

At the time of the move back, I was still dazzled by Cecilia. My earlier 11-year marriage had not left me with a feeling of joy in companionship. My wife was a schizophrenic. Mental illness brings out the best in caring people, but I was not of that saintly band. I had never imagined a relationship with a woman could be both passionate and companionable. But in Cecilia, not only did I find an extremely competent woman, she was everything female I could want.

At that stage, her decisiveness seemed to be matched only by her ability to do what she said should be done. Had she not said, between hump-backed bridges, that we should buy a boat for the children's holidays? And had she not done just that? And had it not been a success, at least for a limited period?

But by 1969, like the *Gipping*, my life was running out of steam.

On the job front, I had seen my zenith, at any rate for the time being. Three years earlier, I had started to search for another job. Unfortunately, my search coincided with a national wage freeze and a business slowdown. To escape the former, executives tried to change jobs more frequently while as a result of the latter there were fewer jobs on offer. Every month during the last half of 1966, I made a couple of unsuccessful job applications. My father, who years before had owned and run Reuters News Agency, had originally got me into the firm as a result of a curious suggestion from his successor, Sir Christopher Chancellor, curious because Sir Christopher really loathed my father and had been the chief instigator of his resignation in 1941. However, time had gone by, and he suggested to my father that I should go into Reuters. I started there in 1955. I saw no favors from Sir Christopher—for obvious reasons. But his successor, Walton A. Cole, had no such inhibitions, admired my father, and was all out to push my career.

I did time in London and Paris as a desk editor, but it turned out I was not suited as a Paris reporter. Cole must have been advised to fire me for failing to see the news value in quintuplets (this was long before fertility pills made them more commonplace), but instead he brought me back to London to work in the administration. Cole's chance on me paid off, for I became a good administrator, mainly interested in the personnel side of Reuters. However, on 25 January 1963, Cole, a hugely fat, but extremely energetic man, took an unusual afternoon nap in his office, just down the corridor from me, and never woke up. His successor, Gerald Long, didn't like me. Nor did my immediate superior, Nigel Judah, the Company Secretary. But Long had decided there should be a much expanded personnel department and had been obliged to appoint me a key member for lack of anyone else who knew about the subject. I had a glorious year or so. The boss of the new department, with whom I worked closely, was Brian Stockwell. While I knew that Brian rooted for me, I could see that I was an embarrassment to him because of Long's dislike of me. Long's obituary many years later showed that I was not the only one to fall foul of him.

I should have stuck it out. I had seen other executives discarded and then cherished. But I did the risky thing: I left Reuters in April 1968 without having found an alternative job. My bargaining position was automatically reduced. As a personnel expert I should have known this.

My departure from Reuters had nothing to do with Cecilia, although she had been complaining periodically of my late hours and the reluctance with which I went on vacation. However, she was no slouch herself, a matter of the pot calling the kettle black, for shortly before I resigned from Reuters, she had opened a franchised slimming clinic in the house in Hove of Betty Montgomerie, half-sister of her former husband, Anthony. It was a small operation and I knew little about it at the time, but by July, Cecilia and I were getting interested in opening another little clinic just behind our house in Westbourne Grove, London. In September of that year, we opened a third operation in Leeds, where many of Cecilia's family lived. I styled myself the Business Manager, but it was entirely Cecilia's money and she ran the operations themselves.

At the outset, it was a franchise, in which the franchisor supplied faradic muscle-toning machines, and all the usual promotion and advertising kit, price structure and so forth. Ladies were supposed to form lines outside to have their fat selectively faradized away. We noticed that one or two women came for other, more sensual, reasons. However, by the winter of 1968/69, we had achieved a negative cash flow of £14,200, and losses were mounting up. Furthermore, we thought we were being gouged by the franchisors and so we bought our own faradic machines, saunas, etc., and broke away. But with no success.

Had I been an MBA at that time — I got it long later in the 90s — I would have realized the folly of trying to run a boutique business in three widely separated locations with no market research.

Around April tax time, Cecilia came back all buoyant from a visit to her tax adviser with the news that the tax man paid for her losses.

I, on the other hand, became frantic wondering how to suture the open vein. So frantic, in fact, that Cecilia took me away for a vacation in the south of France where her father, Bertie, lived, in Menton. He was a sweet man, a people pleaser, who wore white gloves and a saber when he went into battle in the First World War. He was captured forthwith.

He took us to an open-air restaurant in the hills behind the town, where doves pecked up the scraps between our feet. Time went into abeyance as we waited to be served, embalmed by the fluttering vine leaves on an ancient vine against the old house out of which the restaurant had been scooped. Sandals flip-flopped along the sandy streets. Held up to heaven, on a grandstand arching road, we watched the descent of a Mediterranean mountain thunderstorm, as it blotted out a huge ravine, inviolate until suddenly brought back to reality by the slugs of drenching rain as the storm sidled up to us.

Back in London, we decided to shut the clinics.

Since Cole's death six years before, the only bright spot in my life had been Cecilia and her children. I had failed to get another job before or after leaving Reuters. I had so to speak knuckled under by resigning without an alternative; the clinics had been an expensive failure; and now, here we were, sitting on the mud in *Gipping* just mending her up under the Butt & Oyster at Pin Mill and not sailing.

What seems to have escaped our attention — at least, it escaped mine until one of the children pointed it out to me 30 years later — was that the children didn't much mind if *Gipping* couldn't sail. It was a cheap country house on the edge of the water, in a most desirable location in a most desirable village, where the children could do things more suited to children, like biking, sailing little dinghies, fishing and so forth. After all, *Gipping* had been bought for the children, and now that they were getting old enough to spread their wings, a houseboat was quite sufficient. In fact, breaking off from their shore-time pursuits to sail in *Gipping* would have soon become something of a drag for them.

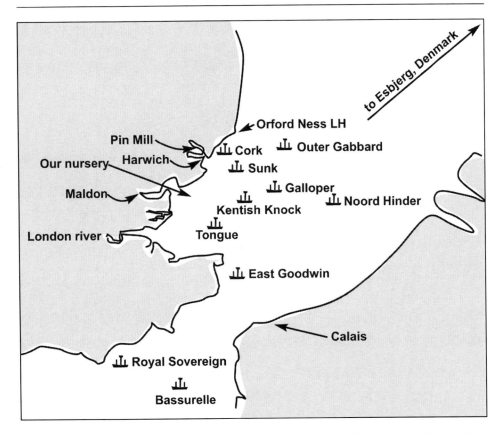

The start of our journey from Harwich to Bornholm to buy what became the schooner Gray, *showing the light vessels clustered around our nursery, to steer us through a maze of sandbanks. The overnight ferry crossing to Esbjerg is about 330 nautical miles (off the map top right). The first British light vessel was commissioned in 1731. They were decommissioned in the 1970s and 1980s (including the* Cork, Galloper, Outer Gabbard, Tongue *and* Royal Sovereign). *The* Sunk *remains in the center of a traffic separation scheme off Harwich.*

Blind to this consideration, when Cecilia produced lists of Baltic traders for sale and said we should replace *Gipping*, I knew she was right.

Of course.

She was the one who drove the whole bandwagon.

I cannot speak for Cecilia. Her motives never came up for interrogation since I was as much in the plot as she was. But I did sound a word of caution this time. Let us indeed go to Copenhagen where these Baltic traders lived, but let us go there with no fixed intention of buying one, I said.

Of course, she said.

I suspect that Cecilia was far too smart to press the obfuscation. I had agreed to come, and that was the next important step. Steps after that could be worried about later. Besides, we were merely using our commonsense. If *Gipping* were too rotten to sail, and if we needed a sailing ship of her size, we knew enough about the barge world to know that a sound version of *Gipping* at a price we could afford simply did not exist. The Baltic traders in Denmark had served much the same coasting trade as the East Coast barges, except that many of them were younger — and probably more sea-worthy — as we could see from Cecilia's list.

We took an overnight ferry from Harwich to Esbjerg on the North Sea coast of Denmark. That is, we traveled in safety, and at speed, over ground that had previously been fraught with anxiety in the barge.

Supping as we passed the Sunk Light Vessel in a powerful overnight steamer bound for Esjberg made the light vessel shrivel in the same way Eton had diminished when I went back to my old school as an adult. The last time we had seen the Sunk, we had been stuck six hours beside her in a gale of wind waiting for the tide to change.

We didn't make love that night on the steamer, but we did, a year later, in surprising conditions, on the way back.

The agent in Copenhagen was smaller and more impressive than either of us had expected. He must have been in his 60s, maybe older. His son, taller and more sensitive, showed us rotting Trader after rotting Trader, pretty as a picture if we didn't look too close, and offered at prices which we knew not to be serious. I was relieved. Did I want another huge wooden sailing vessel? I didn't really know, but if I couldn't have one, it took the responsibility away from me.

So, I thanked the agent's son at the end of the first day of searching for a ship. I didn't want to say they were rotten, but we hadn't found a suitable Trader and should now go home. He began to review the list with us, and concluded that it was time to go back and see his father.

We had to wait for a while. On entering his office, the father asked me how much our hotel room cost. I was taken by surprise, hesitated, then remembered it was 51 kroner including breakfast.

He said he had thought as much, but one never knew what deals the hotel might have struck. He had taken the liberty of having our bags removed from our room and put on the ferry to Bornholm. One way would cost 25 kroner, so we could go there and back for less than one night in the hotel here. Without waiting to see what our reaction might be he continued straight on to say there was one final ship he wanted us to see. She was not pretty, but she was cheap and strong. Only 200 tons. He would see us back in Copenhagen in two days time. He rose. The interview was over.

The ferry arrived in Rönne on Bornholm early in the morning and didn't leave until that evening. We had no alternative but to spend the day on the latest Baltic trader, whose name was *Gray*. She was exactly as the agent had said: a solid ship, but not at all pretty, partly because she had lost her sheer, partly because her bluff bow was even bluffer than usual. The owner, Captain Larsen, had made no attempt to make her more than serviceable. There wasn't even much of a deck to speak of, just a pair of gaping cargo hatches. Two of the three masts had gone, and the foremast had been reduced to a stick of sorts just sufficient to operate the derrick and carry a steadying sail. *Gray* carried anything from rocks to fishmeal around the Baltic under engine.

In our relationship, I always saw myself either as led by Cecilia or as relying on her for a sense of direction. I'm not sure she would see it that way since her leadership was so instinctive she probably didn't even notice it. And her leadership consisted in seeing things very clearly — even if she was occasionally wrong. In this case, she had come to Copenhagen to buy a ship for the children, although I would own it. Better to bankrupt me in the event of an accident as I had less money. Privately, I thought it would only cost me the 10 percent deposit right now. We could go back and think about it — and maybe we could even get the deposit back one way or the other. Besides, it was a lovely September day. Glancing back on our way to the return ferry, we saw the owner and his wife, their hands crossed behind their backs, dancing a jig on the deck. They knew something we didn't?

On return to London I became completely immersed in the clinics and forgot about *Gray*. The Leeds clinic was to be closed later in the month, and the following month the Hove clinic was also to be closed. All the equipment had to be disposed of, and in the case of the Leeds clinic we were still searching for someone to take over the lease. It was therefore a nasty surprise when I got a call from the agent proposing a date for the next step, the inspection of the ship out of the water. One way or another, I made difficulties, finally agreeing to a date early in December, not realizing that by then Bornholm, within a few hundred miles of the Arctic Circle, would have virtually no daylight.

Cecilia was still running the Bayswater clinic behind our house, so I went back to Denmark alone. I wasn't particularly bothered because I felt sure I could refuse the ship on a hull inspection. Why I thought that, I cannot imagine since a moment's reflection would have made it obvious the owner would have taken the precaution of covering the bottom with a coat of tar. Nothing would be visible.

I took the overnight ferry from Harwich to Esjberg, traveled across Jutland by train, then another ferry, and finally to Copenhagen on the other side of Zealand, where the agent's son, Sven, had offered to put me up for the night. It was still a full day's journey to Bornholm.

It was a very small apartment, totally modern, totally wooden, totally shining, totally visible. I could see no dining-room table, no third place set for a hungry Dominick. Apart from food, I needed something else like spiritual care, or aspirin, or support against Buyer's Remorse. In the kitchen, Mrs. Sven picked me up and set me on a high stool like a vase of flowers. She produced a tidbit. Sven produced some beer. They didn't — couldn't — sit themselves in the tiny kitchen, but they gradually served me a smörgåsbord which Mrs. Sven must have spent hours preparing.

Next day, Sven obliged me to go shopping on the way to the ferry to Bornholm. I felt he was continuing the care for me his wife had started. I bought the wool-lined flying boots he pressed on me, but refused a rough Norwegian sweater. A man caring about my body made me uncomfortable.

Arriving in Rönne on the near side of Bornholm, I found the ship, but no owner. He was at Neksö, on the other side of the island, even farther east. Would I like to come over? So, back on another ferry. Everything was dark. It was extremely cold even with the clothes I had bought with Sven which I had topped with a thin plastic coat. By now I had the beginnings of a fever, a runny nose, and no reserves of paper handkerchiefs.

The owner and his wife were childless. They offered to have me sleep overnight before the bottom inspection. It was an inviting idea. Like Sven's, their apartment was neat. But so small that when they offered me a chair, one of them had to stand up. I couldn't inspect the bedrooms, but it seemed likely that the apartment might only be tolerable for Mrs. Larsen on condition that her husband spend much of the time at sea.

So I said I would sleep on the *Gray* and see them in the morning. Larsen drove me over, said I would probably find something to drink on board.

One of the problems about heating ships is distributing the heat evenly. On *Gray*, this problem had not been solved. As I descended the companion ladder into the cabin aft, my feet entered a cube of heat and passed through it as my body and then my head became trapped in it. To begin with, I enjoyed the warmth, particularly in my feverish head. But the temperature gradient was so steep that every time I sat down my face got cold again. And there was no question of removing the cheap flying boots, the only warm garment Sven had been able to force upon me.

I thought a drink might help: schnapps and beer, no wine, nothing long. It was only when I fell over in the cabin that I realized I had gone from sobriety to drunkenness without a moment's intervening satisfaction.

I began to loathe the ship. There was a general smell of diesel oil leaked by the stove, the cabin had the dirt accumulated by men dropping into it exhausted and uninterested in making it a home, just a refuge between turns at the wheel. There was a bench to lie on, but it was unsprung vinyl stretched tightly over horsehair. The vinyl was blue and had a large cigarette burn in it. To the end of *Gray*, nearly 19 years later, that burn remained. The little side bunks under the quarterdeck hadn't been slept in for years, and looked too cold and dirty to clear out.

I wanted to escape very badly. Through the fog of drunkenness I felt I had to have some support from Cecilia in England. I would call her. I carefully got onto the quayside, wandering around hoping to find a telephone. Though it had been dark for hours it was still only early evening. There was not a soul around. My nose kept running. I tried to wipe a drip away. It had frozen.

If I tripped, I would be dead of exposure by morning, no one the wiser. Very carefully, I slipped back onto the *Gray*, realizing that the horrible diesel stove was all that lay between me and death.

It was still dark when Captain Larsen returned to wake me up and take *Gray* to have her hauled out. He didn't wait for me to dress but sprung the ship off the quay and presented her to the cradle of the slipway, still in the dark. It was nearly ten in the morning. Then of course I discovered that the hull of the ship was indeed thickly covered in a fresh coat of tar. Larsen had taken the ship out a few days earlier to have the bottom spruced up for sale, and doubtless to make sure I could see nothing of importance.

I made as though I knew what I was doing, tapping around the hull with a small hammer—and listening. Years later, I learned that a hammer is pretty useless but that a broken hacksaw blade is excellent. It will slip into those unwelcome cracks between oakum and wood and instantly penetrate anything rotten.

A shipyard owner in the south of France explained to me that wooden hulls should be regarded as a series of match sticks wedged apart with oakum. This material became extremely important to our lives. Originally, it had been the byproduct of old ropes and was thus made of hemp fibers. Cordage on ships was generally a natural product in the great days of sail and would become worn out for rigging long before the end of its useful life. So, old cordage would be cut into lengths and then picked apart, a painful and laborious process, in order to

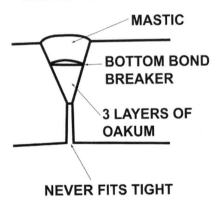

THE SEA OUTSIDE

MASTIC

BOTTOM BOND BREAKER

3 LAYERS OF OAKUM

NEVER FITS TIGHT

The oakum forms the bottom waterproof layer, and is made of layers pounded in on top of each other. This is painted with something soft to break the bond between the mastic and the oakum thus distributing changes in size of the seam over two mastic surfaces, not one. The mastic merely protects the oakum from being abraided out by passing seawater.

form a sort of loose rope which could be pounded into the seams between planks of wood in the hull. Old cordage became scarce when wire rope came in, so in my day oakum was purpose built by mixing Stockholm tar (a resin from pine trees) with jute fibers. It was then loosely twisted together, and folded over to suit the width of the seam to be filled as it was pounded in. Sounds simple, but it wasn't because the seams I had to deal with were never regular, and often rotten on the inside so the oakum fell through. Eventually I could recognize individual caulkers (the men who pounded in the oakum) by the rhythms of their double taps with caulking mallet on caulking iron. *Gray* probably had about half a mile of seams, and I must have re-caulked at least half of them personally before I was finished.

Caulking mallet and caulking iron. This mallet's head weighs about two pounds; the one I used most frequently weighed just over one pound.

But, of course, in 1969, I had never seen a hull like this before. Close to, the shiny black tar curved out of sight like the sea going over the edge of the horizon. I looked at the propeller and thought its two blades rang differently when tapped. The government inspector came to look for cracks and not surprisingly found none. Defeated, I let *Gray* slide back into the water, not having any clear idea what was to happen next. It was dead calm. *Gray* floated self-possessed, probity fruitlessly questioned, motionless on the blue-black water.

Larsen wanted to get me to Copenhagen as quickly as possible to put me through the shotgun marriage with *Gray* and go back to buy the steel ship of his dreams. He was fed up with wood, he had explained. As the years went by, I, too, longed to be able to weld wood.

We set sail for Copenhagen immediately. I had reached that pitch of fever just a shade over normal when I feel at my worst. Very shortly after midday, the sun was blood red and low in the sky. It was a beautiful evening, to be snatched away before it had even started. I alternately clung to the cast-iron pipe coming up from the stove below, a little too hot to hold, then released it for a brief cooler, and back to the hug to warm up again. The paper tissues were getting low, but I had developed a system for drying them one by one on the stove pipe before storing them away in the other pocket of my sheet plastic raincoat and then transferring them back to the original pocket to start their journey again — nose, stove pipe, pocket, and then back to the original pocket in batches. I got to invent small proficiencies in how I did this batch process, and took a special pride contemplating the coming dried nose-wipes every time I transferred a batch to the original pocket. Our small talk had died long ago, the engine was noisy, and whenever Larsen spoke to me it was at the shout.

I calculated. Larsen had said it was some 15 hours to Copenhagen. A snuffle every ten minutes... how many tissues left? Could I make it through the night? And then all those steady-state calculations were upset: it began to snow and to blow. We started to roll.

At first, it was just a roll, but shortly it began to be a roll which required some effort to withstand. Even Larsen was sometimes spun off the wheel, a big wooden affair with spokes, heaving chains past my feet. I sneezed more frequently. The tissues fell off the stove pipe, sodden and dirty. The plastic inside my waterproof pocket began to get grungy with wet and pieces of paper. It was too rough for me to risk going below to find an alternative handkerchief. I just dripped. And gazed at the upended rubber liferaft dripping like my nose just outside the window of the pilot house.

Larsen began to mutter-swear at the steady red and green navigation lights he had seen fine on our port bow (that is, nearly end on), showing some emotion for the first time. I only noticed the lights when he burst out at the "bloody Pole" as he supposed it to be. Occasionally, a red would go out as the merchantman rolled, and then come back to show both red and green.

These red and green lights are placed on either side of the ship, and can only be seen at the same time when the ship is end on. We carried the same lights. The Rule of the Road required that we pass each other red to red.

The Pole was coming downwind pretty fast, and would have had difficulty steering a straight course, because a following sea lifts the stern off course from time to time. Then we saw a single green. We stiffened in panic. If he meant to cross our bows, having seen us, we could make good his error by turning to port. But what if he had not seen us and were simply wallowing off course? With a turn to port, we would collide more or less head on as he wallowed back. It was now too late to turn tightly the other way, to starboard. We were too close. I saw Larsen crouch by the wheel, his right hand low down ready to heave everything to port. He hesitated. Then, back to red and green. The Pole was now end on, wallowing back on course. I looked at the sodden life raft. Taking to it would solve several problems. I wouldn't have time to think of the misery of my nose, and I wouldn't have to buy *Gray*. At that moment, the icy water seemed preferable.

Then: a single red. We were going to pass red to red.

The bulk of the merchantman slithered by under our port quarter, his red sharply outlined above us against a hull so close we could see the rivets holding it together.

I would have to buy *Gray* after all.

A few nose blows later on, I began to concoct a plan. If I were lucky, Larsen would choose to tie up to a lee quayside on arrival in Copenhagen Free Port. The wind would press *Gray* onto it, and it would be easy to step over the side and run. This cheered me up a bit as I elaborated on how and when to make my escape. I would clearly have to arrange to have the bunk nearest the door and to sleep in the flying boots. Then I would get up first to have a pee. It would be understandable for me to pee downwind, on the quayside, without raising suspicions. Just a step onto land... and was it not a Free Port, so the police might not be so much in evidence?

The approaches to Copenhagen brought rest from the incessant rolling. We steered smoothly into the line of sodium lamps which lit the quay. Larsen had us alongside and tied up in no time, no help from me. I got the bunk nearest the door.

It hadn't occurred to me that Larsen might wake first, pee on the quayside, and prevent me from escaping past him. He came back shouting "Come on, Jones." My name had two syllables in Danish, like "Joe Nezz." "Time to get up." I grunted and delayed, hoping to find an opening, but there was nothing. He occupied the entire cabin, and especially the doorway. I think he must have suspected.

Two things had happened to my body during the night. Without a drop to drink, I felt I had had a debauch of such towering proportions that I would have to wait through a characteristically known boredom period to regain the unity of my head and my reactions; and... — my flu was gone.

The rest of the world uses ordinary cars as taxis. The backseat was quite unlike the distant upright correctness of the back of a London taxi. We lounged together in this backseat, in distasteful propinquity. We arrived at the church... No, what a mistake — it was merely the agent's office in central Copenhagen. During the taxi ride I had elaborated my speech. There would be the agent, whom I feared, his sinuous son, Sven, whom I liked, the enemy Larsen, and myself, the money bags. I would make a little speech: I could not go through with the purchase; I would pay all their expenses; I was sorry they had been troubled. And then I would bow out. All very correct.

My only possible ally, the agent's son, was seated opposite me. Not that I had any reason for supposing he might be an ally: he and his father might simply have gotten used to playing good guy, bad guy. Larsen was on my right. The agent was on my left.

They started off in Danish. I know no Danish.

Out of politeness, I did nothing with my growing restlessness.

"Jone-es," the split syllable again: how was my cold?

Something placatory and anodyne from me and they went on in Danish, until I heard "Jon-es" again. Did I think there were four thousand liters of fuel left in the tanks, the agent asked. I had no idea, and I didn't care. Before I could pitch into my speech, they went on in Danish.

Then Jon-es again. They were going to the British Consulate to sign the papers. I would go down to the street, turn to the left, and find a pharmacy. Then I would come out, turn to the right, go back past our door, and a little further on my right I would find a restaurant. All on this side of the street. We would all meet there for lunch to celebrate.

That was that. No opportunity to announce a just impediment. I was not even asked to sign anything.

We all filed out of the door in our two different directions pretending (on my side) that we were all participating in the general bonhomie of a successful purchase and sale.

The pharmacy was huge. It was a relief to find they had paper tissues, to feel comfortable once again, to buy pills to decongest, potions to deconstrict, aspirins to lower, uppers to upper. I came away with a bagful of comfortingly familiar family remedies. Lunch turned out to be a relief. There were no decisions to be made any longer, and I'm good at turning on my social side, a side which is embarrassing when inappropriately brought out for business. But it was appropriate here and allowed no revealing chink of light to fall onto what I really felt.

My only discomfort came from not having emptied my bowels for a day or so.

3

Let not thy left hand know what thy right hand doeth — Matthew 6:3

We could have said goodbye at the restaurant, but the agent's office was so close they invited me back.

I stood in the agent's office while they telephoned. In Danish, of course. I thought they must have some business to conduct before paying attention to me. I began to feel redundant and slighted.

It became clear after a while that they still had me in mind. They put down the telephones. The agent turned to me to say that Captain Larsen had kindly agreed to take me and the *Gray* to Middelfart. It had a shipyard, but they had not been able to get hold of the boss, and so they were not absolutely certain *Gray* could stay there. However, to get the most of the remaining daylight, we would have to leave immediately.

It was said with the same autocratic expectation of unquestioning obedience as he had displayed when he had had our bags removed from the hotel to send us to Bornholm. Larsen propelled me through the door, hardly leaving me time to shake hands with father and son.

For this voyage, it was a day of blue sky and low winter sun. Copenhagen is about 11 degrees of latitude south of the Arctic Circle (that is, about 650 nautical miles). At midwinter, the sun therefore never rises above 11 degrees in the sky — about the incline of a steep one-in-five road — thus casting a perpetual relief across everything it strikes.

The weather was a little hazy. Each ship looked like a cardboard cut-out, stuck on the flat, flat blue water like a stage set. From time to time a cut-out would get up and move, but mostly they appeared to stay where they were, their white wakes as motionless as they themselves. The sun had been pinned onto a cornflower blue sky which shaded into the darker sea, the backdrop for the cardboard ships. Despite the thudding of *Gray*'s damned engine, I felt at peace.

And I realized I wanted to have my bowel movement.

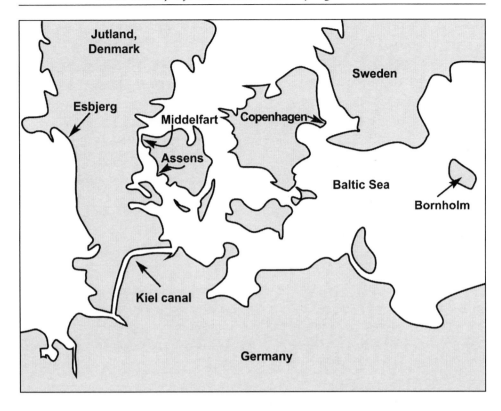

The map above shows the western end of the Baltic Sea, heavily populated with islands, and surrounded by several different countries — Sweden, Germany and of course Denmark, whose capital, Copenhagen, is on the largest of the Danish islands, called Zealand. Middelfart and Assens are on the island of Funen. From Bornholm to Assens via Copenhagen is about 250 nautical miles. The ferry from Harwich docked at Esbjerg, whence overland by rail and ferry to Assens.

Larsen seemed to have scarcely any bodily functions at all. Before we set out from Rönne, he had engulfed some meat balls in sauce. After that, nothing except cigars. He didn't eat, except in the restaurant. I never saw him visit the toilet, an action which would have been difficult to miss as the privy sat there, about half way up the deck, looking rather like the shellacked chairs footmen used to sit in waiting for the door bells of a great country house to ring. It had been made with care from wood, looking entirely unlike the tasteful plastic affairs brought out in ranks for open air public events these days.

I had had plenty of time to work out that it would be impossible to visit the privy without the steady gaze of Larsen. It made no difference that this must have been commonplace to him; to me it would be a matter of embarrassment to have to admit that I possessed such a thing as a gastro-intestinal tract. However, I could see that the hinge was visible, so the door must open to face forward, a silly arrangement in heavy weather but a mitigation for my embarrassment. As usual, my social manner didn't serve me well. I bobbed and grunted to Larsen who of course heard nothing above the sound of the engine. So I just disappeared — without permission.

I sat in the box. I was in no hurry. I held the door open with my hand. The rails of *Gray* rose and fell gently, sometimes obscuring the cardboard cut-outs on the sea, sometimes dipping towards them. The sunlight streamed in almost horizontally, lighting up elbows and beams above me in the privy. My need to evacuate slowly developed, became inevitable and passed to fruition with such total satisfaction that I forgot how I had been taught in childhood to associate the noise of flushing water with the purification of an otherwise sensual, if not salacious, act. There was, of course, no water in the privy.

At that moment, for the first time I began to have an admiration for *Gray*. I noticed that the rail was not just a rail, but a rail upon a rail, a very stout affair, and I noticed that the bulwarks were real bulwarks, looking exactly like the wooden model for a romantic picture, their imperfections tactile, 20 feet away on the other side of the deck.

The hatch wasn't very attractive. It was covered with a tarpaulin kept in place by wooden wedges driven into heavy steel clips around the edges. But I owned this hatch; it was mine; in its practical way it had a certain beauty borne of utility. The hatches would have to be closed in, of course, but for the time being they were admirable. Stepping out of the privy and looking aft, there was even a quarterdeck. A quarterdeck? Yes, a quarterdeck; I owned a sailing ship with a quarterdeck. Not just a little hiccup, but a proper, hefty step onto a stout curving after-deck.

On that midwinter day, I began to develop something near an attachment for this ship. It became the kind of attachment a mother might develop for a defective child. There was never any question of boasting about *Gray*, but she always demanded the greatest effort to try to ameliorate the imperfections (for cure was impossible).

After a while, I could see we were nearing a port.

Trying to remember this period forty years later, I am somewhat mystified that I do not seem to have had any plans for what would happen after the sale to me of this huge wooden vessel. Admittedly it was getting to the coldest part of the winter, a period when shipping tends to move about a bit less, particularly just outside the Arctic Circle where ice could be a problem. But I must have realized that winter quarters have to be found, plans have to be made, a bed found, food bought and so forth. Or, if I wished to sail away, I would have brought a crew with me to do so. In Copenhagen after the sale, I didn't contradict the assumption that I needed to get the ship fixed up somewhere and iced into winter quarters. I took no part in the hunt for the shipyard. I made no preparations to take charge of the ship — it was my good fortune that Larsen volunteered to bail me out. And I hadn't the slightest idea what to fix up or how long it would take or cost. It was a subject which simply had not crossed my mind. This lack of planning seems unbelievable to me now when I can spend three days drawing on my computer before putting a nail into my house.

The port, Middelfart, looked very empty. Larsen heaved the ship round to moor up by himself—he was obviously pretty efficient at doing this—remarking irritably that no one was around to take his lines. The harbormaster didn't seem to be anywhere. But Larsen knew where to look, and found him, a Dane with a long nose and interesting dark shadows around his eyes, a look of intelligence. The port had been closed for repairs, Larsen reported, and, paying little attention to me, they went off to the harbormaster's office.

I didn't quite know what to do. Stay on board and watch for something? If so, what? I decided I was quite unsuited for this kind of work, and went off to find them making telephone calls. They had found somewhere else, they told me: Assens Skibsvaerft. It was a little too far away for us to make it that night. I thanked the harbormaster for his efforts. "A harbormaster without a harbor has time on his hands," he shrugged.

This particular harbormaster was bareheaded, but the owner of the Assens Skibsvaerft was waiting on the quayside next day with a porkpie hat, a badge of rank I have seen other dock owners carry.

Larsen disappeared home almost too quickly for me to have time to say goodbye.

The yard talked English. I hadn't yet learned that it is impolite to go to a country without having bothered to learn a single word of the language and the absence of any Danish at all on my part did nothing to oil relationships between me and the workers. On arriving back in England next summer, I was mortified to find a wooden wedge which bore the inscription:

The yard owner supposed I wanted a new deck. He explained that to cover the existing hatches would be nearly as expensive as a complete new deck as the hatches occupied virtually the whole of the deck area. Besides, the hatch coamings would be in the way and we already had plenty of headroom down below.

We went down to the hold to have a look. It was a round-bottomed ship, a feature of whose real significance I had been quite unaware when I bought the ship. On the barge, I had been used to stepping down a companion-way to a flat surface. The barge, of course, sat on the mud on its flat bottom. I had certainly not expected to get inside the hull of *Gray* and find myself mountaineering, unable to find a comfortable place to stand in any part of the hold. I now began to realize why the ship had rolled so horribly crossing from Bornholm to Copenhagen. Like a football in a pond, there was no irregular shape to slow its roll.

Clambering over the ship, I slowly realized the enormous responsibility of what I had bought, made the more enormous because I knew not the first thing about Baltics, and indeed very little about ships in general. In the barge days, we all had the same thing done, and done by one of the two firms in the business of re-rigging barges—the one in Pin Mill and the other in Maldon. After the initial decision to have something done, there were no consequential decisions, since both these shipyards knew what was authentic and peer pressure forced us to behave accordingly. Besides, we were so thrilled with the idea of having a barge of such great proportions we were not about to argue the toss over some newfangled idea of our own.

With the *Gray*, it was different. The yard needed to know what I wanted, could give me good sensible answers about practicability and cost, but they had no feelings about authenticity. To them, these were just work boats.

For me, an important ingredient of this time in Assens was that Cecilia was due to come over on the Harwich ferry. She hadn't been able to attend the actual purchase of the ship, but that hadn't really mattered since I was merely carrying out an agreed prior decision. The fact that I got cold feet half way through was now of little interest to Cecilia since I had in fact gone through with the deal.

She was much more interested in how we would convert the ship. I needed her ratification of the conversion decisions I had taken, and she had managed to get away to give the necessary support. Larsen and I had arrived in Assens on a Thursday, Cecilia arrived on Saturday, and we both left for London on the following Wednesday, having agreed that we would have a new deck, a deckhouse to go on top and three masts. The decisions taken, I wanted to get back to England to wind up the clinics. Both the Leeds and the Hove clinics had been sold around the time of our first visit to Denmark, but the Leeds premises were giving trouble because the new tenant had immediately gone bankrupt and the lease had therefore reverted to us. The remaining clinic behind our house was struggling along, another cause for worry.

Furthermore, I had just started as a student at the government-run School of Navigation in the Minories in London.

That I was the student, not Cecilia, did not seem odd to me at the time, because it tacitly reflected a fundamental part of our relationship. The argument that Cecilia should have trained would have been based on the obvious fact that she was the driving force. The barge had been hers and her idea; *Gray* was mine but that was a detail. The idea had been hers, and I had trotted along willingly, if somewhat behind. The whole operation was ostensibly based on the fact that we had numerous children, mostly hers. It would have made good sense for her to have been the skipper, and me the owner.

But that was not the way it worked between us, although I didn't realize the potential for trouble. I tended to follow Cecilia mainly because of the difference in our leadership styles, but this covered up the fact that I, too, was a leader.

I had enrolled full time for the Yachtmaster (Ocean) course run by the British government whose school in the Minories (named for minoresses—cloistered medieval nuns— of the Poor Clares) was mainly concerned with turning out officers for merchant ships. Since yachting was a sideline it was usually conducted in the evenings for part-timers. The appropriate evening class was learning how to pick up a buoy with a boathook and push off from the quay. *Gray*'s bow rail was some 12 feet from the waterline; it was unlikely anyone would have a chance of pushing her 200 tons anywhere. So I persuaded the School to include me in the full-time professional courses, mostly for First Mates (Foreign Going), some for Masters (Foreign Going). In any case, since *Gray* exceeded 65 feet, all the basic regulations that applied to supertankers applied to her.

As compared to the yachtsmen, this was clearly a course for officers who would have serious business on their hands, not just amusing themselves at weekends. We didn't spend time having a drink between sessions as the night classes did. We weren't there to enjoy ourselves and yarn a bit towards the end of the evening. We were there because lives and property would depend on what we learned.

And I learned a great deal from this course, even semaphore, although by the time I finished with the sea 18 years later I had never once touched a semaphore flag nor sent a message in Morse Code which I also learned.

My examinations fell too early, so I stayed on for a few months until the next exam period making sure I knew the stuff, but really following a curriculum of my own in which I began to learn more and more about the mathematics of navigation, particularly updating the method of solving the navigational celestial triangle to fix your position at sea. Since the chronometer was invented in the eighteenth century, there had been many changes in how you did the calculations for which special derivative trigonometrical functions had been invented.

- Before the arrival of radio beacons and GPS systems, in order to fix your position at sea you needed to know how far away, and in what direction, you were from a heavenly body. By that I mean something like a star or an agreed bit of the moon or the sun (the agreed bits were either the top or the bottom of the moon or the sun, whereas stars were so small you didn't need to bother yourself with their diameters). Some of the information came from noting the time when you took your sight (i.e., when you measured the angle between the horizon and the heavenly body). If you were where you thought you were, then the information from the clock should corroborate the information from the sextant, the instrument which measures the angle I referred to. It usually doesn't.

Why the clock, or chronometer, is important has been very well described in the book *Longitude* (Dava Sobel, New York: Walker, 1995). It's written for the layman and is a really interesting piece of historical research.

Underlying the measurements you take at sea (time and angle) is what is called the navigational celestial triangle formed by three points on the surface of the earth: your own position, the north or south pole, and the geographical position of the heavenly body, that is, the point on the earth's surface through which runs the line from the heavenly body to the center of the earth.

In the earliest days of deep sea navigation which got into full swing after 1492 when Columbus sailed the Ocean Blue to find that America wasn't the India he had hoped for, all the navigators had were stories from previous navigators, often set down on paper and in some cases termed rutters (French *routier* and Dutch *ruiter*, meaning "something that finds a way" according to Wiktionary.org). These developed into actual maps on which you could make marks to show where you thought you were as a result of dead reckoning, that is, cumulating your course and speed since the last known position and correcting it for tidal currents and drift or leeway. Even with modern charts, tidal predictions and good experience of the leeway your own ship makes, dead reckoning is very approximate, although often the only thing you have.

However, if you had the good fortune to be able to see the sky, the best you could do in the early days was to tell your latitude—how far north or south you are from the equator. You did that by observing the sun around noon, waiting until it stopped rising, and then noting the angle between it and the horizon, the same as your distance from the pole from which you could easily figure your latitude. But, until you could tell the time quite accurately, you couldn't determine how far east or west you were. The problem was solved in the eighteenth century, so by the time of the Napoleonic Wars the ritual of figuring out where you were deep sea was being taught to midshipmen recruited at a young age from their farms, and barely literate.

Two considerations governed how this ritual (called "working a sight") was performed.

Since you were deriving your position from the navigational celestial triangle, why not just draw the triangle on the chart? The problem was that the triangle was usually far too big, unless you were high up in the Arctic with the heavenly body almost directly overhead, not the usual situation. So, a clever solution was found: put a pencil mark on the chart where you thought you were (by dead reckoning), take a sight, and then work out how much error you had made. A good navigator made small errors, so correcting the position from the assumed position to where the sight said you were would then occupy quite a small part of the chart, and be fairly accurate.

The other problem was that if you asked illiterate farm hands to make the necessary trigonometrical calculations to work out the error in position they usually made mistakes in subtraction more frequently than they did in addition. So the next smart solution was to use trigonometrical functions which never resulted in a negative value, hence the use of what were called, until the end of the days of traditional position fixing, the haversine tables. In my day, these were to be found in a substantial book which you then combined with another substantial book, *The Nautical Almanac*, to work your sight. After a good night's sleep, sitting comfortably at a school desk, I was unable to work a sight in under half an hour, even using one of the so-called quick methods which abounded, even with a calculator.

For the technically minded: at least one of the functions of sines, tangents and cosines are negative in quadrants other than the first quadrant . The trick was to construct a new function containing a square of one of the basic three functions—and a haversine is the squared sine of half the angle. If you square a positive number it remains positive, but if you square a negative number it becomes positive. So, it enabled midshipmen to add everything and avoid errors.

When I was at navigation school, calculators with the trigonometrical functions were just coming in—but they didn't show haversines, so they weren't directly applicable to working sights in the same way as they had been worked since Napoleonic times.

To use them, I needed to recapture the underlying calculations for the navigational celestial triangle. So I bought a simple book on spherical trigonometry (called, as a matter of fact, *Spherical Trigonometry*, by J. H. Clough-Smith, Brown, Son & Ferguson, 1966) and mugged it up. Then I wrote the simple algorithms required to solve the navigational celestial triangle for navigational purposes.

Thenceforth, I could work a dozen sights in as many minutes.

My then calculator was the fanciest on the market, made by Hewlett Packard with their special Reverse Polish Notation, a system of operating a calculator so much simpler than the standard way that I cannot understand why it is not itself the standard. This calculator had memories. In those days that was right at the cutting edge. So I devised a system for loading the memories with the awkward numbers resulting from star sights, following instructions I wrote on a piece of stiff paper, carefully kept in the calculator case, which told me which memories to recall, and what to do with them.

I never used standard navigational tables at sea. They remain in their original water resistant wrappings in my basement. The only problem was that I didn't know anything about the computer discipline of backing things up or making a duplicate copy of a program. A few years later on arrival in America someone stole the calculator by this time old fashioned so it didn't much matter. However the loss of the accompanying piece of stiff paper was a disaster.

I went out to the local music shop, and asked for a repeat calculator. The top of the Hewlett Packard line now cost $200 instead of the £200 sterling which I had originally paid. It also had the enticing word "programmable." I didn't know exactly what that meant, but I bought it. I subsequently produced so many navigational, tidal, dead reckoning and estimated time of arrival programs that I used to say in jest that the calculator's bearings ran hot. It was before the days when standard Navpac modules were available. I often wonder who crossed the Atlantic on a calculator without using short methods or haversine tables before I did in 1978.

Although I was still aloof from *Gray*, I nevertheless felt a duty to visit her from time to time. I used the Harwich–Esjberg ferry. Once, when I was alone, there was a fearful following gale. Occasionally, the ferry kicked its screw, racing, out of the water. I went on deck aft to get as much of the wind as I could and gaze at the seas.

They were so broad that neither their height nor their speed seemed particularly impressive until our stern seemed to sink so deep into the trough in front of the advancing wave that I thought the wave might simply walk aboard. Then, as the wave passed under us, our stern was lifted right out of the water, so the screw stuck out in mid-air, raced, and we were flung to the side unable to steer because the rudder was also out of the water. I wasn't frightened, but I watched with curiosity to see how the ship would behave. It turned out to be a useful lesson, for the same thing happened to us on *Gray* some years later.

After a while, the excitement and interest began to wear off, and I went for breakfast which to my surprise was being served despite the conditions. I had been right aft where the movement was most pronounced. In the dining-room, things were calmer until I heard the comic sound of breaking plates, so prolonged it might have been got up specially for a slapstick performance on the stage. There were two passengers for breakfast: a thin respectable old woman, who sat bolt upright in her chair at whatever angle it happened to be, and me. We could not, of course, confess to anything untoward, so we ordered our breakfasts as though nothing particular was happening. However, secretly I was wondering if the waiter could possibly cope with what must have been a shambles of broken plates somewhere towards the kitchen. I watched the old lady, stiff as a ramrod, hands folded in her lap, waiting for her breakfast, and then I watched her, still perpendicular to her armchair, slowly topple over as the chair disentangled itself from its restraining chain and fell sideways on the floor. It would have been impolite of me to have noticed, or moved, so I did nothing as the waiter helped the lady from the floor, re-chained the chair and sat the lady back in it in the same position as before to wait for her breakfast.

One day, sitting at my desk in London paying the monthly bills, I had a call. I heard the familiar Mr. Jon-es.

It was the owner of the yard at Assens who wanted to go into the forest to cut three trees. At first, I didn't have an idea what he was talking about. Then: of course, it was for the masts. We had a three-masted schooner after all. It began to come back to me. To get the height, we were going to step the masts on deck. Just as they do on the Thames barges. I had wondered why this seemed such an innovation to the Assens yard —for me, I was following strictly in the traditional mode, avoiding all adventure, a classic restoration, as it were. Also, if one of the masts went overboard, it would not take a chunk of deck with it, so I reasoned (falsely as it turned out).

While I failed hopelessly to integrate with the Assens yard, I found what surrounded these visits enjoyable. One frozen morning, I looked out through the stern portholes of *Gray* as I lay in my tiny bunk not daring to move for fear of the cold. It was a Sunday. Assens was quiet at the best of times, but this had to be the quietest moment of the week.

The silence was broken by scratching on the wood right outside where my head lay. The porthole was too narrow and too deeply set between the timbers to allow me to see much. As the scratching persisted, I finally persuaded myself that I had sufficient interest in this ship to get up to investigate. From my position of beleaguered blindness inside the hull, I climbed up on the quarterdeck to tower over a pastor, who was unscrewing the name-boards from the ship's stern. He looked up, smiled, said good morning, and went on unscrewing the boards. What was he doing, I asked? Unscrewing the name-boards, he answered. I didn't know what to do with this information, since he clearly had no intention of defending himself against the obvious charge of larceny. After a few minutes' silence, he explained that he always took the name-boards of ships sold here. Maybe, I said, but these ones were still my property. Oh yes, he agreed, but I would have no use for them because I would doubtless be changing the ship's name, and the port of registry would have to be changed in any case. Could he have some coffee, he said, as he was nearly finished and it was very cold out there. He would be up in a minute.

I hurried to get some coffee for him, and only after devious polite conversation did I dare bring the subject round to the name-boards. I explained that I almost

I have no picture of Gray *when she was still in trade. The above is a picture of the* Esther, *a sister ship of the* Gray. *The* Esther *looks as though she is carrying a cargo. Unlike the way I rigged* Gray, *the* Esther *has topmasts which look as though they might have been 70 feet off the deck.* Gray's *were only 65 feet off the deck.*

certainly would keep the name of the ship. He said that would be a break with tradition indeed. He had known every owner of *Gray* since she had been built in 1920, and of course they had all changed the name on change of ownership. It would have been bad luck to do otherwise. He then showed me the picture of *Esther*, a sister-ship to *Gray*, which he thought was taken in the fifties. Then he wrote down all the previous names, and the names of the owners, who their wives or girlfriends were, and why they had renamed the ship — usually, it seemed, to represent the other half of a new conjugal situation. I wish I still had that list.

Finally, he allowed as how he would make me a gift of *Gray*'s name-board, while he would keep the other board with the Port of Registry on it.

During the winter, despite the way my feeling strayed to anything but the ship, it became apparent that in effect we were preparing her for sea with the same kind of inevitability with which one awaits the birth of a child. The event was certain; the outcome was not; but, whatever it was, it would change our lives.

When we bought the barge I had been awed by the thought that anyone could handle so big a sailing ship. Cecilia knew more about boats than I did at the time. In my teens, I had spent three summers fishing for lobsters off the beach near my home at Rottingdean in a plywood dinghy about nine feet long. It had a lot of free-board (the height the water has to jump to get on board), so it could take the lobster pots. The Seagull outboard engine was temperamental. I learned a great deal about how to land a laden dinghy in heavy surf. But that was about enough to train me to become Robinson Crusoe, and by no means enough to give me even the first notion what to do with a sailing barge. Cecilia had, after all, sailed in a sail boat on the open sea, more than I had ever done, except for one voyage. My brother and I had built a sailing boat which sank under me as I tried to make the short trip from my home in Rottingdean to Newhaven Harbor.

When the time came to leave Assens, I had no clear recollection how we had entered the port just before Christmas, other than that the owner of the yard had been on the quayside in a porkpie hat which he doffed to welcome us. In particular, I had no recollection how we could possibly have turned the right-angle bend which protected the harbor from the Baltic. As time went on, I realized we had to negotiate these same bends in reverse. We had to...? We? Me? I had to? Or would it be Cecilia?

But by this time, I had dug my grave. Was I not a Yachtmaster (Ocean), who had passed two days of written tests and survived a three hour oral examination at the Navigation School attempting to demonstrate, face to face with my examiner, that I knew exactly how to handle a supertanker in a seaway?

4

The Minsener Rinne

It was easy, they said...

...from,

I noted,

the safety of the quayside.

Cecilia offered to do it.

Do what?

Take the *Gray* out of harbor... On our own... For the first time.

There would be no Larsen to steer the ship for us. There would be no support group. Just me, Cecilia and 200 tons of Baltic trader.

I never asked her later whether her offer was meant sincerely or was just intended to provoke me into doing it myself. She was always straight-forward, so I rather think she would have been quite prepared to take the wheel herself. I still felt, as I had done nearly five years before when we moved in together, that nothing would be impossible for her.

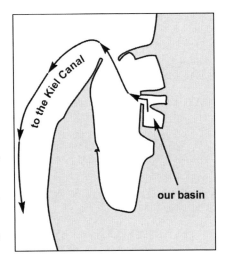

Her children, I found as time went on, admired her leadership qualities — and nerves of steel — much more than mine. And they were not alone in this opinion. Cecilia led by sheer immediate charisma.

But much as I really did not want to take the ship out of Assens, a certain unworthy competitiveness led me to insist upon it. I could see no possibility of making the sharp turn to port to avoid hitting the opposite wall which, frankly, seemed to be getting closer every time I looked.

Plan of Assens harbor where Gray was refitted during 1969–70. To bring her back through the Kiel Canal to Pin Mill was a journey of about 460 nautical miles.

In fact, once actually engaged in the right-angled bend, it turned out to be almost straight. The long exit channel I had expected to get to the Baltic didn't exist. We were at sea immediately.

It was barely daylight, since I had wanted to start early, partly to get as much light as possible, but partly to avoid being watched by the men of the yard. So in fact I never said goodbye to them. I cannot imagine what I was up to, but if any of them reads this now, I hope he will accept my apologies.

Once in the Baltic, I realized for the first time exactly what it meant to run the ship with just the two of us. Before, on the barge, if the helmsman wanted to go to the toilet, there was always someone else to mind the shop for a while. Now the absence of one of us from the steering position dictated the presence of the other. I hadn't experienced this self-reliance before. Even when I fished for lobsters in my late teens off Rottingdean beach, my mentor, Dave Hennessy, a heavyset man with large pebble glasses, would most likely be on the cliff watching out for me. He drove the Rottingdean taxi, one of the last coach built conveyances. As I worked my way down the line of pots, well offshore (for a small dinghy), Dave's glasses were the last thing to disappear. Then, feeling really alone, I would turn back. This time, on *Gray*, there was no turning back.

We had considered the more romantic business of sailing north round the top of Jutland—up the Skagerrak and down the Kattegat as I was made to chant in geography lessons, seeing the passage from the point of view of British aggression into the Baltic. We discarded the idea for the safety of the Kiel Canal.

The pilot—we were obliged to take one on—wore patent-leather shoes. I suppose our huge sailing ship must have been a sort of toy to him, but I didn't understand then, and I still don't, how he managed to get himself spreadeagled with one foot on the quayside and one on *Gray*, at that moment drifting very slowly from the quay. We didn't mention the matter.

The trouble about canals is that the weather at the other end is always different from the weather at the end where you start. The weather at Holtenau, at the Baltic end where we started, was calm and pleasant, and lent itself to such trivia as noticing patent-leather shoes. The canal is very long—53 nautical miles—and took us eight hours. Once we started, we were committed to taking whatever was waiting for us at the other end.

We traveled southwest down the canal into the Elbe, which runs out to sea northwest from Hamburg. We didn't have a lot of trouble crossing the Elbe, heading seaward a little way and stopping for the night in Cuxhaven, near the mouth of the land, though still leaving a series of sandbanks to seaward to negotiate before we could shape a course for England.

The next day we started to lumber farther down the Elbe with all the other ships, some big, some small, all rusty (except us), all going in the same direction, all carrying something for a living. All except us.

We didn't know how fast we would be able to make the passage across the North Sea. If either of us failed, physically or mentally, we would be in trouble. Even if both of us remained efficient, we were taking a big risk in spending two nights at sea, buoy hopping a lot of the way, with no spare resources to deal with problems. Besides, we really hadn't a notion how *Gray* would behave, particularly as we had three trees strapped to the deck for use as masts once we reached England.

- With not even the foremast aloft, we rolled even more rapidly than during the blizzard bringing *Gray* to Copenhagen. The period—the time taken from the beginning of a roll, across to the other side and back to the starting point again—was about three seconds. In heavy weather, it was terrifyingly fast.

  With the masts up, the roll later increased to four-and-a-half seconds. To make the ship more comfortable, and to reduce the strain on the hull, about 12 years later we put 40,000 pounds—nearly 18 English tons weight—of pig-iron on deck, increasing the roll to nearly six seconds. Ironically, after so many years of the old four-second roll, the new one was equally terrifying, if different.

It was only reasonable to start down the Elbe with the help of an ebb tide. But I hadn't counted on a wind — while the ebb tide set towards the northwest, giving us a helping hand down the Elbe, the wind was coming from the northwest — at gale force.

- I should explain. A weather tide is a tide running into the wind. A lee tide is headed in the same direction as the wind. Winds are designated by the direction they come from; tides by the direction they are going to (or setting); thus, a southerly wind and a southerly tide are going in opposite directions and therefore make a weather tide.

  A 15-knot wind is a wind all right, but it's not much of a wind, particularly if it's right behind you and you're traveling through the water itself at, say, five knots. For purposes of illustration only, assume that your vessel is traveling either directly against, or directly with the tide, and that you maintain a constant speed through the water by increasing or reducing your engine revolutions to produce this unrealistic result. Your speed over the ground is therefore nil or 10 knots (the 5 knot tide ± the 5 knots you maintain through the water). So, your speed relative to the wind is either 25 knots (both you and the tide are fighting the wind), or 15 knots (you're going against the tide with the wind behind you), or 5 knots (wind behind you on a lee tide).

  The most usual situation is that the tide changes, but the wind keeps up and you keep going without any change. In our case, going down the Elbe with the tide, but against the wind, we had a lumpy sea and a strong wind but we made progress. The moment the tide changed against us, the apparent wind speed dropped, the sea was less rough, but we stood still.

  The force of the wind on your ship varies as the square of its speed, which is shown in the bracketed figures in the table below

	Wind on the nose	*Wind on the stern*
Weather tide (rough)	25 knots (25 times)	15 knots (9 times)
Lee tide (calmer)	15 knots (9 times)	5 knots (base = 1)

Not having expected the wind to be so strong, we became desperately worried we would not be in the open sea by the time the tide turned against us, at which point both wind and tide would be heading us and we would have to stall around making no progress, just getting tired.

There were various staging points on the way down the Elbe, each of them marked by a light vessel which started where the estuary began to widen on its way into the North Sea. We heard on the radio that the pilots had been moved in from the Outer Elbe Light Vessel to one of the inner ones because of the rough weather.

Just after the Second World War, during the time when I was fishing for lobsters, my mother used to make fairly frequent trips to Dieppe on the ferry from Newhaven. She went to visit her friend Lady Diana Cooper, whose husband was ambassador in Paris. Whenever I went with them, I disgraced everyone by being seasick. It was a particularly heinous disgrace because we were usually treated as VIP passengers.

Towards the end of this period, I had asked a friend to come with me lobstering. I was smoking roll-ups made with coarse pipe tobacco. We were rocking at rest, tied up to one of the pots, gossiping. When my friend confessed to seasickness, I started to hope I had been cured. There was one more trip on the Newhaven–Dieppe ferry when there was a bagful of wind. The captain asked me on to the bridge. I enjoyed the rough weather, hung on to the rails and pillars as the ship rolled, and knew my seasickness was over forever.

Or was it?

Twenty years had passed with no further test of my resistance to seasickness. The time on the Thames barge had been in sheltered waters. Now I watched with horror as Cecilia vomited in the mouth of the Elbe. Could I resist, now she was struck? After all, you have to remember she was still this splendid figure of competence and success. Was I now alone? After all, I knew about seasickness, having been so dreadfully sick myself. I knew it was uncontrollable, unstoppable, impossible to resist. If she had succumbed, would I as well?

Gray was becoming more and more unmanageable. I thought it probable she would capsize if I tried to turn her round and seek shelter back up the Elbe. As the tide ebbed lower, wartime wrecks littering the emerging sandbanks showed me how little room for maneuver we had.

By the time we reached *Elbe I*, the outermost light vessel, the tide was due to turn. We wouldn't be able to make much headway for the next six hours. One option would be to turn round at slack water and go back to Cuxhaven. But as far as I could tell, the seas were still as short as they had been, and some 12 feet high, meaning that we could bridge two green seas wandering on board, one at our bow and the other at our stern. So there was a chance it might not get calmer at the turn of the tide. Besides, going back to Cuxhaven would simply mean facing again the same problems we had faced that morning.

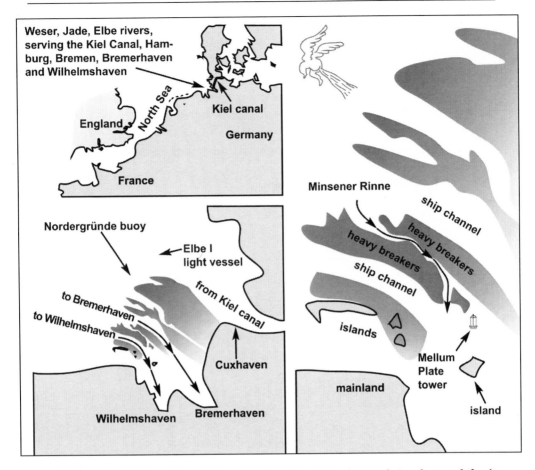

Top left: an overall view of the exit from the Kiel Canal into the North Sea; *bottom left:* the sandbanks at the mouth of the Elbe, and at the approaches to Bremerhaven and Wilhelmshaven; *right:* detail of the Minsener Rinne, the narrow channel between heavy breakers which allowed us to change our mind and go towards Wilhelmshaven instead of Bremerhaven. Zephyr after James Gilray, who drew them in 1797 to lampoon the American artist Benjamin West. Suggested by Alex Kahn to show the northwest gale which was blowing us onshore.

Another option might be to find somewhere to port, downwind and on a lee tide, where we could stop for the night, and thus not lose everything we had gained so far. I knew there were plenty of mud banks, and I would be quite happy to sit on one for a bit.

But there was an additional problem. We had detailed charts of the Baltic and English legs of the trip but none of the central section, where we were now. We were already off the river which leads to Bremerhaven. The best chart we had on board was clearly not suited to navigating between mud banks.

I did, however, have copies of the relevant and admirable Admiralty Pilot books, the Baltic and the North Sea Pilots. They were the modern day equivalent of the early rutters, and almost painfully detailed, corrected at frequent intervals by supplements. Even so, there was still a potential further problem. My mind went back to Navigation School. Whenever our instructor asked, "Gentlemen, what is the first thing you should do upon consulting the Pilot?" we learned to chant with a flourish: "Consult the Supplements."

I had the Pilot on board, but what if we had missed a Supplement?

By this time, we were off the Nordergründe buoy with the tide flooding hard on our starboard bow. Should we stem it for six stationary and uncomfortable hours? We decided to dive in with the tide and the wind towards the rivers, researching the Pilot on the way.

Once engaged in the main fairway to Bremerhaven, we realized it was industrial and unfriendly. But what had caught my eye on the chart was the possibility of being able to cross over to the much quieter-looking channel leading to Wilhemshaven. To my amazement, the Pilot described the buoyage of this channel, the Minsener Rinne (shown on current charts as the Mittelrinne). There was a crucial entry buoy, followed by lettered fairway buoys. But our chart was not detailed and the Pilot did not make the channel look promising under the present conditions.

The Supplement. Consult the Supplement. Even if pressed for time, my instructor had said. Where was it? I found the 1967 supplement, waded through the corrections and found one which seemed to relate to the vitally important buoys I should be looking for. The drift seemed to be that we should be politically neutral and call them German buoys, not German Federal Republic buoys. Right then, I wanted to know if there *were* any and where they were, not how I should address them at a cocktail party.

The absence of a proper chart and the Pilot's warnings about the nasty effects of windy conditions in the mud channels would have told a prudent seaman to settle for a night's discomfort in Bremerhaven. Instead, I changed course due west to clear the extensive sands to seaward of Bremerhaven. I was afraid of being swept onto them by the incoming tide. There were buoys all over the place, so many they were confusing when traveling athwart the shipping channels rather than in them. Hoping I had turned at the right buoy, I changed back in the direction of the Minsener Rinne.

Its channel buoys were small and unlit and I could only find them on the starboard side. Once in the Minsener Rinne we had to keep the Mellum Plates light tower, situated in the middle of nowhere, fine on our starboard bow, the wrong bow, until the last minute, when we should nip smartly round to starboard to leave the tower to port. The Pilot did not say what letter the last buoy bore.

When we turned off the main fairway round the Minsener Rinne C light-and-bell buoy to engage ourselves in the channel, the wind was brought well on our quarter. We picked up speed. Where I thought the first unlit channel buoy should have been there was just a solid wall of breaking surf. Panic I might, but there was no turning back.

The first buoy we picked up was out of sequence. So we had missed a buoy. If some of the buoys were underwater, would we see the exit buoy? How many buoys had we missed? Was this the exit buoy? What with the tide, the wind and our own power, we must have been going nearly 10 knots over the ground. No time to scratch my head. Hesitantly I began to turn to starboard in case there were a break in the line of surf and away from the unseen dangers which must lie at the foot of the light tower. Then a black buoy popped up on our port bow. I realized it had to be another channel buoy and should have been on our starboard bow. It took all my nerve to heave back to port and get the buoy and the light tower once more on my starboard bow.

The light tower seemed right on top of us before the break in the surf came. We dived to starboard, buoy or no buoy. Then, right there, we saw the exit buoy tucked out of sight behind the breakers and knew we were safe. We were almost immediately in calm water.

There seemed no point pressing up river. So we dropped anchor in the middle of nowhere and began to sort ourselves out. The vomit had strained through the uncaulked floor of the wheel house onto our bed; everything was a shambles; we had lost some stores.

Around midnight, I woke to the gentle slapping of small waves on the transom, and realized we were facing the wrong way either aground or sailing around on a weather ebb. It was hard to tell whether we had dragged as there was no land in sight. It took a couple of hours to find another spot to re-anchor. We went back to bed.

The next morning was lovely. There was hardly any wind and a slight fog entombed us in a circle of lucent sea with no horizon. We started to have breakfast, creaking out of sleep, in no hurry to move, pride sitting easily around us. The anchorage had a desolate beauty, but as the lee flood picked up, we started to drag. Let us drag. Flood, mud, no harm. But I couldn't recapture that unfinished breakfast. We got fed up trying not to try, and left for England.

For three full days and the intervening nights, that wretched engine thumped away at its 240 countable revolutions per minute, four to a second. When we were not too tired, it would have been a comfort to chat together. After all, by any standard this was a great adventure. The noise from the engine was never very great, but the shaking and vibration somehow knocked speech to bits in the air: you emitted a sound which didn't make it across. And the fatigue was in a different category. Four hours on was about the maximum either of us could do, so that dictated four hours off, but not really. At least some tea and a wash had to be fitted in. Waking up became a torture, so exquisite through its repetition that I almost dreaded being locked into sleep in the first place.

For the first day, night and the next day, we were buoy hopping, usually in the kind of visibility which leaves you wondering how bad it is, obscuring the skyline and destroying your sense of the horizontal, but not so bad that extra measures have to be taken. Then something would pop up unexpectedly and we would realize that the visibility was worse than we had thought. For most of this time we were in heavy traffic lanes. It would have been easier to have followed everyone else, but they were much faster, and we were constantly being overtaken and then losing our quarry. One ship, the *Star Columbia* of Bergen, looked as though she were light ship she was so far out of the water. So far, indeed, that we were hidden under her bows, and only escaped being run down at the last minute.

In those days we didn't have much more than lead, log and compass — no electronic position fixing system, for instance. We did, however, have a handheld radio direction finder which could tell us which way was up, but not a great deal more. When we could, we used it to home on the next light vessel, until we slavishly followed the Terschelling Bank Light Vessel as she was towed away. She had forgotten to turn off her transmitter.

The second night I began to hallucinate. The steady thump of the engine was irresistibly swaddling. It was dead calm, oily slick calm. We had reached the North Sea proper and were out of the shipping lanes which had hugged the coasts of Germany and Holland. Young men in tailcoats began to gather round the bar, an eddy on the surface of the still water about a mile off to starboard. Young women in evening dress appeared. I shook myself to get rid of the hallucination and to resolve the glint of candles through balloons of burgundy into the red light of a ship ahead to starboard. Gradually, the hallucinations became more real, and I found it harder and harder to disentangle them from what was actually going on outside me.

But there was another bit of my mind which was aware of the hallucinations and set to work to calculate the chances of an accident if I gave into them, like yielding to an anesthetic — the old-fashioned sort of anesthetic which took a while to work. It was a seductive idea.

The lawn and the dance and the bushes and the bar, the men and women circulating round dancing, remained so vivid that forty years later I have no difficulty in re-living that night's hallucinations.

In the morning, we started to get faint signals from the English coast, signals of the light vessels that had been part of our romantic time on the Thames barge. The Outer Gabbard, the Sunk, then the Cork, gone now except for the Sunk. We made landfall at Orford Ness.

I felt ambivalent. This was my first long journey, out of sight of land for much of the time, putting into practice what I had learned at school, not making mistakes. Even then I realized that, to the extent that this was a technical achievement, to that extent it was less exciting, less pleasurable, less romantic, less what I wanted to feel. I had been frankly scared by the Minsener Rinne. I didn't then know that, if that were luck, I was to be very lucky.

There was an additional ambivalence. I remembered how in the *Gipping*, rotten but beautiful and drawing only three feet of water, we had sailed up to Orford, a little inland from our landfall at Orford Ness. Now, in *Gray*, having driven across the North Sea with exactitude, we could not have gone to Orford even had we wanted to. *Gray* drew nine feet, much too deep to cross the shallow bar at Orford Haven and wind up the beautiful river. The door had closed, life had moved on. We were excluded.

Suddenly we wanted to make love. What on earth to do? At the wheel? Not very easy, and yet we couldn't both leave it at the same time. Or perhaps... I lowered the engine revolutions (oh, what a relief), put the wheel hard over and lashed it. For a while we stood on the expanse of main deck and watched us going round in circles. We giggled at the bathos of getting too giddy to make love, and took refuge on the hard deck, our bodies bare to the splinters.

Afterwards, we wondered how much of the deck was visible from the lighthouse.

Six hours later, moored on an Admiralty buoy downstream of Pin Mill, I felt the real exclusion from the club. In the old days, we would have gone right up to the hard outside the pub and sat on the mud. When the hard had been uncovered by the receding ebb, we would have been high above the strollers and stragglers below us. We would have gone about our nonchalant business as experienced seamen and world-girdling travelers, who, looked up to, would have been asked questions, welcomed, silently appraised, pointed out from afar... Pretending to pay no special notice to these attentions, we would eventually have condescended to have left those tasks only real seamen can understand, stepped down the ladder, and gone to the pub for a drink, accompanied by buddies whose own standing reflected familiarity with our luster.

Then we would have gotten drunk in the pub and boasted too much.

Where was our glory now? Returning from a much braver exploit with the stout new ship, we were cheated of belonging to a group who would have understood every detail of what we had done. But that was then. Now was now. And now was different: that nine-foot draft had compelled us to stay away, compelled us to get into our very unsmart dinghy, sidle up to the hard, creep ashore, and be asked: "Haven't seen you in a while. Been keeping busy?"

Our business done, we left for London quickly and quietly. On our way ashore, we passed poor *Gipping*, lying where we would have liked to lie, and about to be abandoned.

Things brightened up a little when we came down the following weekend with the children, who were uncomplicatedly excited by the prospect of seeing our new toy. We had to move house from *Gipping* to *Gray*, with the nine-foot plyboard dinghy I had used for lobster fishing.

The move had to be done at high water, partly because *Gipping* only floated at high water, partly because we needed a light shove from the ebb to get downstream to *Gray*. The dinghy's Seagull outboard motor was the kind of thing now used for fishing when you don't want to disturb the fish. The dinghy was so heavily laden I couldn't reach the motor anyway. Children were on both boats, some on *Gipping*, packing, the others with Cecilia on *Gray*, unpacking. From lack of space in the dinghy, I ferried alone, standing up, sculling with a long oar, largely dependent on the tide for propulsion, nearly waist deep in brightly colored plastic children's clothes, thrown onto dun-colored longshoremen's gear, jumbled up with board games sticking out of cardboard boxes, bits of rope, small anchors...

Our London suitcases looked grotesque among their bedfellows.

• We are probably more familiar with the competitive sport of two-oared sculling than with the ancient system which I was using of single oared sculling. Usually this consists of pivoting an oar on a part of the boat's transom (e.g., through a semicircular cut out), and then maneuvering the handle in a flat figure eight (∞), revolving the oar so that the end in the water provides lift *away* from the boat. A variation on this is to use one of your hands, instead of the boat, as the pivot, but there's a big difference. Lift now is *towards* the boat, enabling the sculler to get out first at a quayside, and help other, perhaps less experienced, passengers disembark. Although sculling is always slow, two-handed, single oared sculling is useful because it is done standing up, takes less space in a crowded boat, can be started on an instant, is totally silent (e.g., for fishing) and can propel the boat in any direction, sideways, backwards or forwards. It works best in a heavier boat with less windage and more stability but it is possible to use it even in a light rubber dinghy provided there is not too much wind.

It was nearly full moon, still, beautiful. A few movements brought me clear of *Gipping*; *Gray* was round the corner, at first out of sight, soon a visible target. It was hard to drag myself back from the addiction of the moon to the reality that if I missed *Gray*, the tide would sweep me past her. And no one on *Gray* could come after me since I was in the only tender.

Seventeen years were to elapse before I moved house again. By that time, I was alone in America.

5

The first winter in England

Cecilia and I had gotten this far along the road: we realized there would be more to do on *Gray* than on *Gipping*. Thus a berth in London would be much more suitable than one on the East Coast. But we had not gotten as far as detailing what had to be done to *Gray*.

The assumption in a commercial dock is that no vessel has much interest in tarrying long. To defray its costs, a commercial vessel carries either passengers or goods for payment and moves them along as quickly as possible. A yacht on the

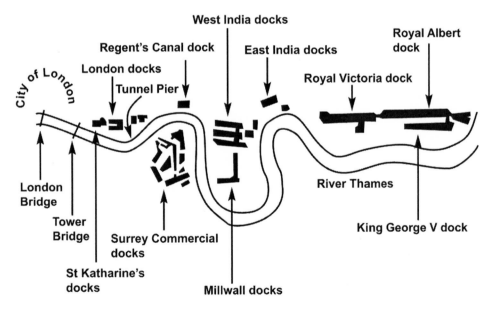

A schematic showing London's docks before they started to be closed in the 1970s. The Pool of London is usually regarded as the stretch of river between London Bridge and Tower Bridge — the Upper Pool — but there was a less well defined area below Tower Bridge, which included Tunnel Pier where we berthed. The river is tidal at this point and flows out to sea to the right on the schematic above.

other hand is subject to more searching scrutiny before being allowed into a new berth where it might want to overstay its welcome.

Gray was a commercial vessel, so it wasn't very difficult for me to say I wanted a berth near the Pool of London, and to get one in the Surrey Commercial Docks. As a yacht, they might have refused in order to avoid the trouble of subsequently ejecting me — as they did.

The Surrey Docks used to cover an area of the East End of London comparable in size to the City of London (the financial district) but on the other side of the river — 150 acres of water, surrounded by five miles of quayside.

For centuries, much of the English trade with Europe had come through London, where relatively small vessels anchored or berthed on one of the wharves in what was called the Pool of London, close by the City of London, the center of commercial activity. The development of steam tugs meant that by the 1830s, many international ports could cater to sailing vessels too large to navigate into them by themselves. That led to the need for enclosed docks into which these bigger vessels could enter through lock gates and stay afloat, rather than floating and grounding on the tide outside. Oddly enough, many of the docked vessels were unloaded into lighters which took the goods back out of the docks and continued to deliver them to the wharves in the river which since time immemorial had been specialists in various trades.

The first wet dock was the East India Dock, operating in 1614. It was followed by a second, opened in 1700, which subsequently became Greenland Dock. With these two exceptions, virtually the entire area of dockland serving the port of London was built in the 19th century. Canada Dock (where the *Gray* was to lie) was opened in 1880, and no further large dock was built until the last, the King George V Dock, opened in 1921. When the *Gray* arrived, dock closures had already started because the increasingly large container ships could not navigate the upper reaches of the Thames even with tugs. The Port of London Authority had therefore moved ocean-going cargo traffic down the Thames to Tilbury. We were the last sea-going vessel to be berthed in Canada Dock, one of the Surrey Docks. Since then, a lot of the docks have been filled in (only the hatched areas shown on the map remain).

The day after moving house from *Gipping*, we chugged round to the new berth, that is, out of Harwich and into the Thames Estuary up to London. But thereafter it was nearly three months before the light began to dawn on me: If I didn't do some work on the ship nobody else would. We were no longer in a position to buy help, there was no Barry, no Webb brothers, and the Assens yard had done its work. There was merely one large wooden sailing vessel, looking very small, tied up to about an inch of quay space in a vast expanse of still water, surrounded by motionless

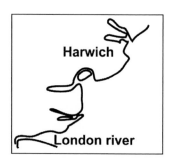

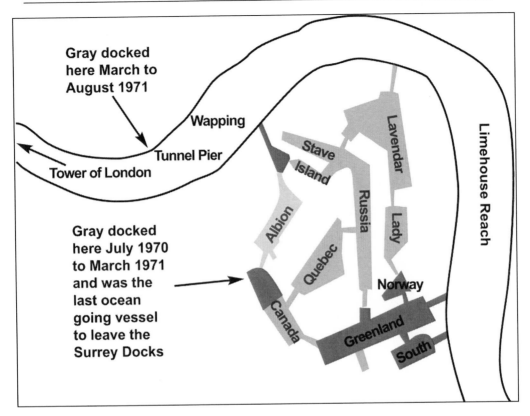

Surrey Commercial Docks in the 1970s showing the extent of the subsequent reclamation of dockland for housing. The dark grey area is what remains water. Albion Dock has been reduced to a gutway to give Canada Dock access to the river.

cranes and the corrugated iron of warehouses. If you stood looking along a quayside, the end of the dock was so far away it demonstrated vividly that perspective consists of the convergence of parallel straight lines in the distance. While there were pockets of lingering activity in dock areas outside the Surrey Commercial, the latter was deserted except for the police. Even to say that would be to imply an activity more complex than what was actually going on, namely one policeman gathering blackberries in his helmet on a hot late summer's day. The waste areas beside the quays had by now become quite overgrown. I even had fantasies of squatting on *Gray* and cultivating the surrounding land.

To begin with after our arrival in London, Cecilia continued to give lunches and dinners as usual for 10 to 15 people, the first nine of them tending to be our family and au pair girl. Several times we bused the entire luncheon party down to the East End to have a tour of *Gray* on a Sunday afternoon when the roads outside the docks were as hushed as the docks themselves. A few other times, Cecilia packed up lunch so that we could spend Sunday day-dreaming with the children on *Gray*.

One fine Monday, the first in October, I decided to go back to work. I had nothing else to do. Two of the clinics had been sold and the third was merely dwindling. I clocked into the docks at 8 A.M. and made a note of it just as though I were a factory worker.

At this stage, *Gray* had no masts. We had had a box built on deck, ultimately to become the galley, but at that time empty. Some flat boards had been put across the curved lining in the hold, so we could walk back and forth. Forward of the hold

was an existing space which held the anchor chains. In the after part of the hold itself, there were two 2,500-liter water tanks, installed in Denmark. We had partially broken through to the engine room further aft, which also housed the two 2,000-liter fuel tanks. That is, we lifted five metric tonnes of water and four metric tonnes of fuel. Right aft was the only accommodation, the old master's cabin, with the steering position above it, protected by a sort of shack that served as the pilot house.

Steel spikes. Recalcitrant unfriendly steel hawsers are placed in submission to these murderous weapons used with vices to make splices.

Up to about this time in my life — turning 40 — immorality really meant sex. You shouldn't actually bugger little boys; far worse, have heterosexual relations outside marriage, or outside your class; never masturbate more than once a week (preferably on Saturdays)... That sort of thing. Drink wasn't immoral because you never spoke of it. It was in the same category as madness: something that happened to other people. Although I had been brought face to face with my wife's schizophrenia during my 20s, I had had little to do with social problems, or situations in which there might be some doubt as to what course would be ethical, or whether, even, ethics existed. At Oxford, I had studied philosophy, specializing in logic, but I had never met a pauper — or a criminal.

Wooden fids for separating the strands of rope and generally getting into soft cuddly things.

Apart from my wife's sickness, I had lived a very sheltered life.

On return to work, the first decision was whether to hire Wally, who said he had served time in prison, as rigger. In the protected life I used to lead, such a decision would have had more or less strong connections with concepts such as whether it was my duty to help someone less fortunate. In the docks, not only did I not have enough money to be able to give myself the luxury of thinking in this way, but Wally would certainly not have worked for me on that basis. Ours was a commercial transaction. He had doubtless figured out that I would find

Serving mallets. Note the hollow to fit the rope being served.

out anyway that he had a prison record. Better to come out with it at once, since trust would be a considerable part of our relationship. In fact, it would not have occurred to me to check his background, so I never corroborated his story of jail. There was not much at that time which could easily be stolen from *Gray*, but eventually there would be equipment like wire, a cooker, possibly navigational instruments. Dockland thieves usually dealt by the truckload, so the odd piece of equipment from *Gray* would hardly even amount to small change. But to me, small change was important.

Since leaving prison, Wally said he had rigged another ship, somewhere on the south coast. He had shown me glamorous pictures of himself with his set-up of wire and wood and vices, tar and rope, mallets, fids, bulls' eyes, spikes and thimbles, helped by some extremely attractive young women, to demonstrate that *Gray* would present him with no problem at all. I felt a little demeaned, but did not say so. He had fallen in love with one of the less attractive young women, but there was a problem. She was of better class, he explained. I gazed at the rather pudgy lady in the picture he withdrew carefully from his wallet and tried to fit her into any version of class which would distinguish her obviously from him. It was such a touching confession. I wanted to believe. I wanted to sympathize with Wally in his aspirations, one of which was to become a Gentleman Rigger, and thus be good enough to seek Madge's hand. Like a young knight in the lists. Consequently, he spent a long time every evening getting the grime off his hands and attending to his coiffure.

Wally had sought the job in such a respectable manner that it came as a shock to discover that he was homeless. He must have seen the calculations marching across my face before I said that of course he should stay on board, only it would be very lonely, as I would go home at the end of the day.

Preparing to negotiate a job with me, Wally had hidden what little he had behind a pile of garbage. He collected it. One of the bags had worn and darkened wooden handles sticking out of the top. A traveling artisan.

At the end of the day, I would pay him. I didn't then know that a daily cash settlement was extremely unusual in this world. Then I would leave Wally alone and go home along the whole of the rough and poorer parts of the East End, passing through historic roads whose names have recurred since the Middle Ages (Watling Street, Tower Street, Eastcheap, if not going the other side of the river through Southwark), into more recently built Regency and then Victorian London until I reached my comfortable house in a secluded street north of Hyde Park. During this journey, my accent and my bearing changed from the string of expletives, larded with a few English words, to all English words, joined together into sentences. I didn't belong in the East End. Although Wally did, I felt guilty leaving him alone every night, and had to resist the temptation to offer him a bed in my house. Not only was he alone on the ship, but the ship was alone, very alone, in a dying area of dockland, a long walk to the perimeter walls, whose gates were heavily locked and barred from the outside sometime in the evening.

I never enquired how he managed to get out to see Madge, whether he had a hole in the wall, or if Madge spent the night on board.

In the morning, I returned, sometimes on the late side, because I frequently had to go shopping for Wally. As he pointed out early on, it was very expensive for me to keep him hanging around because I had failed to secure supplies. So I made absolutely sure there was never a dearth, although it led me into activities which shocked me.

Wire was no problem. I simply went round to British Ropes, such a huge concern that I was surprised it would deal with me, and ordered wire so fat and unyielding I found it hard to see how it could be formed round a metal thimble into an eye. Wally had by this time built three rough wooden scaffolds over the emplacement positions of the three masts. He would stand all day on the top of a scaffold splicing the wire.

I also hired a couple of Jehovah's Witnesses to do the painting, not because of their religious faith but because I thought they could do the work. I became irked at how much I needed to fend off their approaches, which flip-flopped between admiring my height (I was wearing some Danish clogs with wooden soles) and plying me with tracts. Regretting the trade-off, I ensured that paint supplies became unreliable, so they left.

In fact, supplies became my life for a while. Each time I did the arithmetic to establish a shopping list, I came up with something unbelievable. The idea of cutting three trees in the forest for our masts had been a surprise. Then I learned what a board-foot is and calculated how much good wood I would need for furniture and fittings, new deck aft and so forth. The numbers indicated I was looking for another tree, this time a mahogany tree, which I found somewhere in the East End. It was nearly 20 feet long, and the top of it was level with my waist. I bought it, bark, bugs and all. But the most pressing problem after Wally arrived was to keep him supplied with materials for rigging the masts, his job while I shaped the trees and built in the wooden parts, crosstrees and so forth.

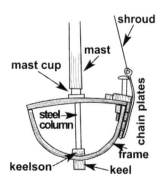

Buy your shackles first, then build the ship around them, was a rule I began to discern.

So I began by listing the shackles we would need, and, of course, the rigging screws and the thimbles. They had to fit into each other, and fit the wire (we had three different sizes) but most important they had to fit onto the chain plates which had been made in Denmark and were attached to the hull at suitable intervals. Chain plates are maybe three or four feet long pieces of three-quarter inch steel some four inches wide furnished with an eye at one end to which the rigging is attached. They are bolted to the hull through the frames. With masts stepped on deck, in what I called egg cups, we were putting a much bigger load on these chain plates than we would have done to support masts penetrating the deck and resting on the keel in the usual manner. What these technical terms mean is unimportant: the message to me at the time was that I could not get by on odds and ends. I needed to have sets, standard pieces each designed for the other. The starting kit numbered 156 such pieces, and that was just for the standing rigging. The running rigging (the stuff you pulled to maneuver the sails) was a whole separate area. I didn't know exactly what I wanted for that, but it certainly included a lot of blocks and more shackles, apart from the rope, which I could buy later on.

I was beginning to realize the implications of the commercial traffic getting larger and moving down river. One was the dearth of commercial ship chandlers. The only one I knew was now trading up from its muckier past into the yacht-chandling business. Just to get Wally going cleaned it out of what remained of its heavier galvanized items.

And there was another problem looming.

In those days, cash was the medium of exchange. A checkbook wasn't much use unless you were already a regular customer. It was long before self service or plastic money, so I took it for granted that I would have to do my shopping with wads of pound notes stuck in my pockets. Most shops had counters which separated the customer from the shop assistant, but sometimes the customer was privileged enough to be asked around the back to make sure the right item was chosen. This applied particularly to shops which relied on extensive inventory such as plumbing supply houses, and ship chandlers. So, visiting the inventory, selecting what was wanted, and then paying for it was done in the company of the shop assistant who, in those days, usually had some specialist knowledge of what he was selling. It became a sort of social effort on both sides, something you did together.

Paper trails are nowadays generated automatically, but in those days, since cash was what you paid with, the making out of the bill — by hand — was an important and sometimes almost sociable operation. When it came to adding up the items to get a total, although it was the shop assistant who did the work, the customer felt involved enough to check, upside down, that the right totals were arrived at.

Accordingly, if the total wasn't quite right, it was something you could talk about with your shop assistant whom you knew quite well by this time.

In this, my first major shopping expedition, the total definitely didn't feel right. It was way too low. And, in addition, there seemed to be a certain urgency about completing the transaction which unaccountably was not accompanied by a bill. In fact, I would say we fled with my purchases, threw them into my van, and I found myself handing over a round sum of cash, no shillings and pence — between my legs as I was inside the van, back turned, sorting things out.

The assistant vanished. I drove back to Wally.

Once back at the docks, I unloaded the stuff. Everything I had asked for was there. Wally came down from his scaffold to see what I was doing. When I told him how much I had paid, I felt a change in the way he looked at me. It seemed a little apprehensive, distancing himself from me. Misunderstanding the look, I explained that I had cleaned them out. I didn't know where else to go for what he needed.

Coubro & Scrutton, he said without adding much more information, and went back to working on the rigging.

About a week went by, during which the first desperate rush of keeping Wally supplied with materials died down a little and I was able to start my part of the mast bargain — shaping the trees which we had offloaded onto the quayside. But Wally was a fast and assiduous worker. He wanted to get the three masts up as quickly as possible with the minimum of temporary rigging so that the heavy permanent rigging could be fitted onto masts already in place rather than calculated in advance as he had to do for the first three temporary bits of wire which would hold them up.

The first mast was stepped less than two weeks after Wally had started work. Although *Gray* was a small ship as commercial vessels go, I had never been involved in an operation of this scale. To step the masts, we needed a crane, ordered by Wally, who didn't trust me to order it myself. It stopped a considerable distance from the quayside. I was desperately anxious to be ready before Wally, and paid little further attention to it, just accepted that it was there.

Slowly, the driver unloaded the trusses from the back of his crane and laid them on the quayside in front of him, each time making the journey into his cab to back off a truss length, so that the trusses were in a long line in front of him. At that point, I began to realize that this wasn't just a crane. It was a CRANE. It was vast.

Having got the pieces in line ahead, the driver began to pin them together. From my distance it was difficult to get the operation into scale until I noted the struggle this brawny man was having merely to maneuver the securing pins into position to connect the trusses. Each pin was about the size of his forearm.

The mobile base of the crane itself must have had eight wheels. Four hydraulic steel hands were flattened onto the ground to lift it bodily into the air, its nose still tethered down way out ahead. The wires on the top of the crane came taught, the driver got out to inspect them for kinks, got back in and began lifting the neck of this animal up into the air. It seemed impossible, but in a few minutes it was transformed from a stupid old chicken tethered to the ground into a praying mantis ready to mate.

The crane imposed an unavoidable discipline. We had to be ready on time. It was not just the wasted money of sending the crane away unused. It was the humiliation of saying to Wally, to the crane driver, and above all to myself that I couldn't fulfill my part of the bargain, that my work on the masts wouldn't be finished. I was haunted by the knowledge that what I avoided today I would have to face tomorrow. I felt like the tortured martyr wishing to be back when he was merely being *shown* the instruments of torture.

The lift went surprisingly smoothly — and quickly. From having been prone on the ground, in a matter of minutes the mast towered above us, flexing slightly as it hung in the air. It now had to be lowered into a steel socket bolted to the deck. Would it fit?

Eight years before, my mother had flown me to New York to see the Broadway opening of one of her plays. I fell in love with the producer's (unattainable) daughter, offered her fish for lunch — which she refused — ate it myself, and suffered acute gastric poisoning in the fifth row of the stalls that evening. My saviors were the tubby cloakroom ladies, sitting around between intervals with their stockings rolled down to their ankles, their black skirts pulled up to their waists, ventilating their groins. It was a very hot evening. To make themselves decent enough to search for gift wrapped salt to enable me to vomit myself back to a fit state for the First Night party, they rolled their stockings back up their legs. Sick as I was, I noticed how there was always a bulge of fleshy varicose vein above the tight roll of the top of the stocking which had to be poked in, captured, prevented from sagging out like the potbelly of a beer drinker.

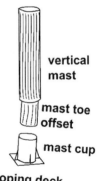

vertical mast

mast toe offset

mast cup

sloping deck

The crane wire holding the mast went slack: the toe refused to slide fully into its steel socket. There was a ripple of wood, a varicose vein, a ring of fat, which bulged out from the close fit I had given the toe. I chiseled it away. The ladies had tucked it in; the only difference.

Wally commented that I was doing him out of a job: I didn't need a Gentleman Rigger. The fit I had made was so perfect that the mast just squeezed in and stood there without support. It became a matter of pride for me to achieve the same fit with the next two masts— so perfect that later it nearly cost me my ship when one of the masts was blown overboard taking with it the egg cup and a large section of deck to which it had been bolted. The irony was that my design objective was a loose fit (to allow a mast to go by the board without dragging a lot of other stuff with it) but I had been unable to stop myself making a tight fit.

The euphoria of stepping the first mast didn't last. Wally was shoving me along to get the two remaining masts ready, which we did in the next three weeks. This time, we had a masting party, and Cecilia came along. Someone filmed it. Maybe we had champagne. The atmosphere was quite different from the private conspiracy that the three of us— Wally, the crane, and myself— had had for the first mast. I found myself being social. It cut me off from Wally. I introduced him to people, including, of course, Cecilia. One wife to another?

Wally had wanted to erect the first mast as fast as possible, with the minimum staying, and therefore with the minimum ironmongery. My first shopping expedition had coped with that. Thereafter he knew exactly what ironmongery he wanted me to buy, drew up a long list and sent me off again.

I had cleaned out the first of the two suppliers, and therefore went to the second, Coubro & Scrutton, who had been rigging the coasting trade forever.

Whereas the first supplier had a somewhat Ye Olde look like a brass and mahogany tavern, Coubro's was strictly businesslike. Steel weighs heavy. Whenever you go into a scrap yard, or a steel stockholder, or a ship chandler of this type, you are at once aware that there is plenty of spare space on the shelves. Try to move a handful of rigging screws and you soon realize that it's one at a time, and you need the space to get yourself on top of the load. You don't just lift it at arm's length like a hair brush. Not at Coubro's, you didn't.

I had my list from Wally. I felt intimidated. Somehow I didn't go to the counter — there didn't seem to be a counter. I approached a man whose attitude to the wire he was slowly coiling showed how unyielding it was. He was massive, with an unbending, impassive, unfriendly face. He was not about to sell me anything. Like a Maine lobsterman, no attempt at good marketing. Just solid worth, salt of the sea.

I began on the list. For me, it was a large order. I felt nervous that I might not have enough cash on me to pay, that it would be too heavy for the Volkswagen van, or that I was asking for the wrong things... I was really asking not for the technical details of money, weight, availability and so forth, but for some nice friendly man to put his arm round me and tell me not to worry and that it would all be all right.

This was not that man. He quoted me a price for the lot — Two Hundred, adding Three ways, and then Cash.

The first time through I understood the "two hundred" to mean £200, but not the rest. Here was this man who knew his trade so well he could add up a long list in his head, add the tax, and tell me: "Two hundred." I stood in awe.

I said I didn't have enough cash on me for that. He told me to come back with it after lunch, kept my list, and went on coiling his wire. As an afterthought, he enquired whether my van was side load or back load. I told him it was side load. When I returned I should back into the alley next his warehouse. They would load it, he said, and I could check it later, when I had returned to the docks.

Dismissed, I climbed into the van, started to drive off to the bank, changed my mind, and went back to Wally. Ostensibly, I wanted to get his view of the price, but I didn't want to admit to him that the nature of the transaction somehow worried me. He said I'd done pretty well to get a price of £200 for all the ironmongery he wanted. But again that odd look as though he was stepping back inside his skin to have a better look at me. He asked me if it would be a rough ride; did I want him to come with me? Without waiting for my answer, he reversed himself. With his background, it wouldn't be good; I could cope on my own.

It was the support I had wanted, not the approval of the £200 I had mentioned.

I went to the bank, presented a check and asked for the cash. The teller handed it to me in large denomination notes. I counted them in front of him. Then I handed one of them back to him, asking for change — in old notes, I added, redundantly explaining that new notes stuck together. Another look, like Wally's. The teller observed there was a big demand for used oncers round these parts as he handed me a bunch of old one pound notes.

I thought rapidly, hesitated, handed him back two of them. Could he give me some coins, I asked. Shillings, florins, or half crowns, he asked. I was at the end of my mental arithmetic and said shillings would do. A lot of shillings, he observed, took a roll, broke it open and counted out the change.

They can sort it out themselves, I thought. Why should I give exact change? This is an ordinary sort of transaction, I said to myself. Once in the car: What was I doing? Just helping them out? Yes, that's it. I'm just paying for some goods I want.

I drove back to Coubro's. As I was about to back in, a good-looking man in his 40s passed me on foot to go into the shed I was heading for. He had a collar and tie on. I noted with disquiet that I took a long time, much longer than usual, to roll a cigarette, and then had to spend a considerable amount of unaccustomed effort to get it lit up, delaying things while the man was inside. I sat and puffed, busying myself with the cigarette. At last the man came out, smiled politely to me, went on his way. I backed in until the door of my van was level with the back of the shed. I could see no one. A man I hadn't noticed opened the door of the van. While two others began to heave heavy hessian sacks into the back, he came to the driving seat, put his hand through the window. "The money," he said. I saw such a forearm as could have plucked me out of the window and thrown me over the roof. I handed him the notes. Staring straight at me, without looking at them, he folded them, and stuffed them in his pocket. I handed over a fist full of coins. Again without looking, he crammed them in his pocket.

It'd better be the right amount, he said, adding that he had friends. I didn't ask for a receipt. The side door slammed. The arm withdrew. I drove out without looking right or left. On arrival back at the quayside, the gear shift no longer had a handle: I had crushed it in a fist which mirrored what was going on in my mind. The pieces were on the floor.

Wally and I loaded the sacks on board *Gray*. Shielded from view by the bulwarks nearest the quayside, we began to unpack them, sorting the pieces of steel into categories. This time, I was having even more trouble pretending to myself that I did not know what had happened, that I had just paid some cash for some goods I wanted, that I didn't do it for a living. Wally went on sorting the goods. I straightened up. We didn't speak for a while. Then Wally said I'd be a first offender, but things would be different for him. With his record, he'd go back inside for what I had done.

He picked up one of the heavier thimbles, and took it to his scaffold where he started wrapping the unyielding wire round it. I went back to my mast, and tried to work on it. He was on board. I was working on the quayside. Between us the water. Silence for the rest of the afternoon.

I could see Wally was packing up. He wanted to be paid. I went to get the cash while he got down from his scaffold. I began to count the notes out into his hand. Would he be coming back the next day, I asked. Yes, he said, adding he'd thought about it, and decided I couldn't have done anything else. Then he left for the night.

In minor ways, however, the same sort of thing kept on happening, while I remained in the East End. I would ask for an item, pay for it in cash, get no receipt, and go away. As time went on, I got to know the retail prices from the old labels occasionally still attached to the ironmongery. There was no proof that the goods were actually stolen, but it began to look as though I was unable to make a straight purchase anywhere in the East End. It was the same with services. There were some small welding shops around where I got work done. I would walk along the quays looking for one of these shops and approach a knot of men standing idle, chatting and smoking. Language was at first a considerable barrier, but I gradually got the hang of the way they spoke, and could make myself understood more easily. I also got to know the specialties of the different shops. But it was always apparent that these shops were merely the service modules for much larger businesses, like the gasworks. They weren't in the retail trade. They could only do work for me on the side.

My next-door neighbor in London was a top criminal barrister. I decided to consult him. After explaining the law to me, he asked if the goods I bought were stacked. Usually, I answered. What sort of discount did I get, he asked. About two-thirds, I answered, and to make the discount clearer I added it meant I paid only about a third of what I thought might be the usual retail price, although it was very hard to say as the goods I wanted weren't generally sold, so I couldn't go shopping around for the best price. He said he might be able to defend me at half price for abandoned goods, but not a two-thirds discount for stacked goods.

So gradually my suppliers got to know that I would only buy stuff which had been kicked around in the yard and that I usually gave them more money than they asked for.

To the end of my time in the docks, I felt extremely uncomfortable, never knowing what the rights and wrongs were. Eventually, I got to know Ken, one of my suppliers, well enough to explain my misgivings to him. Ken had always appeared to me better spoken and better educated than the rest.

He explained that the trade that used to support them had gone down the river to Tilbury, so there was practically no work for those firms which remained. They didn't remain because they were too stupid to understand what had happened. They remained because it was too expensive to get rid of their staff owing to government legislation. He had gone to his boss to ask for a raise the other day, and had been refused. His boss had explained that he knew Ken was making money on the side, and that if he gave him a rise he would merely be increasing his firm's redundancy liabilities.

The light dawned. Redundancy payments, geared to terminal salary, stemmed from the growing philosophy in Laborite England that a worker had property rights in his job, and therefore the right of compensation if he lost it. I knew that this liability could become so high that a firm simply could not afford to fire an inefficient employee.

So in all probability, the bosses knew exactly who I was and were doubtless only too thankful that I was meeting part of their payroll costs. This might be a practical, even an unavoidable, position, but I wondered how it would fit into a course in political philosophy, in expediency, means justifying the ends, that sort of thing.

I was glad when, only too soon, we had to move from our cushy, desolate, thieving corner in the Canada Dock.

6

Battle hardening

Towards the end of 1970, it became increasingly clear that we would have to leave the Surrey. While the developers' plans to revitalize this part of London were vague, they had a common starting point: contractors, innovators, financiers and so forth would be unlikely to be interested in Surrey Docks without vacant possession. So to show they meant business, the owners, the Port of London Authority, moved us over into the Greenland Dock, one step nearer the Thames. It was twice the size of Canada Dock and more exposed to the weather. I think it was the bridge clanging shut behind us after we had crossed the main road separating Canada from Greenland Docks that made me realize I had to search for somewhere else to go.

Greenland Dock exited into Limehouse Reach, a little down-river from the Pool of London, which is bordered to the north by Wapping, home to some of the more ancient of the London docks. Originally, goods brought to Wapping were carried in vessels about the size of mine, or smaller, which were laid up against the various stairs, as they were called, alternately to float and sew on the mud (a technical term for drying out on the mud as the tide goes down: If the waterline has thus dropped a foot, the vessel is said to have sewed — rhymes with food — a foot. It is derived from the idea of "sewer" which drains water away from somewhere). Some of these stairs had been equipped with floating pontoons to become piers a little way out in the river so that a vessel alongside could float at all times.

If we had to leave the comfort of the docks and moor in the river, the tides would be a major consideration. At London Bridge, for instance, a really big tide — just after the full or new moon — could have a range of 25 feet (about the height of a modest three storey house), running at up to 4 knots. Just to level peg with such a tidal stream, *Gray* would have to be making way through the water at about three-quarters of its full speed. By contrast, in New London, Connecticut, where we finally wound up, the biggest tidal range was only a couple of feet.

Cecilia and I were wandering about Wapping rather dismally one Sunday afternoon in early 1971. The place was derelict like everywhere else in that part of London. Half-hearted municipal efforts had cleared some green spaces and edged them with concrete. But there was still an atmosphere of wartime devastation and not much of anything went on. That's why we were there, searching for a berth that no one else might have wanted. The warehouses were mostly Victorian, but there was an occasional Regency building. We came across six or eight Regency houses in a terrace on opposite sides of a small basin which gave onto the Thames. The basin would have been just right for *Gray*. Buy one of the adjacent houses and look out on my three-masted schooner, I fantasized.

We inquired of a young man, who invited us into tea in one of these Regency houses. It was clearly a bachelor apartment as there was only one chair in this huge room, two sides of which looked out on the Thames, one set of windows straight across and the other as far as the eye could see upstream to Tower Bridge and beyond. Cecilia sat on the only chair, while he boiled some water in an electric kettle. I was so excited by the room and its situation and the rising hopes of living there, that it was a while before I noticed that the middle of the room was occupied, from end to end, by two rolls of paper, a foot and a bit by some twenty feet long. With nowhere to sit, I had been stretching my legs wide in order to cross and re-cross the rolls. Each bore a graph, one in a red, and the other in a black. There was a timescale along the X-axis of each.

The young man explained that he was a psychiatrist and that he was giving a paper the next day at the Maudsley Hospital. One of the rolls represented the activity of a catatonic schizophrenic, the other the nursing activities as measured by the amount of medication administered. There was some evidence to suggest the nursing activity actually precipitates the next episode of agitation, as well as being the result of an onset of agitation. His paper examined the evidence either way.

For some reason, I said nothing about my former wife, in another hospital, under just this routine. My fantasy of living thereabouts in a beautiful Georgian house overlooking my three masted schooner vanished. We had our tea and left without bothering to ask who owned the little basin.

Forty years later, I couldn't be sure, but I think it must have been Pier Head off Wapping High Street, less than half a mile from St. Katharine's Docks, the heart of the East End tourist trade. Quite a change from living in Cambridge, Massachusetts.

However, we found a nearby vacant pier. It was called Tunnel Pier. The next pier upstream, just below Tower Bridge, was reserved for the police. Unlike in the Surrey, we had to pay dockage: £5 a week. We kept on being reminded by the local residents that the previous occupants of the Pier had been Elizabeth Taylor and Richard Burton. They had paid ten times our rate, apparently because they had a little dog which was not allowed ashore. They also had a red carpet, which no one offered to lay for us.

I quite liked the Pier, although it was less easy to work on, since we were exposed to the wash from passing ships, and the tide often ran strongly, so I was repeatedly anxious whether my warps would hold in a gale. A lee tide in a fresh wind might be just fine when I went home in the evening, but what would happen when the tide turned a-weather late at night? Then there were the urchins who liked to throw stones and smash the windows of the wheel house. I don't think they were malevolent. That was what you did when you were bored: you smashed the windows of an abandoned warehouse; and when you ran out of warehice, you went along to the nearest old boat.

But despite these problems, I was back in live water. During the winter in the closed-in Surrey Docks, it was all too easy to see us degenerating into a houseboat. The peace and quiet had been essential for the delicate operation of stepping the masts, but that over, I could carry on the work despite a little rocking around from time to time.

Wally had gone — he completed the rigging by about Christmas. Heating engineers had installed the plumbing for space heating, wash basins, a shower, but I still had to find and install the fittings. We also had a new stove, fired by diesel rather like an Aga cooker. Though it could usually be got to work eventually, it was to prove a persistent thorn in our sides.

In the spring, we began to take little trips down the Thames, blinding ourselves to the river's ugliness.

In some ways, this was a high point in my career with *Gray*. When I first berthed with her in the Baltic, skipper Larsen had used a small sail on the foremast to counteract *Gray*'s weather helm. Otherwise sails had become a thing of the past. Now I was going to turn the clock back. *Gray* was going to be under sail, unassisted by an engine. I had confidence in the ship at that time, although it evaporated in a hurry when we tried to leave London in early summer 1974, after nearly four years building.

From Tunnel Pier, we got used to the London River, the seaman's name for the Thames. We followed the old barge habit of tiding down a little way — to get fuel, for instance — and then tiding back up again. We visited Gravesend one weekend. It poured with rain. And it blew. Five of the children were on board.

During the Gravesend trip, I began to realize the windage of *Gray*. We had not a stitch of sail, but her hull was so high out of the water — 12 feet odd right in the bows — that the wind really pushed hard on it. We were moored to a buoy. Two strands of a three-inch (the British measure by circumference) polypropylene mooring warp chafed through in about a quarter of an hour. It was the first time I had met the type of situation which, at sea, can only be diverted from disaster if anticipated. In this case, I should have fitted these heavy warps with some kind of anti-chafe device, something I did later as a result. This time we were lucky: We managed to take the strain on other warps. But the problem was so immense —

chafe at a quayside — that eventually each of the six cast-iron hawsepipes was equipped with a chain plate bolted to the deck, attaching a chain strop which went through the hawsepipe and terminated on the outboard side in double rope tails which could be laced around the mooring warp.

We collected our first three sails in June 1971, the year after we had brought *Gray* back to England. The first two were bent on in July, the third at the beginning of August. We had enough sail to point in roughly the right direction. The children had started their summer vacation and were restless.

For me at least, the holidays started when Romily, then 15, and I staggered down the gang plank at Tunnel Pier with two of the largest plastic dustbins we could find. We were doing something together, father and son, for once. The bins contained pork and beef joints in a strong brine solution. *Gray* lay below us — it must have been low water. I leaned back to carry my load in my hands in front of me; it obscured the gangplank treads, I stumbled; so much food nearly lost, six months at a blow, but I recovered. It gave me a thrill to have salt meat on board. It meant autonomy, less dependence on shopping ashore. And it meant history, Nelson's Navy, my great-grand-uncle Tom, who served under Lord Cochrane, founder of the Chilean Navy, and who spent forty years at sea in the Royal Marines. I ate the last piece of pork with Jim Lawrence, the sailmaker, six months later, thinking of Tom.

It was lovely weather. The children were beside themselves with excitement at going sailing again, this time in a three-masted schooner, capable of much greater things than the dearly beloved old barge, which was pretty but dripped and leaked so much.

I felt pressed, and began to forget simple rules like working the tides. I thought I would risk going off that night after dinner and damn the fact that it was low water. It would soon get deeper out in the river.

We had put no more than a few feet between us and the pier when we went hard aground. I had intended to swing out my stern and back into the river, keeping abreast of the pier. But I misjudged the strength of the ebb and allowed us to go downstream enough to strike the shallow ground I knew was ahead of the berth. There was still an hour to low water, and I could imagine the police on the next pier up the river laughing their heads off at me. I don't suppose they even noticed, but nonetheless I got out the dinghy and started to inspect the hull as it slowly uncovered, pretending that I had gone aground on purpose.

Two days later, I was still learning the differences from *Gipping*: I went aground twice in the day. However, as with the barge, going aground had compensations, even in *Gray*. There's no longer any worry about navigation or hitting something (we've already hit it), and no one needs to be at the wheel. Once aground, we could enjoy a meal all together, something I enjoyed again many times that summer.

There was a further problem with the diesel cooker, which had immediately started to break down. It continued to do this for the next month. There was no redress. It was a custom-built item, bought from a well-known firm, but I couldn't stop the ship while I exchanged angry letters. We never changed it for several reasons, some of which were inherent in being at sea, where there's no corner shop, no postbox, no luxury of delay.

There was a continuing discussion among us about safety. It was obvious that what we were doing was risky. One course would have been to have stopped doing it, and to have spent the children's holidays like any conventional family. But nobody wanted to do that, so the question resolved itself into what procedures were practical, and the consequences of the impractical.

One of the doubts was the extent to which I could turn the ship round in heavy weather to rescue someone overboard without endangering everyone else. In the Elbe, I had thought it would have been impossible without laying the ship on her beam ends.

We had practiced picking up cushions. There was a maneuver called a Williamson turn, invented by an American during the Second World War which consisted of putting the wheel hard over one way until the ship was a given number of degrees off course (how many depended on the ship), and then putting it hard over the other way until you were on the same track, but in the reverse direction. It worked perfectly — but only if we were motoring.

Once alongside the cushion, we could see the real problem was how to raise it (or a body) the six feet vertically to clear the bulwarks at their lowest point.

A scrambling net was a possibility, but would only work with a conscious active body. Parbuckling was the only other stratagem with even a remote chance of success. Ropes (at least two) would have to be made fast inboard, let down into the water, led round the body and up again to people on deck who would then roll the body up the sides. In even remotely heavy weather, the derrick was useless because we had no means of controlling it. Consequently, not only could we not use its considerable power to get a sodden body out of the water but, more critically, we couldn't use it to launch our dinghy in order to get ropes round the body ready for parbuckling or for dragging the body into the dinghy.

Another method might have been to send a swimmer into the water to fix the ropes, but then we would have two people at risk, not one. Besides, a swimmer would really have to be a swimmer, probably in a wet suit, and physically tough. I would have been a good candidate, but it's not wise to lose your skipper.

For this reason, we obliged ourselves to wear harnesses whenever our feet were off the deck, and at all times in heavy weather. Harnesses had two clips spaced along a lanyard so that you could shift one clip while remaining attached to something solid with the other when you wanted to move around. I wasn't supposed to leave the deck at all, but I often had to.

We therefore never wore life jackets (life preservers) — why float if you can't be rescued? This is what one of Conrad's retired lighthouse keepers thought: it's against the Will of God to swim. When your time's come, it's come. A harness is much easier to wear, eat in, sleep in, go to the toilet in, than a life jacket, so a harness was more likely to be worn.

No. Once over the rail, fine or foul, that was likely to be the end. Hence, the harnesses. The children understood all this.

For our summer vacation, we had decided to leave the shelter of our East Coast nursery school, where we could tide around among the sandbanks from one little hole to the next little hole. We would venture round the corner to Newhaven, the start of the big wide world. I had been brought up a few miles away, at Rottingdean, and I liked the port.

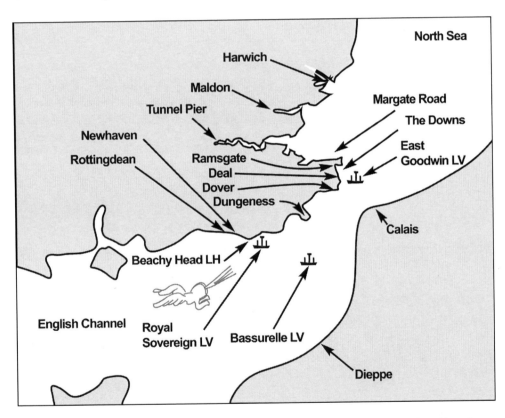

For sailing ships, trading from London to America, there was always an essential problem: how do you turn the corner when the prevailing west wind that will blow you out of London is exactly the wrong wind to sail you down the English Channel? The answer was to wait for a favorable wind by anchoring in Margate Road, or The Downs, often for weeks on end and often in company with several hundred other ships waiting to go one way or the other. Depths in The Downs were around 12 fathoms which would have been a struggle for us with chain on our anchors, but in the age of sail, ships usually had rope which was not so heavy to haul up. The Downs is protected by the offshore Goodwin Sands (East Goodwin LV above). From Tunnel Pier to Calais is about 100 nautical miles. From Ramsgate to Newhaven is 75 nautical miles.

With our three staysails we could proceed, more or less slowly and more or less in the right direction, under sail, given a favorable wind. In unfavorable conditions there was of course the engine. Our first stop round the corner was Ramsgate, and then it would be but a hop and a skip to Newhaven. After that, who knew? Maybe we would just keep on going west.

In Ramsgate, the benign weather we had been having that summer continued. I should have taken the rare easterly that blew on our last day there, but didn't feel the pressing urgency. Who knows what tomorrow will bring?

Tomorrow brought not just a return of the prevailing westerlies but a Channel gale, which decided to beat its way towards us as we pressed into its face in the opposite direction down Channel. We could have waited in Ramsgate, but we had a stout ship, a reliable engine, and anyway, as I was to discover three summers later, waiting for the right wind could be a long drawn-out affair.

So we left.

The first little bit of the journey was south by east. The wind, off the land, was in the northwest, a soldier's wind, abaft the beam. Fine fellows we thought ourselves, too. But as our course veered southerly, and then southwest, the wind backed to the southwest and we had to take down the sails to motor. Ahead, I could see the high cirrus clouds of a wide depression, streaked with the gold of a hazy setting sun.

One by one, the coast towns lit their municipal lights, and slid by fairly rapidly until around midnight. By Dungeness, we would be half way to Newhaven. Wide storms move slowly. Even when the tide turned foul and Dungeness was well behind us, the coastal lights still slid by, slower it is true but by they went. And pitching (as we were) is a good deal more comfortable than rolling. You never know: the storm might have been dissipating.

I had settled down to the slog — uncomfortable, but we would get there. Lights clumped together as towns formed everywhere along the coast. It was impossible to distinguish which town we were passing, and therefore to gauge how far along we were. It would be slow going against a foul tide until daylight, but the loom of the Royal Sovereign Light Vessel was dead ahead, that is, the glow we could see before the light vessel actually appeared in person. We would have to pass it close to. How far ahead I could not tell, and it was not so reassuring also to see the loom of the light on the Bassurelle Bank which was halfway to France.

Someone else took the wheel and I went below.

Cecilia and I slept in the after cabin, not the most comfortable place in the ship. There was a lot of noise from the heavy steel rudder clanking back and forth, and the propeller itself was right below us. Rolling had the same effect throughout the ship, but our cabin was the worst for pitching, being at the end of the ship, which rose and fell several feet every few seconds.

I was shot out of a doze by a tremendous roar under the bunk itself. The ship shook, and then the roar stopped. I lay suspended, waiting for a recurrence, as no one else seemed to be alarmed. Perhaps I had imagined the roar. Sleep wasn't easy. The bunk was rising and falling more than ever.

Then it happened again — a tremendous vibration which shook the entire ship. We were pitching so badly the propeller was coming out of the water. I had heard the same thing in the Esjberg ferry on the way to buy *Gray*, but I thought this sort of thing happened — like cancer or insanity — to someone else, not to me.

You know how something complex can become apparently simple in a feat of intuitive visualization? I realized that the half wave length of the waves must now be comparable to the length of *Gray*, and sufficiently steep to expose her propeller on the downhill side. Quick calculation: might be 20 feet high. (The height of a breaking wave does not exceed one-seventh of its length; our keel was 75 feet long; say, the last five feet out of the water; double that to 140, divide by 7 = 20; problem only ceases if waves are bigger or flatter.)

The consequence chilled me: slowing down would do no good. Alternatively, we could increase the apparent wave length by going diagonally at the waves, whereupon we would roll, perhaps dangerously. Either way I was caught.

So, I tried reducing the engine revolutions. It didn't really help, just as I had thought, but the propeller raced less fast. So I edged her over to port, and the rolling started. Perhaps I should call it what it was: corkscrewing, a most uncomfortable situation, but possibly the best compromise for the time being.

However, it would surely soon be over, as the loom of the Royal Sovereign below the waves had now become a light showing above the waves.

In the early hours of a bad day when shapes begin to be more discernible than they were, any lights you can see are a great comfort. It's hard to gaze at the compass hour after hour and keep it where it should be. Besides, our compass errors had been determined in the Kiel Canal only for a level ship and one heading. I had no notion what the heeling error might be, and the compass needle was dancing around all over the place. This type of error can really set the most careful compass correction to naught. Looking at it from the point of view of the compass, heeling the ship is indistinguishable from swinging a magnetic pendulum beneath the compass: on one side it deflects the compass needle one way and reverses that deflection on the other side. Correcting this error is not easy since it only shows up when you're in trouble.

First the shore lights went out at the appointed time when municipalities considered their responsibility to the public was over for the night. There was too much spray and haze to see the shoreline itself. But there was still the light of the Royal Sovereign dead ahead until, two hours later, that too went out at its appointed hour. We were left in the murk with none but a perilous compass to steer by, abandoned to our fate. It is a dismal time when man's friendly lights have left you, and celestial light has not yet reached you. Neither God nor Mammon to plead to.

I was tired. There was nothing to do. I slept. The Royal Sovereign went past. I didn't see it. Others did. By the time I got up again, Beachy Head was abeam. The wind freshened and the sea increased. I was surprised by how small the light seemed to be, set at the bottom of a towering cliff of white chalk. We had just rounded the headland, and gradually this tiny red-and-white masonry candle slid seaward of the headland.

Then it stopped.
Then it began sliding the other way.
We were losing ground.
The tide had turned foul against us. It had the meager compensation of calming the seas. I went back to bed leaving Cecilia at the wheel. I dreamed we had rear-ended into the Royal Sovereign.

A couple of hours later, I was awakened by a throbbing succession of racing propellers. Up at the wheel, Cecilia shouted down that we had been hit by a squall. I could hear the wheel jerking her around the wheelhouse, the soggy thump of flesh against a bulkhead. Beachy Head disappeared, probably somewhere ahead now, blotted out by the rain and scud. The ship corkscrewed.

I was fed up with waiting, didn't care any longer whether we sank or swam, couldn't bear to wait in these terrible conditions for another two hours for the tide to turn.

I increased the revolutions. The propeller kicked out, but no worse than before, just as I had calculated. Between squalls, Beachy Head light came out from behind the cliff, stood still against the background, and then slowly started creeping towards our beam.

I knew Newhaven must be ahead, not far. For half the distance, we could probably get glimpses of the cliffs, but for the last bit the chart showed the coast receded and lowered. We might not be able to see it. By the time we were level with Newhaven, the tide would be running heavily in our favor, and would kick up a tremendous sea, punching to weather as we were. I did not fancy the prudent course of keeping out to sea until Newhaven was abeam, risking that maelstrom beam-on as we followed the deep-water ferry route at right angles to the shore. We might overshoot Newhaven for one thing, and for another it would take longer to go round two sides of a triangle.

We should go direct, keep the seas on our nose, and get into the lee of the Newhaven mole that much the sooner. But the direct route lay over some shallow patches, just before the entrance to Newhaven harbor.

As we picked up speed over the ground, so the apparent weather became worse and worse. We began shipping serious seas. Some of them were sufficiently high that, even in the wheelhouse, normally 12 feet above the water, I couldn't see over them. That figured with the occasional 20 foot waves I had calculated. Cecilia, who is smaller than I am, was now being hurled around by the wheel, so I took it and she went below, feeling seasick. No more navigation. But you can't function seasick, any more than you can walk around with a broken leg. It's not a question of will power. Romily came up from the hold. He had been feeling seasick in his hammock which had hit the underdeck several times, he said. Then he went back to the hold.

Thomas followed him out of the deckhouse door. Victoria wasn't anywhere around.

Thomas, calf deep in water in the fathom-long waist between the aft-facing deckhouse door and the quarterdeck step, took off his thick glasses, and started to polish off the spray. Under the shelter of the deckhouse, he was reasonably safe. He had neither harness nor life jacket. He gazed round the deck rather absently, and saw that the plastic Minisail, a little sailing dinghy we carried on board, was coming adrift from its mooring on the side of the deckhouse. I could see that he was letting go some of its lashings so that he could re-do them and keep the Minisail from going overboard. He was working on the weather side. A huge green sea came stalking over the three-foot-high bulwarks and soaked him. We rolled heavily to weather again and another green sea came on board. Our rail went under this time. We must have been 35° over. The loose Minisail lashing was nearly free.

I watched him. I was safe, relatively speaking. If he were swept over by the next green sea, it would be my decision not to turn round.

I didn't call Cecilia. Too much noise anyway.

Between seas, Thomas took a heave on the lashing, then a turn, then sweated it up, stole the slack, sweated again, belayed it, wiped his spectacles with care... And went back into the deckhouse. He was 16 at the time.

This 200 ton ship was no longer behaving like a ship but like a dinghy. We must be over the shallow patches—the waves were being tripped up. I was no longer able to steer as such because the pressure of the water was too great on the rudder. But I was able to feel for a slack in the weight, steal some slack, and then prevent the wheel from turning back. As far as I could, I luffed up to the bigger seas, and then payed off to keep the way on us, then luffed up again and payed off. Dinghy fashion.

...Cecilia couldn't have done this anyway, even if I had called her up. She would merely be hurled around by the wheel again.

...or, would she? Was I merely justifying my failure to call her up when Thomas was on deck without a harness?

Something seemed to be ahead of us in the murk. Not sure what. Stand on grimly. Little by little, it got more solid. Stand on? Into danger? A glance at the compass. It was swinging, but seemed to be in the right place.

No reason to change course; no reason not to; terror to stand on.

It was the mole, but not what you might have expected of the mole. It was a giant mound of tumbling water. Calm water in its lee? Does calm water still exist? Yes, calmer, but not calm.

We belted into Newhaven unable to stop. An official with a loud hailer ran alongside us as fast as he could, rapidly losing ground, and yelling at us where to moor up.

Victoria came on deck. She had been sitting on the chemical toilet for the last several hours to prevent it from upsetting while her whole world crashed around her. Lid down? No, up: to make a more secure connection. Inside the hold, oily bilge water had shot through the listings (the gap in the lining left for servicing the hull from the inside) and onto the bunks and food. Somehow a box of nails got into the brine crock, which still had its lid on. Some oranges bobbed around in the bilge water by the keel.

...Thomas ...Williamson turn ...Thomas ...harness ...Williamson ...harness ...Thomas ...W —

...Out, damned spot. Out, I say.

Later, we heard the low crump of the maroons being fired to call out the lifeboat. Some other poor sod.

The Newhaven Watch had recorded a steady Force 7 (28 to 33 knots, a moderate gale), with gusts up to Force 9 (41 to 47 knots—up to 54 miles an hour—a strong gale).

7

From pillar to post

The weather remained lousy; the children waited for it to change; they gave up, went back to school; whereupon the weather changed to fabulous.

It stayed that way for the month of September.

There was a gridiron in Newhaven. I decided to sit on it.

A gridiron is one of the cheaper ways of getting to the bottom of a ship. It consists of a stationary platform which dries out around half tide, the exact point being a compromise: the lower, the deeper the draft of vessel able to get on; the higher, the longer it remains dried out, but the vessels able to use it have to be smaller. The trouble is that the ship floats free of the gridiron twice a day and has to be tended back onto it each time the tide goes down; has to be listed against the dolphins at the inner side of the quay — too much, and the weight damages the ship's rail; too little, and you fall outwards causing dreadful damage. Furthermore, nothing dries out, so there isn't time for any serious repairing or painting. And, the keel lends itself to the blocks which means twice a day the ship is bent out of shape. It results in doors not shutting and the triatics (the wire between the tops of the masts) going slack. It also strains the ship no end. At the time, I was unaware of all this.

This is the other sort of dolphin.

Apart from seeing *Gray* exhibited on a railway in Denmark, this method of getting to the bottom was all I knew about. It was exactly the same principle as the blocks used for the barges, only the barges needed no dolphins to lean against, since their bottoms were flat. We had used the blocks over a weekend for *Gipping*, but they did not form a serious part of our lives, and when other barges used them it was with an implication of terminal sickness. Now I think about it, the reluctance to work on the bottom of a barge must have stemmed more from the terrible conditions crawling around in the mud than from any judgment on the condition of the hull. At that time, I didn't think too much about the bottom of a ship.

Cecilia helped me on to the gridiron, and then left me to myself while she put the children back to school. It was a leisurely two and a half weeks: The ship was only dried out on the gridiron for about four hours a day, which meant that every day I was getting up later and later to work as the tides moved on, until the wrenching day when I had to back up a tide, and start very early in the morning. At that point, I felt like a good muscular Christian back in my office routine full of self-righteousness; redeemed once again from the sluggardly habit of sleeping later and later in the morning. My mother came over from Rottingdean to visit me. So did my sister. But most of the time I was alone.

It was fine autumn weather, no one was bothering me, I enjoyed casual conversations with the port employees, and above all I was relieved to be at rest for the first time since leaving the Surrey. The five months on Tunnel Pier had not been restful. However, the gridiron was a complete waste of time and money. I didn't dare do anything serious to the bottom of the ship, either because of the short working day, or because I simply knew too little to dare make a hole in the hull. Nor did I appreciate that all the paying (what handymen call caulking) had come out because the ship was working, that is, the planks were sliding over each other when the ship changed shape in a seaway, thus spitting out the caulking. So the time I spent re-paying the hull was pointless. I should have caulked it first to prevent the planks from sliding over each other. (Caulking is the name shipwrights use for the oakum forced into the joints between planks protected by the paying on top). Not only pointless, but when the bitumen paying all fell out again, it left the old caulking (a vegetable product) exposed to the worms, who found it delectable.

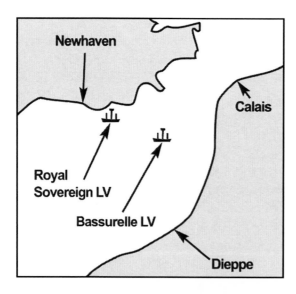

Newhaven to Dieppe (direct) is 65 nautical miles.

I had two of the most romantic sails I can ever remember before returning to winter quarters, which we thought could be up one of the East Coast rivers. I swung off the grid alone using the tide to float me across the river facing in the opposite direction. I was enormously pleased with myself, and fascinated by the quiet with which 200 tons of wood could be moved so gently around. The maneuver raised a small cheer from some of the dock workers.

Cecilia joined me and we decided to sail to Dieppe irrespective of how long it took us to get there. We had the three first staysails, which pulled us along at no great rate but were enough to stop us rolling. We were also able to use them to self-steer. This was a complete change from the time when the two of us had brought the ship from Denmark, shuddering from the engine, rolling like a pig, and steering every inch of the way.

I had always thought of the Channel as something you crossed. It was normally jam-packed with vessels doing just that, if they weren't going up and down. Nobody seemed to want to stick around. This time, I learned that outside the established routes, thick with traffic, there was really nothing much doing. We spent most of the first day going only vaguely in the right direction, and were completely lost by the evening, no one in sight. So we did the old-fashioned thing, we hove to, took a sun sight, and then crossed it with a moon sight an hour later, filling up the time in between with chat, food, a drink, altogether very amiable.

The two sights showed we were well out of the shipping lanes, so why not have a good night's rest? Which is exactly what we did—both of us, neither on watch. The next morning, we were sitting in the deckhouse having breakfast sailing along slowly all by ourselves. A storm cloud darkened our plates, alerted us to return to our duties, gaze through the porthole...

...at a big tanker, right alongside us, stopped in the water, as the crew took pictures. We were too ashamed to go out on deck.

About mid-afternoon the next day, we decided we really ought to make Dieppe by nightfall, so we gave up this leisurely existence for the crashing thump of the engine, found the French coast, asked for directions from a French trawler, and then smelled our way into Dieppe. The Dieppois were having dinner, and well out to sea the mixture of garlic and wine was unmistakable. We went to a restaurant that night.

You get to Dieppe through a narrow crack in the cliffs, round a hidden bend and from there reach the Avant Port in which nobody tarries because of the huge range of the tide—and the ressac we were to learn about later. (The words ressac or scend are the words in French and in English which we—and everyone else except the dictionaries—used to describe horizontal movement of water with virtually no vertical movement, typical of swell waves created by distant storms, that is, a very long wavelength). At low water, our provisions had to be lowered to the deck on a gantline whose block, at the hounds (30 feet off the deck), was little above the quayside. Tending the mooring warps was a constant preoccupation so at high tide you go through a lock into an inner tideless basin. There were never fewer than a dozen people on the quayside gazing at us, and the crowd swelled to about 50 when we went through the lock gates. Part of the interest may have been due to the small crew—just Cecilia and me.

This was when I learned my weakness as a master, a weakness I never managed fully to conquer during the whole of the time I had *Gray*. I can't shout, I have a low voice, nobody ever believes I'm in command. In those early days, indeed, of course I wasn't in full command. A couple of fishermen must have sensed this, came on board, and took over the ship to get her into the tideless Bassin du Canada. Having been brought up to be polite to strangers, I didn't dare tell them to mind their own business. Instead, I thanked them for their help. *Gray* was several times bigger than their own fishing boats, but with an engine a quarter the size of theirs. So they presented themselves to the quay at an awkward angle and then handed *Gray* back to me to have the honor of finally coming alongside. I didn't make a good fist of it and moored up rather heavily.

As time went on, I began to understand the full extent of the dangers of being unable to be seen as a commander. In all other respects, I eventually became very good at my job, but I could never persuade nervous passengers, and helpers on the quayside, not to feel responsible for mooring up.

Later on, when I was better at it, I would gather those on board who were going to pass the warps and chalk a picture on the deck of what was going to happen, whether we were going to back in (my favorite, which was so unusual a maneuver it threw everyone into a panic), whether we needed to launch the dinghy and use it as a radio-controlled pushman, or whether we would go in bows first.

I virtually never did this operation without the engine, partly because we would have the engine going anyway to get into the port area, and partly because we could do so much damage if I made a mistake. Besides, we were never insured.

Backing in was the easiest, a maneuver I learned later in La Coruña. I could see how far we were from the quayside, and I could usually control the person with the stern warp. But even that was difficult. They longed to throw the thing (which was very heavy), and it always fell short. This they would do despite me spelling out very slowly and distinctly that it was my responsibility, not theirs, to get the ship close enough to the quayside so they could hand (not throw) the warp to someone on the quay. If I made a mistake, I would try again, I tried to reassure them. I used to have nylon warps all round, but nylon sinks, and a nylon stern warp accidentally dropped in the water means that the screw has to be stopped at the most crucial moment for the warp to be fished out of the water. So I changed the stern warp to something which floated, a nuisance because synthetic materials which float usually chafe more easily.

The behavior of the people on the quay was sometimes uncontrollable. If I were going in bows first, Cecilia handled the warps forward. In the early days, she would ask someone to walk her warp aft. With monotonous regularity, they would take the warp in the opposite direction, forward. If there were a wind off the quay, this left me incapable of controlling the ship. So Cecilia and I decided that if ever I docked bows first, she would hand some light bit of nothing to the person on the quay, and tell him to go anywhere she thought easiest. Then, with a satisfied helper on her hands, she could usually get him to take the vital spring warp aft. This made mooring more predictable, though slower (one of the reasons I preferred backing in).

This visit to Dieppe was to stand us in good stead later on. At some point, it was going to be necessary to haul *Gray* out of the water at least to clean the bottom, if not for repairs. On the English side of the Channel, Sheerness, Chatham and of course London were shown as having dry dock facilities, but the Belgian and French coasts seemed to be dotted with them — Ostend, Dunkirk, Calais, Boulogne, Dieppe, Le Havre, Cherbourg. No one in England had urged us to use an English dry dock, possibly because they were now into steel ships. So we took a brief look at the Dieppe floating dock.

A large proportion of the Dieppe fishing fleet was in the same size league although smaller and made of wood. They used the floating dock routinely. Essentially, it's a big floating steel platform with high sides, open at both ends. Imagine a piece of paper folded in three as for a business letter and then opened up into the shape of a "U." That's approximately the shape of a floating dock, except that the bottom and the sides are hollow. The air in them provides sufficient buoyancy so that the dock will normally float high enough out of the water so that the platform is high and dry — no water sloshing in from the open ends.

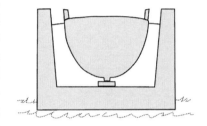

If you start letting water into this hollow enclosed space, the platform slowly sinks until the surrounding water starts coming into the open ends. As more and more water is let in to the hollow enclosed space, the dock sinks deeper: The hollow platform is now full of water, and the only buoyancy remaining comes from the pockets of air left in the sides. This air is allowed to escape until the platform gets deep enough sunk for a fishing vessel to float in. After the vessel is secured to the sides, water is pumped out of the hollow spaces in the dock, the dock rises until it starts to take the weight of the vessel, and goes on rising until the platform is clear of the water.

An elegantly simple solution it would seem, but inherent in the whole operation is that top and sides of the dock must not communicate with each other. If they do, so long as there is an internal free surface, water will collect on one side giving the dock what is called an angle of loll as it is pumped dry. Floating docks tend to be large in relationship to their loads and are therefore reserved for modest sized ships.

From a language point of view, I found the term "dry dock" more loosely used, even to include floating docks, but the term "graving dock" I found to be reserved for the hole in the shore with lockgates to let the water and ships in and out.

The second lovely sail was our return to Harwich, and on up to Butterman's Bay, just downstream of Pin Mill. It must have been a record — for slowness (an average of 2½ knots). But I could easily have stayed at sea a great deal longer I enjoyed it so much. Of course it was the wind, which kept shifting in our favor each time we had to make a wiggle in our course.

One of the reasons we took so long over the journey was the discovery that *Gray* really could self-steer with its sails. I wasn't about to give up a minute finding out as much as I could about why and under what conditions the ship could do this. For 15 ensuing years, every time we put to sea, the tyranny of the wheel forced us to have more people on board than we really needed, rendered us less mobile, and obliged at least one person to be absent during meals, except when I could make the ship self-steer on the sails alone. It was ironic that when I finally built a self-steering arrangement which actually worked — that is, I took a couple of short calm journeys with no one but myself on board — it was really too late. The ship was becoming pointless with my family gone, and me too old.

Anyway, I didn't then know that this early ability to self-steer under sails was largely luck. It was so enthralling that we followed the wind's moves whenever we could, gazing out at the moonlit sea holding our breath at the incredible fact that this huge lump of wood and flax could take us home without human help. She became like a living creature, a tame obedient creature, but with a will of her own all the same.

Most of the time, the weather was clear and bright, the moon full, but for about an hour or so between the Inner Gabbard and Harwich the sea looked grey and unpleasant with bursts of sand churned up by the tide ripping across the shallow sandbanks.

Even when the wind started to head us, and we had to heave to off the south Inner Gabbard, waiting for the tide, so we could weather the Galloper Bank, it was a challenge we enjoyed. To this day, these coastal names thrill me — the Cork, the Sunk, the Gabbard, the Galloper, the Platters, Biscay, Finisterre, Sole, Shannon, Fastnet, Rockall, Malin, Bailey, Hebrides, Faeroes, Fair Isle, Viking, Cromarty, Forties, Dogger, Fisher, German Bight... Poetry such as this need not be understood, although it is in fact a jumble of real weather forecast areas and real sandbanks.

When I stepped ashore at Pin Mill, intending to lay the ship up for the winter, it was to spend my first night on land for more than two months. I felt generally pleased with the summer. We had survived our first severe weather with a house-keeping mess but no worse. I erroneously thought we could develop self-steering on the sails to be the norm, and just use the engine for dock maneuvers. Imperceptibly, I was coming to identify my life with the ship, although I had absolutely no plans to live aboard permanently, or even semi-permanently. One way or the other, I had come a long way since Denmark, had become more expert, but I was still a long way from being in charge. I took it for granted that it was Cecilia's job to decide where we would go next.

Quite suddenly, just before Christmas 1971, this leadership was brutally withdrawn.

At the end of the summer, our intention had been to leave *Gray* on the Admiralty buoys on the Orwell just downstream from Pin Mill. We had left her there before with no problems. Pleasure craft on the whole didn't like them: they were too big and too out of the way from Pin Mill itself. *Gray* wasn't leaking, and I had no intention of returning to the London River.

However, around the end of November, I noticed some heavy-duty service barges and a wreck-lifting vessel moored to what I now considered to be our own personal buoys. I tried not to notice when they began lifting the immensely heavy and dirty mooring chains for inspection. They worked their way down the trot of buoys towards us. Finally, the commander, a navy man, visited me to tell me we had no right to be there. They were Admiralty moorings. Besides, they needed to have them all clear for inspection.

We had nowhere to go. It was well past the sailing season.

We shifted to the other trot (there were two parallel lines of buoys) to let the wreck-lifting vessel work around us. Then they plodded away to find more filthy buoys to lever out of the muddy bed. I was beginning to hope that all would be forgotten when a surveyor from the Ipswich Dock Commission came on board to give us notice to quit immediately. I knew the Navy was not only within its legal rights, but the buoys were part of the Navy's emergency arrangements, and had to be kept free for emergency use. But I didn't know what else to do. The river was used for commercial navigation and was too narrow for us merely to slip our moorings and anchor nearby.

One night at the beginning of December I was waiting for Cecilia, who was driving down from London. The routine was that she would flash a lamp from the muddy shore, the signal for me to pick her up. The motor barge *Silver* had junked up with me. She was an owner-operated commercial vessel, but work was slack in the winter, and *Silver*'s skipper had had the same message from the Ipswich Dock Commission when he was on buoys in another part of the river.

I waited and waited. I ran out of things to talk about with *Silver*'s skipper. Then I decided to go ashore before the tide got so low I would be incapable of meeting Cecilia anyway. By the time the Butt and Oyster closed I was extremely anxious. They had some sort of uninformative message that Cecilia had been delayed, but no one could make out exactly why. I started calling the police and located her in a nearby hospital. When I got there a taxi ride later, I almost stumbled over her being wheeled on a gurney from one room to another. She looked quite cheerful and said she had had a car accident. Sorry about the car, she said. It was probably totaled, but she had a dislocated hip into the bargain, and wouldn't be back to help me for a few days.

It didn't ring true. She was almost fainting with pain. I found the doctor who had looked at her. He had the comforting lilt of an Indian or Pakistani when he echoed my word "dislocated." No, he explained, the hip has not been dislocated, not at all, he said, adding that the head of the femur had been driven right through the acetabulum [the hip socket] and that it was "rubble in there, just rubble."

It was clear her injuries were beyond the scope of the hospital. By chance, Cecilia knew the name of an orthopedist in London. She went there, alone, two days after her accident while I was frantically trying to get *Gray*'s ground tackle to work so that we could get off the Admiralty buoys.

The London surgeon took his time. It was evident he wanted to get it right. CAT scan was new in those days. He took several 3-D pictures with it, and then sliced right up into the waist and far down into the leg. Some months later, when she could stand, the children were happy for a talking point to guests ("Would you like to see my mother's zip?").

The fact that the operation took place on the eve of the Christmas holidays made the inaction thereafter even more oppressive. She was in traction — I learned a lot about traction and why it was done. One of the lessons was that it was slow. The leg had to be kept in extension while the muscles round the knitting bones wanted to shorten themselves. How long would the knitting take? Some months, was the answer. In traction all the time? Yes. Where? Here, in the hospital, they supposed.

This seemed to be a nutty idea and, despite insurance, very expensive. I cross-examined the nurses, and then tried it on with the surgeon. On being pressed, they agreed that the only specialist help Cecilia needed was the traction machine — and good nursing, of course, but that wasn't critical, it turned out. Why couldn't I build a traction machine? I wanted to know. It didn't look complicated. Oh, no, they said. I pressed. Well, they supposed it might be possible, but expensive. Not a fraction of the cost of keeping her in hospital, I said.

So with at first grudging and then increasing support from the hospital, I drove to somewhere in the Midlands to take delivery of a traction bed, complete with weights and pulleys. I installed it in the drawing room, where Cecilia was then moved. Total cost? The equivalent of a few days' stay in the hospital even with the cost of a resident nurse. Cecilia was out of action for five months which, instead of being spent in a lonely hospital, was spent with masses of children and friends to look after and amuse her. At some point, a formidable Sister Wellbeloved came to take the traction pin out of the bone just above the knee. She conducted the maneuver as though she were lecturing her usual classroom of several hundred students instead of just the children. Thereafter, the traction was applied to the flesh and with decreasing strength.

The operation on Cecilia's hip took place on 16 December 1971, when I spent nearly two weeks in London. Thereafter, until the middle of April, six days was the most time I spent anywhere consecutively.

The Admiralty was correct. They wanted to have their buoys in case of emergency — that is, a national emergency, not just for me getting into a mess. I could understand that.

So I moved off the buoys to a rather narrow anchorage downstream from Pin

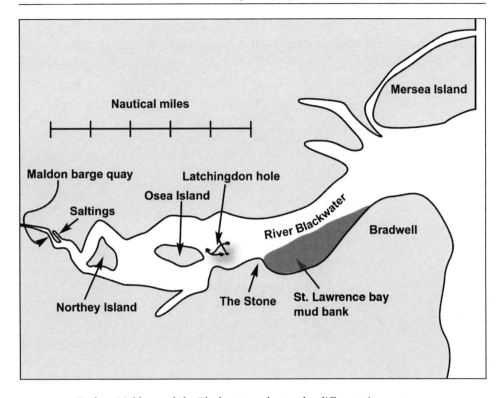

Back to Maldon and the Blackwater — but under different circumstances.

Mill. There was very little traffic in the Orwell at that time of the year, but you could depend upon it: Someone complained.

I moved again. By this time, it was late January 1972, not a month for pleasure crafting. With the help of the sailmaker, Jim Lawrence, I went down the Orwell and round the corner into the Blackwater up to Osea Island on the way up river to Maldon, the other sailing barge capital.

My first anchorage, on the Maldon side of Osea Island, was liable to dry out on mud but was reasonably sheltered by its shallowness from the fetch of an easterly gale up the wide estuary. Two brothers were accustomed to dredging for oysters thereabouts. The weather was so unappealing that the only two boats in the river were mine and theirs. Within two days of my arrival, I was told they had complained I was on their oyster bed. Another fisherman in Maldon told me this was public ground. The chart seemed to corroborate him, for it was a very large area of shallow water to be owned by one fishing smack. One of the brothers told me to go to Latchingdon Hole. And then I was threatened with fines by Maldon officials if I did not leave. Meanwhile, the fishing smack started dredging as close as possible to me, running over my ground tackle and one way or another reminding me with abuse of their vital interests in the mud right under my keel. The weather was foul. I had difficulty in finding crew.

It was not until early March that I could move to Latchingdon Hole, and then I was immediately marooned on board for three days by an easterly gale sweeping up the river full on to the new anchorage, which was in deeper, more exposed, water.

Although I could usually get someone to help me shift berth I was alone a great deal of the time. My recollection is of work constantly interrupted by gales shooting up the estuary, gazing at the enemy fishing smack through drizzly poor visibility, hauling the dinghy on board when it was too rough to leave it afloat, sailing around at anchor, lifting my mooring tackle periodically by floating it up on the tide underneath my dinghy, strengthened for the purpose with a strong-back. The anchors were always dragging—except in New England Maine mud, it was a worry right through to the end—even with two and sometimes three anchors down. Two of the stockless anchors weighed 3 cwt and 4 cwt, and a big fisherman which came up to my neck weighed about 6 cwt. The chains were the heavy items. We had four shackles (a shackle is 15 fathoms, or 90 feet) on each side totaling about 47 cwt.

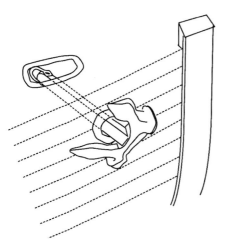

Our two stockless anchors regularly jammed in their hawsepipes, and regularly dragged.

That is, we could put three tons of steel on the ground and still drag.

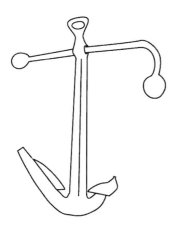

Our fisherman down, we usually didn't go anywhere, but to get it down in a blow was dangerous hard work. On a pitching and rolling deck, it had to be lifted three foot up on a derrick to get it over the rail.

• A hundredweight or cwt is 112 pounds—that's why it's called a hundred, of course—and 20 of them go to a ton, by which I mean a good solid English ton of 2,240 pounds, not one of those mingy American things of 2,000 pounds, rightly called "short." And not of course one of those register tons of 100 cu ft used to measure how much wine a ship's hold could carry.

This is what Wikipedia has to say about anchors:

The Admiralty Pattern, "A.P.," or simply "Admiralty," and also known as "Fisherman," is the most familiar among non-sailors. It consists of a central shank with a ring or shackle for attaching the rode. At one end of the shank there are two arms, carrying the flukes, while the stock is mounted to the other end, at ninety degrees to the arms. When the anchor lands on the bottom, it will generally fall over with the arms parallel to the seabed. As a strain comes onto the rode, the stock will dig into the bottom, canting the anchor until one of the flukes catches and digs into the bottom. Developed in the late 19th century, stockless anchors represented the first significant departure in anchor design in centuries. Though their holding power to weight ratio is significantly lower than admiralty pattern anchors, their ease of handling and stowage aboard large ships led to almost universal adoption. In contrast to the elaborate stowage procedures for earlier anchors, stockless anchors are simply hauled up until they rest with the shank inside the hawsepipes, and the flukes against the hull (or inside a recess in the hull).

When the weather permitted, I went ashore once a day to call Cecilia. The nearest civilization was at The Stone, essentially no more than a shingle beach, overlooked by a desolate pub, about a mile away on the far side of the river. On a calm day, I could skim there in about three minutes, but it could take a wet quarter of an hour or even 20 minutes in heavy weather.

One time, I was marooned on *Gray* for six days by the weather. By that time, Cecilia had recovered enough to take a vacation in Rhodes, so there was no one for me to call when the wind abated and I could launch the dinghy again. I might have listened to the radio perhaps, but it's not my style, so I spent the time without uttering a word or hearing a human sound. Except once. In the middle. Without noticing its approach, early in the morning, a sailing barge was abeam. Silence. Outward bound on the ebb, sails well filled, a single figure at the wheel. The skipper (Tommy Baker—I was still in awe of him) hailed me. I tried to hail back, but the words would not come. Instead, an ill-defined croak. I cleared my throat, tried to start again. By this time, the barge was a silhouette. Some eddies in the water were all that was left of this meeting.

I had another few days of silence before going back to London.

In April and May, I spent longer periods in London because I needed to do some blacksmith work.

I set up a portable forge, an anvil and welding equipment in our back garden, and had a lovely time making believe that I was back in the era just before the Second World War, when there were enough horses in Rottingdean to justify a blacksmith. Then, being small, I could only just see over the edge of his forge, a large brick affair spread with pockets of smoldering coals. The blacksmith allowed me to work the bellows which fed the forge, but the handle lifted me off the ground—it must have had a counterweight. He said I was blowing straight: I had to learn how to blow crooked. I was deeply impressed and promised myself to learn how to blow a forge crooked when I grew up.

Where pain was concerned, Cecilia was always hard to read. Over the 21 years we lived together, I eventually learned this lesson, but in the early days I didn't always recognize her courage for what it was since I didn't know the underlying pain she had to surmount. All I saw, after the car accident, was a woman who cooperated with the innovation of leaving the security of the hospital for some traction arrangement to be built by me; who was perfectly happy to have Sister Wellbeloved remove her pin as a public demonstration; who appeared to start to do things for herself sooner than she was really able; and who, at the end of May, said she felt well enough to come on board.

During her convalescence, I had had to fend for myself, not in the security of winter quarters, but out in the open river, hounded from pillar to post. Neither of us had had an easy winter, although my problems paled into insignificance beside hers. Would she ever walk again was a far more serious fear than: Will *Gray* sink?

That May 1972, after six months of reverse after reverse, at last there seemed to be light at the end of the tunnel. We might get to sail that summer after all. Cecilia said she was better. I took her statement at face value.

I had been toughened by months of winter hardship in the open Blackwater estuary, and drove my equipment to its limit. I was no longer the paunchy, sweating figure who had first sailed *Gipping*. I was in my early 40s, an age when men have lost the ability to sprint but have reached the peak years of endurance. I was definitely tough.

I had got wet as usual on my way ashore to meet her. It was blowing across the river this time, southwest, rough by *Gray* but at The Stone, a mile downstream of *Gray*, where I berthed the dinghy on the beach, it was completely calm, sheltered by the land from the wind.

My landing place was a small beach, an isolated patch of shingle, rare in those parts, where it was mostly mud. On the shore at one end there was the public house with the telephone, the object of my trips ashore during the previous months. I had no car because I used to go by train to Maldon, five miles up the river. Then, I would get into the dinghy for the last bit down river. In good conditions, it only took a quarter of an hour, and much of the way it was sheltered. The road leading inland from the landing spot was therefore unknown to me. It terminated right where I was standing waiting for Cecilia. The pub was there beside me gazing down the river. Over the months, it had become completely identified with the calls to Cecilia. I used to have some beer there, it is true, but it was partly to delay the moment of telephoning. After all, before putting the call through, I could live in the expectation that I would reach her. Once the call had been started, I might have to suffer the disappointment of a busy line.

I didn't quite know what to expect. Emma was driving. Cecilia got out. The car was stuffed with stores. I would make two trips: Take Cecilia and then come back to fetch Emma and the stores.

So on the beach with Cecilia, I hauled the dinghy into the water, Cecilia already aboard, and, without breaking the momentum, steamed off at full throttle. As I expected, the seas got steeper and we began to slam. Cecilia was on the thwart ahead of me. She squealed with pain and anger. I dropped the dinghy off the crest of a wave dead in the next trough, no power, appalled at what I had done. I had a vision of her hip coming apart again. She thought I had done it on purpose. Of course not but — and here was the troublesome bit — while Cecilia had cooperated in being treated like the object of an experiment (hyperbaric oxygen and the traction bed) I had come to believe in her as almost invulnerable. Hence, the first seasickness in the Minsener Rinne and the fact I could actually hurt her came as a great and unpleasant surprise to me.

Emma brought Cecilia's elbow crutch as part of the stores on the second trip. Cecilia could get around the deckhouse virtually unaided, but the truth of the crutch she needed on deck showed how far she still had to go. They stayed for two days. It was still another month before Cecilia could come and go, and a further month before she could stand in the water, knee deep, directing the re-provisioning of the ship at anchor offshore, and shaking her crutch at me for my failure to have the ship ready to sail on time. Didn't I have a date in my head? Didn't I realize the six children were about to start their summer vacation?

While I had been very good at producing a few smart solutions, I had never crept inside the mind of a mother with many children who has been so badly damaged that it might jeopardize her role as a matriarch. This was the crucial difference between the two accidents, since the finger could never have threatened her role as a mother, while the hip might. If she failed the children, she had no reason to believe that I could, or even would if I could, take up the slack.

I ran a resource: The ship, and it wasn't serving its purpose. I hadn't been known to cuddle children.

8

Who says France faces west?

During the first six months of 1972, I made 18 visits to *Gray*, spending a total of 15 weeks on board. On three of the visits I had a friend to help me shift berth. And of course there was the short visit from Cecilia and Emma. Otherwise, I was very much on my own. There was a little transistor radio on board, but I didn't bother it much. My anxiety to get ashore was limited to calling Cecilia. There was no shore life to speak of.

While realizing that circumstances were forcing me to be penned in closer and closer to *Gray*, I had thought that we might spend a reasonably quiet construction winter on the Admiralty buoys near Pin Mill, but the Admiralty thought otherwise. Cecilia's accident had had the effect of making me realize that the buck stopped with me from now on.

One consequence was that my point of view began to shift: instead of looking at *Gray* from the shore I started to look at the shore from *Gray*. I asked myself questions I might not otherwise have asked myself.

One of them was: Did I observe the right time? I concluded that I did not.

As the days got longer, I was increasingly waking after daybreak, thus losing the daylight at the beginning of the day. At the other end of the day I had to go through the messy business of lighting oil lamps, and spending depressing hours in the darkness waiting for bedtime. This seemed idiotic. It was all the fault of the way I had been brought up. Certain clock times trigger certain rituals (for instance, meals and shaving).

So, the obvious solution was to alter the clocks on board.

I tried putting my clock an hour ahead for a day or two. It wasn't sufficient. Another hour, and then another, until I was three hours ahead of winter time, or, later, two hours ahead of summer time. To begin with I was getting up in the dark, but quite quickly, in those northern latitudes (the whole of continental America is further south), the day was becoming so long that I could get up and go to bed in daylight.

One of the smaller cabins with two bunks is shown on the left. You will notice Cecilia's quilts. On the right is a detail of the bookcase and shelves to the left of the entrance doors to the main cabin. Oil lamps could be hung in the oval spaces in the middle of the fluted columns, but we rarely did so, as we had electrical lighting.

Why on earth didn't the whole world follow suit, I wondered (and still wonder). As far as my life on the ship was concerned, it was an end to those messy, if beautiful, oil lamps. And it was the beginning of seeing the shore life wake up around me, the first birds stirring, an animal on the prowl, a peace later to be destroyed by those wretched other animals in their motor boats. By that time, I would be thinking about lunch, having put away a decent morning's work.

When the time came for the children's summer holidays, I had been alone so much that every fault on the ship stood to attention when it saw me. The entire familiar faulty landscape would be upset by six children. They would want food (how would I get it on board?), water (was there enough of it? would they waste it?), and worst of all something to do. They might even want to go ashore, and then they'd have to take my plastic dinghy with the huge engine. Or, worse, they might want to stay on board.

No, I thought, that won't do at all. They can take my other little lobstering dinghy with its little engine. It didn't plane, and would be far safer.

Lucy, 12, and Victoria, now 14, were the first to come with Cecilia, and quickly knuckled under to this regime. Besides, being helpful girls they spent a lot of time helping their mother prepare for the other children.

But when the boys arrived they immediately resented having to take my little plyboard dinghy to cover the mile to shore, particularly when they saw my speedboat moored off *Gray* doing nothing the entire day.

So, bit by bit, I had to give ground. I agreed they could take the speed boat provided they didn't plane, forgetting the fact that the boat was designed to go fast or slow, but nothing in between. However, they agreed until I saw that the returning loaded speedboat was so manifestly unsafe waddling around in the waves that I had to give in on that, too.

One night, I was woken up at one in the morning by the children obviously planing, having been to the pub. I was furious the next day at them coming back in the small hours of the morning at dangerously high speeds. "Small hours of the morning?" they queried. Pubs close at 11 P.M. they pointed out—I had better stop that silly time I kept and get real.

Of course, they were quite wrong about the time being silly. But, I was forced to compromise on only one hour ahead.

In other ways, I was obliged to enlarge the zoom lens of my life which had for months been stopped down to the weather, my work in hand, the mudworms, seagulls, and Cecilia, possibly in that order of relevance. We had to set sail. And how did you do that? You scrubbed the bottom first. And who did you do it with? You did it with the children, of course.

There are several ways of getting at a ship's bottom. The most immediate is to dive in full diving gear (what is called SCUBA diving or diving with a self contained underwater breathing apparatus—the air tanks divers carry on their backs delivered to a sort of teat in the mouth). Disaster can be averted, but it is hard to do a great deal of useful work. I was to learn to dive later, impelled by necessity rather than zeal, another of the competences imposed by owning a ship this size.

You can do more work if the ship is allowed to dry out on the mud (that is, sewing on the mud) or on a gridiron (as at Newhaven). Although it can be done afloat, a ship is normally careened when high and dry, the word careen being derived from the Latin carina, a keel. To careen is to lay the ship over on its side in order to get down to the keel on the exposed side. This used to be done by laying an anchor out on one side, and then heaving down the topmasts, but it can also happen inadvertently when the ship merely falls over, as it did two years later. Barges could sew, but they could not be careened since they were flat bottomed. While quite complicated repairs can be effected, essentially the ship has to be rendered watertight every tide.

Finally, the most satisfactory (and expensive) method is to take the ship right out of the water. It can be hauled out of the water on an inclined carriage running on a railway, or it can be floated into a dock, the gates closed, and the dock pumped dry, or it can be lifted by a floating dock. Part of the expense with all three methods is that the ship idles sophisticated machinery while the repairs are being made. To get over this problem, there are travel lifts which lift a small vessel out of the water and leave it on a spare bit of land, thus liberating themselves for another vessel. Unfortunately, the travel lift was not suitable for *Gray*, partly because of her 200 ton weight and partly because she was already sufficiently old and weak to need to be supported at fairly close intervals along her straight keel. The usual travel lift might have two or three slings; *Gray* needed support at least every six feet along her 75 foot keel — that is, about a dozen supports.

Gray had been on the Newhaven gridiron the year before, but I was so inexperienced I did not realize I should at least have painted the bottom with an antifouling paint (a paint which slowly leaches poisonous chemicals, often based on copper, into the water). Almost a year had gone by and the marine growth on *Gray*'s bottom was now formidable. It would slow us up considerably. St. Lawrence Bay just down river from The Stone was a large sheet of mud at low water, but we drew too much to get onto it. And the edges shelved steeply enough to make it difficult for us to go aground near the edge, except in the best conditions. There was nowhere else handy. Plenty of other drying mud banks existed but mostly the mud was too soft for walking around.

The moment I decided we should try to sew on the edge of the St. Lawrence Bay mud, the wind turned easterly, blowing up the river. We would have to go aground on a choppy weather tide since the estuary was open to the east. Going aground on a weather ebb (that is, when the water is ebbing into the wind) is never easy. Apart from the choppy conditions, the ship starts sailing around at anchor, sometimes casting off to port and then to starboard. Under bad conditions, it is not at all difficult to sail so far up on the anchor as to sit on it. Even under moderately good conditions, it is impossible to sit on a precise piece of mud of just the right consistency, previously located, patted, petted, smoothed, and generally loved up. I made several attempts before achieving a good stable position.

A good grounding in sunny weather can be great fun. It starts on the first contact with the bottom. Great anxiety. Are we straight? At the right depth? Will the mud be firm enough? Too soft? Will we fall over? Once firmly held at the keel, but still supported by the water, the ship often starts to teeter, rather like many tiny rolls, until more weight is taken by the ground and less by the water. I always disliked teetering. Then an hour or so with nothing to do but wait, get the buckets, scrubbers and scrapers prepared, and wait again. Finally, you can see the mud through a layer of water. And then the excitement of seeing how the ladder will hold in it.

Under ideal conditions for a scrub, there will still be an inch or so of water which can be used for rinsing off. Even without that, the scraping can be muddy fun, followed by frantic scrubbing as the tide returns to provide rinsing water. One by one, we are forced up the ladder by the tide until maybe one or two of us swim round the ship to finish the scrubbing.

It is one of the few jobs afloat that requires little skill and can involve everyone. So, that's how we started the summer holidays.

In the days of sail, leaving the east-facing Thames to go down Channel was always difficult for it involves a turn of 180° into the prevailing westerlies. From the Thames Estuary a course can be shaped direct to the north Foreland but, from where we were—near Maldon and further north—the long Gunfleet Sand prevented us from going direct. In the good old days with *Gipping*, we could have threaded our way through a little gap in this sandbank called The Spitway, but no longer in *Gray*.

Insofar as we had a plan for that summer, it was to go round the corner again, that is, to sail eastwards, then turn south round the north Foreland, and instead of

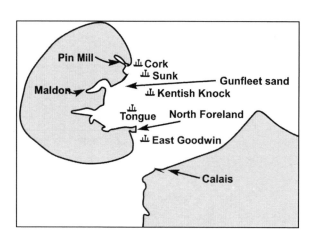

keeping close to the English shore, thereby risking fighting the westerlies (as we had done going to Newhaven the previous year), we would keep on south and reach the French coast somewhere like Calais.

I could hardly wait to test further *Gray*'s ability to self-steer under sail. If that could really happen, our autonomy at sea would be limited by our provisions and not by fatigue, since the ship was large enough and comfortable enough, despite the lack of proper cabins, for us to get a good night's rest. In addition, a sailing ship pressed by the wind was likely to roll a good deal less than if she were motoring. All in all, the promise was terrific.

By the time we sailed, the wind promptly turned westerly. It would have been all right if it had remained north of west, but instead it backed to the south, slap in our path to Calais by the time we reached the Kentish Knock, the outer limit of East Coast sandbanks after which we could pay a little less attention to exactly where we were. It wasn't blowing badly, just blowing enough so that we could not make progress against it.

We were a good ten miles from the traffic lanes to Germany, so there was little risk of bumping into anyone. I hove to (that is, backed the sails) for the night. With her long straight keel, *Gray* lay quietly. We might make a little progress, or we might lose a little, but what did it matter? We could all have a good night's rest, and start off again in the morning. Maybe this was the strategy to follow in the future.

We had a comfortable night. Then it began to blow harder and get rougher. The strategy might have an undesirable flip side: Heaving to and waiting for a better wind might also mean not getting out of the way of a worse wind. I was not anxious to repeat our experience off Beachy Head the year before. I decided to turn back.

Seasickness was worse than usual. I expect this was due to the sandbanks. But we certainly started to roll. Victoria was in the cabin aft, and said the auxiliary compass hit the stops on its gimbals several times. Afterwards, I measured the stops—it meant we had rolled at least 50 degrees over. Romily, in his hammock in the hold, hit the deck beams three times. It was to happen to him again.

Instead of the quick little sail to Calais, we reached Pin Mill in the early hours of the morning two days after starting out from downstream of Maldon. We had gone north instead of south. In some ways, the worst discovery was the extent of the mess in the hold. Once again, oily bilge water had slopped up through the listings, ruining a lot of stores. This kind of mess every time we were in a seaway would render the ship virtually unusable except in fine weather, which was not at all what I had intended.

Furthermore, the cooker broke down again.

We rigged a seventh sail (one of the three outer jibs), and a week later tried again. This time, poor visibility meant that there was little wind so that again we had to run the engine as well as navigate by radio beacons so as not to risk slopping around losing position and perhaps creeping into some dangerous area.

We had a couple of fishermen from Maldon on board with us, and I suppose I was showing off. I went to bed the second day, giving the helmsman the appropriate course and saying that I would get up when we closed the shore near Dieppe (what wind there was made it possible to aim much farther down the French coast, but we began to learn the depressing lesson that to sail the seas you have to have a good engine—*il faut un bon moteur, pour naviguer à voile*). I must have been out of my mind to close the land in thick weather with no one but a helmsman around, but it worked. I got out of bed, ambled sleepily onto the bridge, said all too nonchalantly, "Ah, there's the French coast"—and tried to stop my fingers trembling with the anxiety of knowing how reckless I had been. Never again, I swore to myself. But, like an addict, I did it again many times.

On that part of the coast, the tidal range (that is, from the bottom to the top of two succeeding tides) can exceed 20 feet. Although, Dieppe harbor is well protected, it develops a dangerous ressac or scend in a stiff northwest breeze and certain tidal stream conditions. And the scend can develop suddenly. On the second day of our visit, towards the top of the tide, we were sitting on the rail with oysters and wine, gossiping to the sightseers milling around the cobbled quayside. There was a commotion on a fishing boat two or three down along the quayside. There'd been a collision. But with what? Then I realized: the crews were piling into their boats and getting off the quayside to avoid getting their gunwales smashed by the scend, which had started without warning. We were a good deal slower and suffered some minor damage before following the others into the mêlée of fishing boats backing and filling in the Avant Port waiting for the lock gates to open, so that we could dock in the inner harbor out of reach of the tides.

> • Originally, to turn a sailing vessel round to the opposite tack, you had to *back* the headsails to help it turn through the position in which the wind was dead ahead. You then *filled* the sails on the other tack. If the maneuver failed with the wind dead ahead, you would start making stern-boards and would be said to be in irons. You then had the opportunity of wearing ship, which meant passing your stern through the eye of the wind instead of your bows (which refused to go). We used both methods in *Gray* which often ended up in irons.

We hadn't any particular plans for a long stay in Dieppe — that was to come later — so we lifted (a technical term for loading provisions) a ton of water, and 100 liters of wine, changed our propane cylinders (used as insurance for the cooker breaking down), walked and biked in the rain to a nearby town, got bored, and left Dieppe for Cherbourg, where we got bored again.

I always thought of France as a country facing west, the vanguard of Europe opposing the great Atlantic. Except for the Mediterranean, it doesn't have an east coast. Or, does it? Somehow, I don't know how, we discovered that a tiny piece of Atlantic France not only faced east, but even southeast. We must have been pretty sure of our quarry, because Cecilia and I left one day on the Lambretta I kept on deck to have a look at a port called St. Vaast-la-Hougue, about 30 miles from Cherbourg on the other side of the Cotentin peninsula. It was at the west end of the stretch of coastline where the Normandy invasion took place.

We arrived around low water: No port to be seen, until we realized that it had

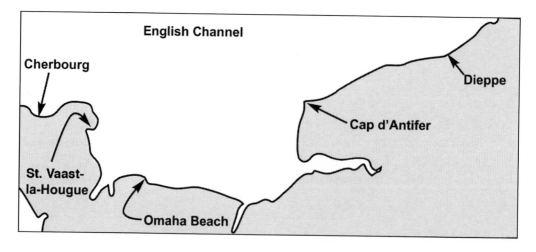

dried out. There were a few fishing boats propped up against the jetties, no yachts, some old women in black, not much else but a gloomy harbor master.

I explained to him we were in Cherbourg and would like to come for a short visit. Where could we go? The harbormaster pointed to a patch of mud. By this time, I was a real expert on mud. I knew the squashy stuff so soft you just sank in, the stuff which looked like mud but turned out to have damaging rocks under the surface. I knew how to shove an oar in and listen to the plop as it came out.

I had never seen better mud.

It was firm enough to walk on, but an oar could be plunged in several feet. I spent the rest of the time there removing the odd stone, measuring up, and generally admiring my mud. We would lean on the jetty and the view looked magnificent.

The harbormaster gazed at me. Said nothing. I talked plans with Cecilia — which way round, how long afloat, when we would start, that sort of thing. We went to say goodbye to the curmudgeon.

Où sont vos béquilles? he asked. I considered *Gray*, all 200 tons of her, and wondered what size of crutch we would need to take her weight, for that was what he was asking: the small fishing boats I could see were prevented from toppling over by planks — béquilles, the same word as a crutch for an injured foot — lashed vertically to their sides.

I said we didn't have any. Then you can't come here was his response, as though I didn't have the right paperwork. After all the time and trouble and excitement I had spent loving up my mud, the gloomy old fellow was going to prevent us from coming.

I began to explain issues of hydrostatic stability and the way in which the weight of a vessel is transferred from the water to its keel when it grounds out. My French had not acquired the technical vocabulary that was later forced upon me, and it was evident my explanations were carrying no weight. After a bit, there was a clear misunderstanding — some word I used reminded him of the name of a ship.

He wanted to know if we were like her. Since I had never heard of the ship, I began to admit ignorance. Cecilia interrupted me to say, Yes we were very like her. The harbormaster immediately saw the light. Then, in that case, there would be no problem at all, we didn't need a wall though it might be a convenience for going ashore, and as for béquilles? He opened his hands palms upwards.

Gradually, it became apparent that he was reminiscing about World War II. St. Vaast was the first port available to the invading Allies, who went ashore on beaches stretching from there towards Le Havre. Since the port dried out, it was abandoned immediately Cherbourg was available three months later after heavy fighting, and the brief moment of fame for St. Vaast was over.

So, it further appeared that we would be the biggest thing St. Vaast had seen in nearly 30 years. I started to assure him that I would not fall over... Cecilia quickly shut me up, and we left. She found me pretty dumb sometimes: she had herself never heard of the ship, but explained we had better be like her to get permission to come.

We left in rather different frames of mind. Cecilia was quite simply ecstatic at the prospect of being there; I was beginning to heap up all the technical problems which would face me: finding the place, getting in at the right state of the tide, listing the ship, heaving it hard enough against the jetty so we wouldn't fall inwards, and possibly dealing with the unexpected, like the wind in the wrong direction, or a stand in the tide, a bad scend...

Encapsulated into our different worlds by the wind of the scooter, we had consolidated our different positions internally by the time we were back in Cherbourg. I listened glumly as Cecilia spread the good news to the children. I needed my hand held.

This part of the Channel no longer has the comfy mud banks of the East Coast. This is an area of rocks (nonchalantly marked by a small cross on the chart) and fast tidal streams, like the Barfleur Race through which we would have to go. The Admiralty Pilot says that "the sea breaks heavily, especially at springs when the wind is against the stream." We were at springs, the stream in the race was nearly five knots, and the tidal range in the harbor of St. Vaast (which the Pilot says should not be entered without local knowledge) was 19 feet. The Pilot also notes that "fresh winds from between northeast and southeast cause a heavy scend."

While the Channel doesn't normally suffer from the dense advection fogs common in the summer on the North American Atlantic seaboard, visibility can be quite awkward. Because of the off-lying dangers, we would clearly have to stand out to sea, and would be unable to identify landmarks as they slipped by. In clear weather, it is desirable to make a deliberate error in the landfall up tide, so you know which way to turn along the coast to look for your harbor. The previous year, smelling our way into Dieppe, I failed to do this. In fact we had more or less hit Dieppe the first time but didn't recognize it, turned the wrong way and had to ask for directions. But, if the visibility were poor, approaching the land in the wrong place could be hazardous.

I was definitely not the life and soul of the party with such worries circulating in my head.

When we left Cherbourg for St. Vaast-la-Hougue, the wind immediately blew northeasterly, an unheard-of summer wind. In no time flat we were at Barfleur, born along against the wind by a heavy tide. The Pilot was not misleading about the rough water in the race.

Then we ran into the age-old problem: poor visibility and no buoys. Since nobody but small fishing boats had been to St. Vaast since the war, buoyage was not a high priority. The chart marked offshore rocks. So here was my dilemma: aim for the wrong side of our destination and strike a rock; or take the risk of getting it right first time. I think I must have been developing a kind of sea sense which fortunately never left me. I decided to aim for Île Tatihou, which shelters the harbor mouth, and there it was, right there, as though I need never have bothered my mind.

> • Bothering about poor visibility and buoys seen from the present must seem almost quaint. Today (2013), we not only have the GPS, but most likely a real time screen showing the local topography together with way points and such like. All this was beginning to come in when I stepped ashore for the last time in 1987. It transformed navigation. However, I made it a rule always to buy electronics (for instance my LORAN) in pairs so that an equipment failure would involve replacement, not repair, at sea. There wasn't room or money for two radars so we had none. When we did most of our sailing, the only piece of electronics available was the radio direction finder which could give you a very rough idea of the direction of a radio beacon. At the end of an Atlantic crossing that was the only way to identify Antigua, for instance—a single beacon. Apart from this electronic help, try to imagine (if you can) a world in which all navigation was done with reference to what you could touch and feel: mud with a lead, the stars with a sextant, stopped down to only the compass if nothing else were available.

These sturdy night vision binoculars served me for twenty years. They were probably 10 × 50 but the markings have rubbed off. They weighed nearly three pounds, and were about 10" long.

I had worked things out for our passage from Cherbourg with some precision. Owing to the swift tides, we didn't have the luxury of hanging around off shore. I had therefore calculated our departure time from Cherbourg with a pretty exact arrival time in St. Vaast in mind. And that arrival time was not much before the top of the tide, since we had an outer bar to cross, which the harbormaster had told us two days earlier might be too shallow for us. I thought he was wrong, because my own calculations were that the bar would indeed dry a couple of feet (as he had said), but a 19 foot range would give us plenty of water at high tide — maybe more than 15 feet compared to our draft of only 9 feet. Nonetheless, the extent of the divergence between the local expert and me was worrying — perhaps I had missed something significant.

> • The *range* of a tide doesn't tell you much about the height, since you really need to make precise calculations on the *heights* at high and low water which I didn't have. So I had assumed that drying a couple of feet would mean a height of 17 feet (19–2 = 17), knock off a couple feet because I didn't know what kind of tide the harbormaster was talking about and you get 15 feet, still 6 feet of margin of safety.

On arrival, I had to turn the ship round, and I knew I had no time to lose before going aground. I had started a little late, and was trying to do a tricky operation on a falling tide — not to be recommended. With the unexpected northeast wind blowing us onto the quay, turning round was not easy for a start. Then we saw that there were two fishing boats on the wall with the space between them only a little greater than our length. It's possible to go in sideways, but extremely difficult without a tug or something to keep the bow from crashing into the quayside. The Commandant du Port was there to receive us, but didn't seem to realize that we needed something like a bollard or two or a ring bolt to grab hold of not already precluded by the fishing boats. When forced by time and the falling tide to do something, he pointed out nothing our size had been in the harbor during his time and went off to lunch.

We did the best we could, and were in any case pressed up against the quayside by the wind. For a while, I didn't notice the dense crowd of fishermen he had left behind. Maybe it was because they were completely silent, a silence occasionally punctuated by the word "béquilles." I imagine it would have been the biggest excitement any of them had ever had if we had fallen over into the harbor. I sensed the crowd had a substantial hostile minority, probably no more than that or the harbormaster would not have let me come in the first place. But his disappearance meant that he was clearly not going to root for us.

None of them smiled, and none of them offered to help — like giving us a little more room to berth in. They watched.

I had no time to do a public relations job. The ship had to lean against the wall, not too much and not too little, and had to be fendered, again not too much and not too little. The ideal was to list the ship against the wall sufficiently so that when she took the ground she would exert no more force on the quayside than if she had been moored in the ordinary way, tightly enough to squash the fenders a little. If, for example, we were too far out, or too greatly listed, or both, when we took the ground, the ship would fall towards the quayside with sufficient thrust to start breaking things. If there were any sort of a lop in the harbor when we came up again, we could teeter and do ourselves a great deal of damage.

In two feverish hours, we filled everything we could find with water — two dinghies, dustbins, water carriers, the life raft cover — to give ourselves a list of 2½ degrees to starboard (towards the jetty). Why 2½ degrees? Anxiety, I would say — better to crush our bulwarks than to fall off the jetty.

• The harbormaster had been concerned that without béquilles we might fall *outward* into the harbor, but I was also concerned about the damage *Gray* might suffer falling *inwards*. When sitting on her keel, I obviously wanted *Gray*'s center of gravity to be between the keel and the quayside. That could be achieved by putting weight on the deck near the quayside. But, if we grounded out on the mud with a big gap (e.g., through inattention or because our fenders were squashy) between our gunwale and the quayside, *Gray* would lean inwards towards the quay, putting a great deal of force on structures, such as the bulwarks, not designed to take loads of any substantial nature. In Cherbourg I had been doing pretty simplistic calculations just to get an order of magnitude. If we weighed 200 tons, assumed the center of gravity was about halfway vertically between the keel and the bulwarks, and listed the ship 1°, the load on the bulwarks might be 1½ tons if it followed a sine wave, rather than a ton if it were merely proportional to the angle of heel. Each extra ½° would put more than half a ton on the side thrust from the quay; 2½° looked like being 3½ tons, getting right up there.

Two factors stopped the work of listing: we had run out of containers, and we wanted to have lunch.

Cecilia had many times demonstrated the same ability: to be hard at work with everyone else and to have produced a decent meal while no one was watching. So we sat down in the deckhouse galley. We were hot. Someone pushed open the roof hatch to get some ventilation. The tide had already fallen enough for us to look upwards, not sideways through the windows, at the crowd of silent fishermen on the quayside, waiting for us to fall over. We couldn't shut the hatch again. It would have been rude. But it certainly cramped our style to have to eat with those gloomy faces peering in through the hatch. However, there was one good side to it. I was more afraid of public opinion than I was anxious for the ship. If I had made a mistake, I knew there was nothing I could do. I didn't want to be seen by the crowd fussing around on deck, so when I first looked we had already sewed a foot and a half. We hadn't fallen over; we hadn't broken anything.

For a little over a week after that, we had a vacation which justified every moment of hard work on the ship.

We discovered we were news. A stringer from the newspaper *Ouest-France* came to visit us and we duly had an article. This was the first of several which were published about us while in France. They were always on the same lines: the happy family going round the world on a romantic sailboat. I suppose there was nothing much else readers wanted to hear when faced with the picture of the ship which usually accompanied the article. I wasn't thrilled to be a caricature of reality in this way. Oddly, we attracted little newspaper coverage outside France, either in England or later in America.

Several of the days were spent getting to know the food shops, in particular the butcher, who clearly thought Cecilia to be a great catch. As the queues of locals grew longer behind her, the butcher kept her in thrall while he trussed the joint he had cut and trimmed for her so frequently I could barely see meat for string.

He eventually handed over the elaborately tied and wrapped package with, "*Eh bien, madame, la conference est terminée*" (the lecture's over), presumably to reassure the waiting line that he had only a professional interest in Cecilia. I didn't object to the delay. I gazed at the butcher's wife, but I was too timid to talk to her. I also gazed at the butcher's absent middle fingers, the victims perhaps of previous encounters with attractive customers.

One day, without preamble, a bearded young man asked us to come for drinks with his parents. He would fetch us the next day by car. He barely waited for a reply: the invitation seemed to be more of a command than a request. Cecilia and

I were in the second car load to drive to his parents' house. We recognized it. We had walked past it when we arrived and wished that our lives brought us into contact with such people. The father wore the ribbon of the Légion d'Honneur in his lapel, the furniture was lovely, the atmosphere somewhat formal, the whole reception being terminated somewhat abruptly by the older man getting up and saying, "*Eh bien, mes enfants, à table*" (time to eat). The next day, the son, Denis, took the children to the Normandy beaches.

I should have gone, too, but a situation which became all too familiar arose. We were in an easterly squash, that is, pressure was low over Spain (quite normal for the time of year) but high over Ireland (a good deal less normal). Because the two systems revolved in opposite directions, they produced a strong easterly air flow through the gap between them. It produced quite a slop in the east-facing harbor. High water began to become a nightmare, since the ship was being damaged against the quayside. We had fenders, but not enough. A holiday maker went off and fetched us enough old tires so that we could make up six, very heavy, double fenders. It was a horrible job. The tires had steel mesh inside the rubber and were extremely difficult to pierce. The only tool in the least effective was a punch. Romily's job was to attempt to bend the tire a little so that I could get a heavy straight blow at the punch from the inside of the tire. I was worried my heavy mall would miss and I would mangle his hands. Even now, decades later, I sometimes squirm at how my better judgment had been distorted by panic. The tires had to be suspended this way, or the rope would be chafed through quickly if it was merely tied outside.

So I refused to go with Denis to the Normandy beaches because I was afraid for my ship. There was very little I could have done to improve matters, but I couldn't bear not to be there, anguishing, in case of a catastrophe of some kind. It was thus that I was becoming slowly trapped by the ship. Cecilia's attitude was always different under these circumstances. She saw there was nothing further to be done, and went off to the beach to sunbathe instead. It was a beautiful day — but not for me.

St. Vaast was like many small French country resorts–cum–fishing ports, although it seemed more of a tourist resort when I visited it with Romily in July 2008. The port is protected by the Île Tatihou, connected to the mainland by a large area of land which dries out. Way back when we visited in *Gray*, on this land, covered twice daily by the sea, was a well-maintained shellfish conservation system. Every day at low water, women in black came down with donkeys to work and mind their business in the system of streets created through the shellfish fishery. Here was the lost city of Atlantis. Fish crates formed the buildings, laid out like a city grid. The women sorted the shellfish, loaded it into crates, and onto the donkeys... I was amazed by the complexity of what they left behind each tide, each object, cart, tool, cage properly attached to something to prevent it from floating away from this miniature underwater city.

We had not visited the island because it would have meant staying there for the whole of a daytime high-water period, the low waters being morning and evening. They were springs, bigger and rougher than normal. I was not anxious to be a prisoner on the island watching my ship being damaged.

But the day before we left, the easterly squash was breaking up, lessening the danger to the ship. I consented to spend the day away from her. So we walked through the underwater city, shortly before it was flooded by the incoming tide, and spent the day on the island with a picnic, playing games with the children. No one else was there. In fact, for six hours we knew we would be undisturbed, we knew we had to have organized fun, no one could suggest it was time to go home. And, for six hours, the underwater city's gates remained closed to us. We were locked into the fairground, obliged to be happy.

The three girls, Emma, Victoria and Lucy, had had enough of the summer vacation by this time and left by ferry from Cherbourg to be in time for the oyster race in the Blackwater. I was a little disappointed at their attitude to the flesh pots. No sense of loyalty, I thought to myself, off to the next distraction. Romily and William stayed behind with Cecilia and myself to get us back to London, and into the Albert Dock, a former commercial dock like the Surrey which was now being turned over for private use. It was a little downstream of the Surrey.

We would pay for our berth, but not very much. It was sheltered, safe, and I could get on with the conversion. I had been on the move for 18 months. I was looking forward to having a bed on dry land and commuting to work again. I was looking forward to the stability I needed to get the steady work of conversion of the inside well under way by the following summer. I had slipped quietly into thinking *Gray* was my job, at any rate for a while.

After we had docked *Gray* in London's East End, I spent the night between clean sheets at home in Bayswater. The next day, I visited *Gray* and found a considerable amount of water in the bilges.

9

The Royal Albert Dock

As we motored up the dingy London River toward the Albert Dock, I had reflected on what we had so far done—and what I hoped for in the future.

Undoubtedly, the ship had shown it could go from one place to another, and I had shown I could operate it with the help of family. But the key seemed to be whether the ship could self-steer under sail and make some ground to windward. With those two capabilities, all of a sudden the need to go from one place to another on time would diminish. On a yacht, the need for promptness is partly generated by a lack of autonomy both in provisions and in manpower; on a larger ship, this need is propelled by economic considerations. In our case, since our way of life was very cheap and the ship was comparatively large, neither of these two constraints would apply. Provided we could make to windward, even if slowly, without being tyrannized by the need to keep the wheel manned day and night, we could take our time on a passage and enjoy ourselves the while.

This may have been the logic, but the experience of the two previous summers had been mixed. Beachy Head had shown how uncomfortable and tiring the ship could be under motor in a seaway, while in this past summer we had set out for Calais under sail to find that not only had we been beaten back by relatively light winds but that once again the ship had been reduced to a shambles inside. When we had finally reached France, it was, once more, courtesy only of the motor.

On the other hand, there had been a couple of sailing passages when the wind was just right, and these at least had given me a glimpse of what might be.

The last 18 months had been exhausting, constantly on the move, and unable to get down to the business of converting the ship which I knew to be a nine-to-five job in a quiet spot somewhere. Nonetheless, as I neared the lock into the Albert Dock, instead of looking forward to a period of solid construction work, I was regretting that I could not carry out just a few more experiments to see how well the ship could sail. The result might have determined whether to continue with the conversion. I felt depressed. My mood was not improved the next day when I found the unexpected water in the bilges.

The Albert Dock was rough, to be sure, but it was roughness we only heard about, not a roughness we took part in. A reputed mobster, for instance, notorious at the time in a gang murder investigation, arrived one Saturday morning with a stunning companion to buy a cigarette boat for cash — used notes. He took it straight down the Thames, and came back complaining loudly to the dock owner that a police helicopter had followed him all the way, both ways. Didn't give him even the privacy to lay the girl. He dealt in refrigerators. Did I need refrigerators? It turned out his minimum order was a shipload.

Meanwhile, the conversion of *Gray* had really become my solo job. Of course, Cecilia and I talked about it a great deal, but while I went to the docks she went back to running a very full household, entertaining family and friends at least once a week, sometimes on quite a large scale. Sitting down 20 for a meal was a squash, and it usually only happened at holiday times, like Christmas or Easter. But since our own family was eight, only a few guests would bring us up to 12 or 15 for a meal. Cecilia's center of gravity was understandably therefore in our house.

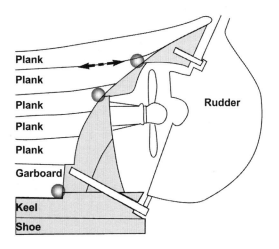

By the time I had organized a young man to help me and had started to take some big bites out of the agenda which lay ahead, Christmas was hull down over the horizon, waiting to interrupt the flow.

My first inkling that there was

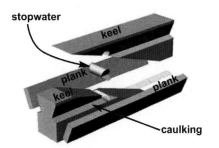

Leaking from somewhere aft overshadowed the whole of my life with Gray. **Top:** *The arrows show where I found the massive leak when we later left the London Docks never to return. But, even after repair, there continued to be sporadic leaking from the area. Where the keel is joined to bow or stern there are massive blocks of wood (shown shaded). To prevent water seeping across their joints, a piece of soft wood, called a stopwater, is driven across the joint at any point where it passes under the ends of the planks. Candidates for stopwaters are shown as shaded balls. The top one was replaced shortly before I left Gray for good. The log does not mention leaking so the repair probably worked.* **Bottom:** *The lower diagram shows an idealized exploded scarf with its stopwater which completes the waterproofing from the caulking.*

anything wrong with my attitude towards Christmas occurred at the very late age of 23 or 24. Instead of having the usual modest Christmas with my small family, I went to stay in Scotland with my wife's large family, probably just after getting married in December 1954. I speculate there might have been upwards of twenty staying under the same roof, for it was a Scottish castle. I had, of course, brought presents for everyone, but I sat in a corner and shed tears for the inadequacy of my response to the growing pile of presents I received.

During those early married years, festivities in our house returned to being modest, owing to my then-wife's worsening illness. Now, with Cecilia, I was plunged back into a crowd. Most of the time I thought it was terrific — except at holidays of obligation (my flippant version was birthdays and Christmas in contrast to the Roman Catholic list which Cecilia's children groaned about).

So... I was surly whenever Christmas was mentioned.

Cecilia accordingly evaporated my Christmas problem. She was going to take the children to Port Meirion, in north Wales, the fantasy Italianate village designed by Clough Williams-Ellis. I could come if I chose. My bluff was called. I followed meekly, still in a latently belligerent and uncooperative mood, made worse by being unable to find anything to complain about.

We lived a kind of pæan, groaning boards, agreeable other guests, ascending to the summit of Christmas Day itself. Cecilia, a Roman Catholic, was going to take everyone to mass. At last I found something I could get my teeth into. I refused to go. It was not that I had anything against the mass itself. I happen to be a lapsed Anglican (né Presbyterian), and I found the bells and smells and sophistry of the true church highly attractive, and a good deal more muscular than the Thirty-Nine Articles. No, I was still smarting at how neatly Cecilia had outmaneuvered me over the Christmas holidays.

The Tory party decided to go to prayer in their Anglican church at the same time as the Catholics. I wandered round the empty streets wondering why the architecture was so pleasing. I hung a beer mug on the end of a string attached to an arch and measured the angle of the support from the vertical. Craning over at one point, I was bumped into by a man on a brisk walk.

He paused expectantly. I explained I was measuring tangents.

He walked on. Later, I found out he was a senior official at the Victoria & Albert Museum.

I noticed that wherever possible in the village a right angle had been avoided, but I also noted that the tangent of the angle from vertical or from horizontal never exceeded 0.3, the tangent of the incline of some steps I liked (ten along and three up, an angle of 16.7°).

What I learned had a profound effect on what I was doing on *Gray*, in particular on the design of the cabin doorways which I wanted to be 15 inches deep to give an impression of massiveness. Before Christmas, I had been thinking of aban-

Above is the main part of the hold, about 45 ft long, which I was converting into sleeping cabins. On the left of this picture is a doorway, showing its depth, but not so much the angling of the two boards making the uprights. The picture at the right shows an overelaborate internal ventilation aperture. It caused family trouble because I dallied on this feature rather than getting the ship ready for sea.

doning this design because of its tunnel-like oppressiveness; after Port Meirion, I designed the door frame like a funnel, still 15 inches deep, but the outer half being angled away from the inner half by an angle whose tangent was 0.3. It worked well but was difficult to make in quantity—there were 10 such uprights.

After Christmas, I settled down to a couple of more months' work. Then the leak I had noticed on arrival in the Albert Dock the previous September began to open up. At first, I tried to disregard it, but I had gotten so used to the idea of a dry ship that this was difficult.

We had been knocked around at sea for the previous couple of summers without seriously worrying about how to remove the bilge water which collected. I anticipated a change in this situation and had built an extensive new bilge pumping system based on the fact that we had very dirty bilges, something which caused a lot of housekeeping problems after Beachy Head and after the abortive sail to Calais.

Electrical power had been installed at an early stage in the Surrey Docks. In order to avoid the continual noise of a generator, I had decided to rely on banks of car batteries giving 24 volts, charged from a hand-cranked Lister diesel engine which I ran for an hour or so two or three times a day. Equipment for a lower voltage (for instance 12 volts) would have been easier to find, but voltage drop over the long power lines would have been significant. Even with 24 volts, my calculations of voltage drop had led to some awkwardly thick copper wiring. What little household electricity we needed (for work tools, kitchen equipment and the like) came from a transverter which put out usable domestic household current from the car batteries. Heating loads were, of course, impossible from car batteries, but were supplied quite well from the diesel oil which we carried on board in quantity.

Nowadays, commercial vessels have their engines running all the time they are at sea. The bilge pump driven by the main engine is therefore an incidental byproduct of the motive power. I planned to avoid running an engine all the time. Scarce electricity was therefore the only alternative for the bilge pumping, apart from a hand pump on deck.

To conserve power, I had to have a float switch. The commercial ones I could find were either too big to fit between our timbers, or broke down in adverse conditions, since they were designed for use in houses. I therefore built my own from a piece of copper wire with a champagne cork fitted at the end. It was surprisingly reliable, and, of course, very easy to service. The only trouble was that when the rising bilge water floated the cork upwards to flick its supporting wire against another electrical terminal as the ship rolled, the signal could be dirty and inconclusive. So I had to have a series of relays to clean up the signal, operate a time switch, and finally a power switch.

My eldest stepdaughter, Emma, later scoffed that she had never met a leak freak (I was to become one) who needed half a dozen relays to operate one measly little pump. She exaggerated, of course. The system only needed three relays.

During the winter, I had been building twinned filters to protect the pumps from abrasion or blockage due to the filth in our bilges. Only one filter operated at a time, so that the other could be cleaned without interrupting the pumping. I calculated that the filter system could handle a ton of water every three minutes. If we were not hand pumping for some reason (at night, shorthanded, etc.), the smaller electric pump would automatically take over. There was a much larger pump driven directly by the Lister, also through these filters, and a third badly filtered so-called "catastrophe" pump (pronounced katastroff by the Danes) on the main engine which I never got to work satisfactorily because it really needed a great deal of water slopping around to suck effectively. It was a centrifugal pump — they are difficult to prime.

While I had made all these preparations to stay afloat, I surely did not want to put them into operation in a quiet dock. It was not until March when the water was getting really cold that I reluctantly decided I had to have some help from professional divers. If they were not successful, I would have to start hunting for a dry dock and I would never get on with the conversion.

At the same time, Cecilia took Romily, Victoria, Lucy and William off to ski in Andorra. I didn't go. It was an indication of how my path was becoming less and less mainstream.

While I was attending the School of Navigation in the Minories three years earlier, I was also going with Thomas and Romily to a club to learn how to dive. The conditions were perfect for we dived in the clearest water in a heated indoor swimming pool. The only trouble was that when practicing rescue operations, I did not welcome being kissed on the lips by a stubbly chin (which seemed to enjoy it) as a means of resuscitation. All three of us found this tiresome and eventually gave up.

The conditions in March 1973 in the Albert Dock were quite unlike the heated swimming pool. I consulted some Port of London Authority divers who pointed out that I could not operate a ship like this without knowing how to repair it. That meant under, as well as above, the water. They didn't have the time to keep diving themselves to search for the leak, but they said they would teach me. There were two divers and their boy, a man of around 70 who powdered their dry suits, helped them on with their weight belts and so on. I only had a wet suit.

The cold struck me with such force that I lost control of my breathing and nearly drowned before they could get me up. It was not merely the cold. They had to teach me how to tell which way was up by watching which way the bubbles traveled so I could follow them to the surface. I don't believe the diving club taught me that blinded by murk I could easily dive deeper in attempting to surface. These practical working Port of London Authority divers also taught me how to hang on to a foul bottom to make repairs, and how to dive alone (something strictly forbidden by all reputable diving authorities and therefore not taught, although, for all the 15 years of diving that followed, I never had the luxury of a buddy diving).

Then they left me to gaze at the dead cat and the plastic sheeting through which I would have to reach the appallingly cold and blind and lonely abyss that was *Gray*'s hull. Searching for a leak is a laborious business, and in fact, I didn't find the leaking stopwater which was causing part of that particular leak for 15 years, just before I sold *Gray*. All I could tell with certainty at the time was that the leak was coming from somewhere near the propeller shaft, an area where a lot of timbers come together making it very difficult to see from the inside what was going on behind them. However, after spending some three months more or less preoccupied with the leak, I managed to find some doubtful seams near the propeller shaft, smother them in black sticky tarry mastic and reduce the inflow of water enough for me to get back to work above water.

Naturally, at this stage, and indeed for many years, I did not suspect the leaky sternpost stopwater (it's a piece of softwood designed to stop leaks between two sections of the rudder post and is buried from sight under the hood ends of the planks).

It was enough to deal with what I could see: the doubtful seams in what turned out to be roughly the same area. By this time, it was May 1973 and the summer was coming up once again.

All six children were either living away from home at school or university or were just about to be. I felt that if I held out that the children's summer vacation could be spent afloat and then failed to deliver the goods, there would be a lot of family trouble. I foresaw quite a while being spent packing up the work on the inside, getting my mind to bear on the navigational aspects of a summer afloat, charts, sails, and so forth. And the leak worried me. It was not increasing, but it was too large for comfort. The moment we moved it might open up. I had good reason to believe that I would be thought of as a fusspot, a leak freak as they came to call me, and be given little sympathy. Besides which, Cecilia had a problem. If the children were all assembled on board to go sailing and we remained in the gloomy docks in London, without moving, what could she do with them? I couldn't or wouldn't be a help because, like it or not, I would have to be working overtime to get the ship ready. In any case, Cecilia knew perfectly well that I was not given to sharing her burden of child care. There had been delays the previous summer, the one following Cecilia's car accident. Rather than go through that again, I simply refused to try to take *Gray* to sea.

I was a little surprised that Cecilia didn't make any effort to persuade me out of this point of view. She quickly reserved flights for Crete and arranged with the help of a friend, Peter Ryan, to get an apartment in Palaiokhóra, the then top hippie resort. Cecilia and I were twice as old as any of the vacationers and our children, William and Lucy, walked on two legs. Everyone else's child was slung from the hip in some fashion. To mark us out more completely we were housed in rooms, with beds. Everyone else slept on the sand. I felt suburban, middle class, unsuccessful and out of it. Things brightened up when the *meltemi* started to blow. The wind drove the sand, and the sand drove the hippies into our apartment for shelter, bringing a lot of the sand with them. But Peter's reluctance to consort with us was not lost on me: he was one of *them*, while *we* were having a family holiday.

- The meltemi results from the combination of a high pressure system north of Greece and a low pressure system over Turkey producing a squash of northerly winds, rather like the easterly squash we experienced in St. Vaast-la-Hougue. Both squashes produce strong winds in clear weather.

I didn't enjoy myself. Try as I would, it seemed to me I was merely putting by so much time before I could get back to the ship in London. I don't think Cecilia felt this way. In fact, since her accident, *Gray* had been becoming less and less a part of her world. It was far from being a passionate commitment for me, but I had little alternative. I no longer had a job. I didn't see how I could turn my back on the ship, even if I had wanted to. We needed to get to a point where we could sell or use the ship as a going concern, but going concern it had to be either way.

Apart from the continuing problem of leaking aft — a problem which increasingly sapped my confidence in the ship — there was also the problem of the wharfborers. The first year we noticed anything, we thought that cow dung from the surrounding fields was responsible for the beetles which flew around our hold as we cruised around the East Coast rivers. That was in 1970, the year we brought the ship from Denmark. The beetles were slow flying with brown wing cases. I had a lot of other things on my mind during that first brief sail round the English East Coast estuaries and didn't think about it again until the same thing happened the following year. Then the children told me the hold, where they slept, had been full of the flying beetles, obviously much more than the master's cabin at the stern where we were. The expert to whom I took a beetle identified it as *Nacerda melanura*, the wharfborer, whose larvae were quietly munching away at our ship. It was the black wing tip which distinguished it from the dung beetle. Except for a period in May, June and July, the beetles were in their dangerous larval stage, feeding on the wood. In the summer some of them emerged as adults and flew around to mate. The expert explained that only as adults could we kill them, by fumigation. But as the years went by, there seemed to be more rather than fewer bodies to count after fumigation. I hoped that the increasing numbers were due to increasing infestation with eggs before we had the ship; I hoped our fumigation policy would pay off down the road. So that summer, isolated in the docks, I felt surrounded by sinister problems flying around, or welling up, in the hold.

The expert told me larvae lived more than one year, but he could not say how many years — could I expect a dozen years of munching our timbers, like the Death Watch Beetle?

- I have records covering five years of fumigating the boat at the sight of the first wharfborer of the season (usually in early May) and then counting the bodies in a specific area of the ship. The third year looked as though we were having a success. Then the last two, the body counts increased. The strange thing is that I have no further records of body counts. I remember the infestation stopped suddenly and it could have been in 1978 which would indicate the larvae spend five years munching wood before emerging as adults.

After our return from Crete, things had come to something of a head between me and Cecilia. It was obvious that the children were going to grow up and leave us. We had, for instance, only taken the two youngest children to Crete that summer. The other four were off doing their thing somewhere else. I told Cecilia that when they were all gone, we might face each other as strangers. There had been so many of them, they had been such a preoccupation, that Cecilia and I rarely talked of anything not in some way connected with them. Not only that, we rarely talked of anything but plans and arrangements. At that time, to be fair, there was not the slightest pressure on me to do anything else. Left to my own devices, I would have bored her, as I was boring myself, with endless talk about *Gray*.

As far as children's education was concerned, I hardly did a thing. Since Cecilia had run a school with her former husband she knew a great deal about education and I didn't even try to understand the intricacies, except when it came to claiming tuition grants, which I was very good at. So while I complained that we were becoming strangers, Cecilia complained that I had failed to understand, or even to sympathize with, the constant pressure she was under to bring up six children. The whole point of *Gray* was that it was for the children; sometimes, she thought I couldn't see the wood for the trees.

On 30 April 1974, Cecilia moved on board, all the children having left home. She was very good at quick changes of direction, when circumstances changed. The ship was now looking more ready for sea, and her arrival meant we could both work to get the ship ready for the summer. Even at university, children still get vacations.

Cecilia said later she had made the move to become part of the ship once more. I didn't have to commute any longer and in fact it was another 13 years before I slept permanently ashore again. We were in a very poor part of London, so our standard of living went down to the level of the goods available in the local shops, in the main limited to food. The locals didn't own major appliances, for instance, and so they didn't need to repair them and create a local market for spare parts. But that didn't matter. I enjoyed being two adults playing with our own toys, instead of the children's. Besides, I was dimly aware of, and not very enthusiastic about, the way in which, like the children's game of Snap the Whip, I had found myself out there in front.

By June, the children's summer vacation was coming up again, and we got ready to move out of the dock, with the intention of coming back at the end of the summer, and resuming our life in a large house in a better part of London with our three-masted schooner docked waiting for us in the East End.

• What had I accomplished during the previous 18 months? Here's the list I made in the rough log the month Cecilia moved on board (looking at this list years later, it brought home to me how much I must have felt under attack at the time, particularly as it doesn't now appear to be much to boast about):

After-galley removed from behind the steering position and a new deck of 1" mahogany constructed over steering chains

Steering re-built to provide twice the purchase; rudder raised one inch so that load is taken on a bronze sacrificial collar on top gudgeon instead of the skeg of the keel; extra gudgeon provided

Mizzen boom, horse and large oak bitts constructed

Sole boards completed throughout hold [these were to enable me to inspect the bilges and clear them if they got blocked up]

After half of hold converted to bulkhead stage (no interior fittings)

Decks and all coachroofs re-payed throughout and decorated to complete tightness

After hawsepipes re-fastened

Topsides raked out where drying had ruptured mastic, re-caulked, all seams payed

Bilge pump system completely re-built with easily accessible twin strainers, capable of being serviced while in operation, and pipe sizes sufficient for 80 gallons per minute (about 20 tons per hour), supplied from a choice of two motor pumps, an electric pump on a float switch and a hand pump on deck.

The Schooner **Gray**— *internal layout. The deck-house is just forward of the engine, and on the upper deck you can see where the companion ladder runs.*

Forward toilet fitted out, together with main salt water intake and washing water waste

Two deck hydrants installed (for washing decks and for fire)

Navigation light system re-built (based on oil)

Re-decoration of master's cabin aft and all enclosed spaces in hold except food store

New engine room hatch and ventilator hatch for forecastle

New foremast derrick constructed

10

The Lappel Bank

As we were being locked out of the Albert Dock in which *Gray* had been for 21 months, the lock keeper made the usual sallies about going round the world, to which I modestly replied I would be glad to make it to the end of the river. I had loaded our small car onto the foredeck, so this must have sounded a little hollow. Cecilia was, of course, discussing with the other lock keepers which part of the world to have at our feet. We spoke with two voices while we waited for the water level to sink from the dock to that of the Thames outside.

I strolled past the engine room hatch. It was the end of a beautiful day, the end of a tiring and in many ways dispiriting 21 months, the beginning of a night on the tiers outside, smelling the river, secretly confident that we would, in fact, go round the world...

- A row of mooring buoys is usually called a tier when talking about commercial vessels, or a trot when talking about yachts, the main difference being that larger commercial vessels often use two buoys to moor fore and aft on a tier in a river to prevent their swinging around and obstructing traffic, while yachts, being smaller, can swing to a single buoy in a trot. Mostly in France we also met *"une tonne,"* designed for warships, most uncomfortably big. I have not met a specific English translation for this hostile buoy.

A routine glance down the hatch: There was water everywhere, pouring in from somewhere astern, and being chucked all over the place by the flywheel, which was now deep in water. I told the lock keeper to fill the lock again: we had to return to the basin. I couldn't bear to leave the deck and go below to get my diving things. Cecilia staggered up the narrow companionway with a mass of unyielding rubber, the lead weight belt, the clanking air tank, goggles, fins, pressure gauges and all the rest.

As soon as I could, I started to back the ship very gently out of the lock into the basin, deeply apprehensive that the wash of the reverse slipstream from the propeller would scour out more seam.

There was going to be a thunderstorm. The water was now less splashy. For a moment, hope. Then I realized deeper water doesn't splash so much. It was clearly coming in fast. I decided not to waste time mooring the ship. The thunderstorm would blow us onto some quayside somewhere.

When I got down beneath the ship, I knew where to go. The winter before, it had always been difficult to pick out the exact spot when revisiting it to stuff up the seams. This time, the seam a few inches in front of my eyes was visible because it was clean and empty. I worked along the seam a little. Empty in both directions. Should I establish how empty? Should I start work anywhere I could? Immediately? The quantity of water coming on board was clearly huge. The bottom was covered in weed which swayed this way and that as we moved gently in the storm. On the fringes of the open seam, the weed lay down neatly like combed hair, a slightly different color, sucked towards the seam by the flow of water. I knew the rush of water must gradually be scouring each end of the open seam, making the hole longer.

The ship's keel shuddered as we connected with the quayside. I collided spongily with the hull.

Cecilia had just finished tying us up when I got back on deck. I asked her to collect the tarry bitumen paying for a quick smother of the leak.

- The paying is normally a soft water resistant layer with no structural integrity on top of the caulking. Mostly we used something like roofing cement, but we also experimented with a mixture of cement and tallow. Landlubbers call caulking what we call paying.

I thought I could probably mix it with oakum to stiffen it. From the outside, I had no means of knowing whether I was being successful. This is always the problem with leaks. Someone on the inside has to signal what's happening — by tapping on the wood, or some such — while the diver works on the outside. For that, the leak has to be small, and not buried by bilge water, and of course the signaling system has to be set up in advance together with all the planning for the repair of the leak.

None of this was in place. In any case, the leak might be invisible inside under bilge water. It was my first catastrophic leak. I was not to know that twenty years would go by before the next catastrophic leak, six years after I sold her. It sank her.

This time, I controlled the panic breathing, remained underwater, smothered the leak step by step, and surfaced to find the pump gaining on the bilge level.

The lock staff was about to go home. Without taking my diving suit off, proud of my conquest, I waddled over, the crutch flap of my wet suit swinging awkwardly between my legs, to tell them we wanted to leave after all.

As I waddled, so I reflected, then turned round, and found that indeed the repair had pulled through the empty seam and had started up all over again. Heavy thunder clouds made it so dark it was difficult to see even above water.

The only alternative to diving again was to turn my back on the ship and walk away. I knew from previous experience that I was the best placed to effect the speedy repair required to avoid sinking. I had seen a wooden barge with neglected open topside seams fill up enough with rain to immerse these open seams and go down in a hurry, just across the basin from me. I had also seen the immensely powerful machinery which had been brought to raise the barge so that it could be towed away to sink in a more congenial spot, the ship cemetery I fantasized about for the next 13 years. They brought huge airbags, pumps of a size I could scarcely imagine, and a wreck-lifting vessel which listed so badly with the effort that it demonstrated without a doubt what a vast and expensive problem it was to remove a wreck. If I walked away, that was what would happen, I would be found, they would hunt me down in my comfortable London house. I would have to pay up — and lose the ship I had worked on for years. Maybe lose the house, too. The ship was uninsured, though not from choice: We could never get cover of any sort.

So I buttoned up the cold wet rubber, saw the air tank was now so low that it, not me, would book-end the operation in success or failure. The air I needed to breathe from the tank would give out before I did. I had an alternative idea of how to build on the previous repair to make it more secure, with lead tingles (patches of lead or copper to cover damage to the planking) on top, so that even if it started to leak again, the flood would not be so bad, and the pumps might be able to cope to get us through the night.

I had not used lead in the first place, because it is difficult to work with. A strip of lead is soft enough to mold itself to the side of the ship, but it's heavy and doesn't want to stick to the tarry stuff in the seam. I really needed three hands: one to hold the lead against the side, another to hold the copper tack ready to drive through the lead into the wood of the ship, and a third to hold the hammer. With only two hands, I got some of the copper tacks started into the lead, but they didn't like to stay there and some fell out before I could drive them into the wood. It was depressing to see that I was not the first to have driven copper nails into the hull at that point. There had been trouble before. Slowly, I worked in bitumen paying and oakum, and tingled it over with lead, hoping that the rot was not so extensive that the copper nails would go right through the hull. And to keep my body pressed up against the ship's side so I could work, I had to keep slowly finning with my legs, as the PLA divers had taught me.

Inch by inch, I repaired the seam, trying to make the soaking oakum stick in place first, paying over the top and then fixing it with the lead sheath, the tingle. Apart from the problems with the lead, the seam had pulled through because of the rot inside, and so the oakum had nothing to get wedged into. Besides, the wet oakum had by that time swelled in the water. It was better than nothing, but not much better.

As I finished the repair, it became a little harder to breathe. The pressure gauge confirmed the bottle was nearly empty. Slow suck, another nail. Steady not to drop them. No second chance. Slow suck, hammer it in. Harder to suck now. Time to inspect the repair? Slow suck. Work my way along. Now too hard to breathe. Must come up.

I would have liked to have known immediately whether I had succeeded enough to stand down for the night. Could we have dinner? Could we have rest? Could we pause to consider the next step? Could we consider the longer-term implications? Should we just gaze at the leak from inside? With my mind on the level of water, my ear gauging the frequency with which the pump was triggered, I could not withdraw myself from the crisis sufficiently to do anything but waste my energies uselessly, knowing as I did so that the most prudent course would have been to consider rather than to fret.

Cecilia had had time on her hands while I dived; she employed that time to make dinner; there was food. I needed it. To the end, I never understood her ability to release herself enough from the anxiety of the moment, the preoccupation which in my mind meant life or death, or something pretty near it, in order to accomplish some task which would be needed only later. I was never able to do this—I envied her the ability to be practical under stress.

It gradually became clear that the repair had succeeded enough to allow us to doze the night away, though constantly aware whether or not the automatic electric pump was beating the leak. Things got better towards morning. There were longer gaps when the pump was not triggered. It might be clogging up (a bad sign for sea-going work), or merely taking time to drain out the last drops from the filthy bilges (a better sign). We slept at last.

I had my own diving compressor on board. I never dived for pleasure round coral reefs in clear, limpid water, not I. But I had heeded the PLA divers' advice to be able to repair any part of the ship at any time, even when there was no support from the land. As the diving bottles filled with air, so I crept nearer the treadmill of heroic measures to save the ship. For, you see, the heroism of diving in the thunderstorm the previous day had now resolved itself into a commitment for another heroic act. I went in three times during the day after the leak to establish just what I knew and just what I didn't.

One cause for a little hope was the discovery of a rope round the propeller shaft whose free end must have given the seams real punishment. Usually the smaller ropes which get wrapped up round the propeller shaft are so pulverized there is nothing left to remove. But the bigger heavier ropes survive, and, obviously, are the hardest to remove. They have to be cut. By definition, the rope is usually wound round the shaft so tightly it is only just short of breaking. There is no slack to allow the knife in under the coils. Removing this particular rope was no easier than any other rope I have had to remove. That is: very difficult and somewhat hazardous, wielding a knife with force.

After about four hours spent mostly underwater in the filthy conditions of a locked-in basin, I thought there was a reasonable chance I had made a medium-term repair. I could do nothing further afloat.

The pressure just to keep the ship from sinking had been so intense I had not considered the next step, either alone or with Cecilia.

Cecilia, however, had.

First, she pointed out that I was cold and needed to warm up in a shower.

At that point, the shower space was planned and the pipes were in place to deliver water, but there was no shower bottom. Part of the reason was that an ordinary shower cabinet would have been too tall to fit, and part of the reason was that I was still trying to find some way to avoid draining the shower into the bilges. Since the ship had thus far had a history of being dry, I was less worried about it interfering with pumping results than about whether fresh water would cause rot. Nonetheless, at this stage it was possible to get hot water onto the body, wash and rinse, and that's what I needed, although under present leaking conditions I was reluctant to confuse matters. Cecilia pointed out the shower water was nothing compared to the amount which had been leaking in.

As the hot water coursed over my body, I felt inside its cocoon which was itself inside the cocoon of a now unreliable ship, but nonetheless preferable to the hostile outside world. When I emerged, Cecilia had it all figured out. We would leave next day at the first high water of the day, and sit on the tier for twenty four hours. If the repair didn't hold, we could go back into the lock, otherwise we would go down river.

It's hard to imagine nowadays (2013), but this leak was something that had happened in our own world, the two of us. No one else. Even the lock keepers had gone home. There were some sheds with corrugated iron rooves, some weeds, some broken concrete, the water in the lock, the lighter on the other side of the basin. There was otherwise no life, no telephone, no computer, no email. There was no way of sharing our world with the children, tweeting them or some such. And they were expecting to spend some of their summer vacations on *Gray*.

So I went into some technical detail with Cecilia about what I had actually managed to achieve. The real problem was that I suspected there was internal rot I could not see, and had therefore not been able to wedge anything into the seam. My repairs had been laid over the seam rather like a sticking plaster. When I said I didn't want to leave it was an emotional reaction to do with remaining in the cocoon, unsafe, but safer than outside. She pointed out that the leak was not like skin: it wouldn't heal itself under the sticking plaster I had put on. We'd better find some mud, she concluded, as quickly as possible.

It had been a common occurrence with the barge to sit on the mud. In fact, they were built for this kind of life. I had become more accustomed to looking for patches of mud than for quaysides, which were not plentiful.

Nevertheless, my heart sank. We obviously needed a dry dock, but on arrival in the London River I could find nothing suitable for our size on the East Coast. It had been worrying me for some time. Careening on the mud was the only answer. So here I was, one heroic struggle completed, facing another consequential upon it. When would it ever end?

So we locked out the following morning and sat on the tier. It was awkward as the buoys were too far apart. They were intended for much bigger vessels than us. It took a lot of effort getting warps on the fore and aft buoys in the first place and then tightening them up sufficiently so we would either not swing too far into the fairway or go aground inshore. I had difficulty concentrating on anything but the pump being triggered by bilge water, but we got out the charts and found some mud.

It was near Queenborough at the mouth of the Thames, and it was called the Lappel bank. Google Earth makes it look (2013) like a parking lot but at that time it was mud. It would be easy to locate the ship right on it, provided the ebb was a-lee with a westerly or southwesterly wind. At that time of the year, easterly winds are rare, so a patch of mud open to the east (this was open to the northeast) would likely be in calm water as the tide ebbed. We had briefly visited Queenborough in 1970 and 1971. It was a sleepy little village with an excellent butcher. (With no refrigerator, meat is the most perishable food, so butchers were important to us unless we wanted to eat from the brine crock.)

Cecilia and I started down the Thames, with the engine revolutions around the usual 240 per minute.

We took a couple of hours to get to a fuel station where we had to come alongside in a strong current to bunker diesel. By the time we reached Gravesend three hours later, the leak had started up.

Diving in a current is a virtual impossibility. Now that we had left the Albert Dock, there would only be a small diving window every six hours when the tide turned. I had no experience of how long this window might be, but it was certain that I could do nothing if we sprang a catastrophic leak between whiles.

We arrived at Gravesend just before slack water. I hurried into my diving gear and hung the diving ladder overboard. It was a heavy steel affair designed to hang down into the water about six feet so that a diver could get a foothold while still mostly immersed. I could see the remains of the ebb making little ripples past it. It seemed very slow and gentle to me ten feet above the water, so I started down the ladder. The tide took my body and swung it astern nearly wrenching both ladder and me from the ship. I got out again hurriedly, looked at my watch and saw that it was about half an hour before slack water. If there were the same time after slack water, the window would be less than an hour.

I waited for a while and tried again. It was 15 minutes before slack water. The tide, imperceptible from the deck, still tugged hard at my body. I had tied the ladder onto the ship, and had a lifeline from me to the ladder. It seemed a hard struggle to stem the tide once in the water. And to work at the same time...

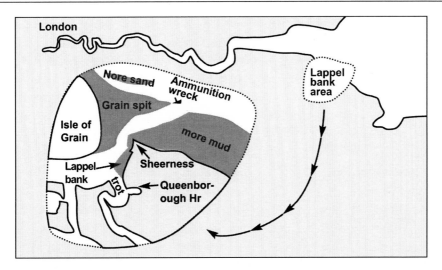

On the map above, the Lappel Bank looks fairly insignificant, but in my day it was a completely deserted stretch, mostly dry at low water, nearly a mile long parallel to the shore, and about a quarter of a mile deep, more than enough for us. From Google Earth, it now (2013) appears to be one vast parking lot.

I found the tingling had been lifted, presumably by going into reverse at the fuelling station while bunkering. I patched it up for the night, concluding unhappily that I could no longer blame the rope for the damage to my repair. I really needed to sew on that mud to do a better repair.

The next low water was in the middle of the night, but the following afternoon, with more of an idea what it was like diving in a tidal stream, I managed to get about an hour in the water. It was much harder work because I had to keep finning just to keep still. It used up the air bottle much faster, but that didn't matter because diving was only possible for a much shorter time than in the tideless dock.

When we were not watching the leak, we tried to concentrate on more enjoyable things like hanking on sails. For brief moments, I forgot the sickness below, the dread secret we bore, out of sight, like a communicable disease, and then I would land back on deck with a thump remembering to remember to feel the guilt of the leak I concealed.

On the sixth day after the catastrophic leak, we gingerly started off down the Thames again for Queenborough. I felt I had to drop the engine revolutions still further (to about 180, which means three distinctly audible engine revolutions per second). We displayed a D flag to advertise to those who could still read flags—a dwindling minority—that we were maneuvering with difficulty. It might help our defense at the inevitable court of inquiry but I doubted if it would help keep ships clear of us. And there was, by now, quite a number, ploughing up and down the murky Thames minding their own business.

We were getting down to the Nore where we would have to turn in to Sheerness and Queenborough. It was in any case a tricky section of our journey because it was necessary to arrive at the Nore at slack water so that we could then take the flood into Sheerness. We were not doing much more than drifting around on the tide for fear of opening up the repair, such as it was.

The visibility closed down further. I gave Cecilia a compass course. Coolly, she said she wasn't going to steer quite that, and gave me the course she thought best — about 12 degrees away from what I had told her. Without looking up from the charts, and by this time nervously exhausted by the diving, I became icily, coldly, quiet and ordered her to steer the course I had given her.

Something in the tone of her reply made me look up and see we were steering slap into a power station, plainly visible out of the murk. Our compass, left to its own devices for a couple of years while building was in progress, had developed a large deviation, that is, instead of pointing north it was pointing somewhere else.

I needed that compass, and I needed it right now. I wanted to take a shortcut to Queenborough as we were running late on the tides.

Just after the Nore Sand lay the wartime wreck of an ammunition ship, plainly visible out of the water. No one was allowed in the area, so we would either have to go round it keeping to the deep-water channel, or to cut inshore of it, either way giving it a wide berth. I wanted to go inside because we were losing the ebb and I didn't think we had a lot of time before the flood would push us back up London River the way we had come. There was a buoy which showed where we should start the shortcut across Grain Spit marked in places on the chart "sand, shells," not good for going aground. There was nothing to mark the spit thereafter until we got to the other side and the fairway buoys into Sheerness and Queenborough. Without a good compass, we risked going aground, since the fairway buoys at the other end of the shortcut had disappeared in the murk.

I knew enough about the theory of compass work to know that if we changed our heading (in this case by about 90° to leave the London River to get into Queenborough), the 12° deviation would mostly likely change, too. I had no idea by how much, or in which direction. The worst case scenario would be steering 24° off course — that is, by the time we had gone a mile down the course, we might be nearly half a mile from where we had intended to wind up, not counting leeway and tidal currents.

In silence, we turned for the shortcut, noted the compass reading and stuck to it as we steered across the unbuoyed spit, unable to see anything, knowing that we had reached the bottom of the bran tub, the lucky dip: if I had got it wrong, we had no alternative solutions to offer to fate. I watched an eddy of sand over the side. We were close to the bottom.

Somehow, we got to Queenborough and lay on one of the buoys in the trot. It was evening.

Once more, heroic efforts had brought us to the end of a stage. Some days before, it had been keeping the ship afloat, this time it was getting to the safety of the Queenborough buoys. But each heroic objective reached is but the launching pad for the next heroic effort. And so it was at Queenborough: The tides dictated that I be off the Lappel Bank in a dinghy with measuring equipment and marker buoys well before four the following morning, low water. After surveying and marking the berth in some detail, I scuttled back to *Gray*, shaved, had some food, and brought *Gray* over the mud berth by a little before midday.

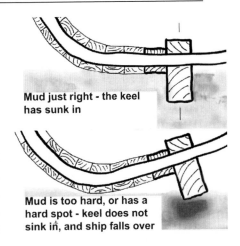

Mud just right - the keel has sunk in

Mud is too hard, or has a hard spot - keel does not sink in, and ship falls over

The wind was right, and everything else was right, but for the one piece of information which can only be gathered on site: the hardness or softness of the mud. The bank was a little steeper than expected; the mud a little harder. We touched bottom, but never dried out. The next tide, I shifted us a little inshore. This time we took the ground all right, but fell over a little, not much, some nine degrees, but enough to make it a concern that the mud was too hard to let the keel penetrate so that it cradled the bottom planks properly.

For five days we lay on that mud bank, shifting around a little, but not really being able to do much work because the mud was so variable, lovely and hard to work on, but too hard to keep *Gray* upright, or so soft it was impossible to move around to do the work. Besides, the children started arriving. We had to make arrangements to meet them on the shore, and to ferry them out by dinghy, all of which took time. Victoria arrived first, followed the next day by Thomas and two friends, but only for the night, so that meant two trips ashore. Then we had to move back to the trot because of an easterly forecast, which would have meant going aground on a weather tide. Emma and a friend arrived for the inside of a week, and left. Thomas came back. It never seemed to stop. The children had all gotten to an age when they wanted to make sure of their summer delights, since by now they had alternatives to a leaky old boat that didn't move.

With Thomas's return, the forecast changed back to southwest — a lee tide once more. We rushed back to the Lappel Bank.

This was it. Time had run out. If I were to keep the children, I could no longer wait for better conditions. A repair had to be made which would last us at least through the summer.

The tides had moved round to a more comfortable day time area. We took the ground in what seemed to be the right place. The tide receded. Thomas, Cecilia and I got ready. As soon as the bottom of the light wooden ladder we used for careening stopped floating away, we poked it into the mud. I got down to have a look. The area near the propeller which needed repair was well clear of the mud, and the latter was firm enough to walk on. Matters looked ideal, except that we would need trestles to get up to the repair, out of reach above my head because the keel had penetrated the mud even less than usual.

As I gazed, the ship slowly fell over towards me. There was no way I could move to safety, sucked in by the mud. But I was near the propeller. All that happened was that the repair lowered itself to come within easy reach.

I didn't have time to assess how far we had fallen, but I thought it was suffi- ciently far that we could fall no further. I started work: an immense horse bandage of lead, held in place by copper tacks, to keep the bitumen and oakum in place, and more lead to keep the lead which was keeping the bitumen and oakum in place from being disturbed, and then more lead on top of that just in case.

It was a terrible repair, but there was nothing further to be done but finish and wait for us to lift off.

We tried to sit in the deckhouse chatting, reading, but it was difficult. We were a long way too far over to be able to sit down without sliding. Using the cooker to make tea, for example, was impossible. I tried to measure the heel. We didn't have a proper clinometer, so the obvious thing to do was to get a bit of string and a beer mug, in just the same way that I had measured the angles of the arches in Port Meirion. I pinned the string onto the side of the deckhouse, measured its length and then across to the side of the tilted deckhouse. Thus, I had the tangent of our angle of heel — and it turned out to be about 0.3 or the same tangent I had found for the flight of steps in Port Meirion. No wonder we kept sliding off our chairs.

It was a nice amusement for me while we waited. The tide was rising. We would soon be up. We went back to trying to get comfortable in the deckhouse.

In a while, I got bored, and went outside to watch the rising tide. No one asked me anything. I said nothing. Thomas got up and spent rather longer watch- ing. He also came back saying nothing. Then he watched again. He said the rising tide had nearly reached the gunwale. I knew he knew, as well as I knew, that this was way higher than the usual waterline. We worried in silence, sticking to the facts, not knowing too well how the ship would come up, having heard tales of ships stuck in the mud.

After a while, neither of us could resist it: we just leaned on the rail watching the water rise. I had mixed feelings about Cecilia's ability to get on with something useful, for she was not with us at the rail.

Thomas asked if the covering boards were tight. He had a slight, and very attractive, stutter at the time, so he spoke slowly to articulate his question clearly. The gunwale (rhymes with tunnel) was now fully immersed, and the water was crossing the covering board towards the deck.

I lied that the joint between them was tight, but I knew that these two sets of

powerful boards, forming the edge of the
deck, and the top side of the hull, were the
only two planks on a wooden ship to be spiked
together on their sides—and the spikes inter-
fered with the caulking. Furthermore, without
any tumblehome (that is, a curve inwards to
the covering board so that the fattest part of
the ship was nearer the waterline), the joint
took all the punishment from the quayside.
Gray had suffered from all this want of design,
and the joint was, to say the least, doubtful.

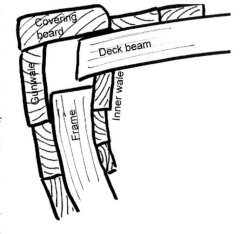

I also knew that the moment the water
lapped over the covering board, the righting
lever (that is, the buoyancy on that side of the ship) would start falling fairly rapidly.
If the water rose too far across the deck it would start pouring in through the door
to the deckhouse which was on the side we had fallen over. The ship had racked
(think: medieval torture) on the mud: the door would no longer close, since the
door frame was no longer square.

Our feet began to get a little wet on deck. I went down below and gazed at the
now fully immersed joint between the gunwale and the covering board, visible over
the inner wale between the deck beams. Water was certainly coming in. Then I
looked through the listings, a few feet further down, and I could see the whole of
the inside of the ship was wet from topside leaks. Enough to be dangerous? I had
no means of knowing.

Back on deck again, I stepped out of the deckhouse door into water now ankle
deep. We must be losing righting lever fast, and the tide had but a few more inches
to go to pour in over the foot-high cill, which resulted from building the deckhouse
in Denmark on top of the massive hatch coamings, instead of clearing them away.
I had not foreseen this particular eventuality—sucked into a muddy grave.

Neither Thomas nor I spoke. Cecilia was still occupied elsewhere.

A pushman and a barge were coming up from Sheerness. I had seen many of
these weird and efficient contraptions going up and down past our buoys at Queenborough. The pushman was all huge engine in a small box with a steering position
on top. It simply strapped itself onto the back of a barge, the couple together looking
like a perfectly ordinary ship. When the barge was heavily laden, it would swim
sedately through the water without much fuss. But when the barge was empty, the
pushman was capable of a rare turn of speed. And it was certainly not aerodynamic.
The heavy draw from a passing pushman had often caused me concern on our
buoys.

This one was light ship—that is, its barge was standing high out of the water,
probably empty—and it was going fast. I feared the worst. And, indeed, I could

see my fears being confirmed as the wave from the barge reached us, first of all drawing the water off *Gray*'s deck, then flooding back on board nearly up to the bottom of the open door, and then sucking as rapidly back…

…sucking *Gray* clean out of the mud.

We popped up, righted ourselves, green water poured from our deck, just like a submarine surfacing as you see on the movies, the bilge pump triggered and the fears of a moment before seemed like so much cobweb gathered up into a tiny ball to be thrown away without remark.

We had gone onto the Lappel because of the benign southwesterly forecast. It had begun to blow while we were on the mud, but the wind rose further once we had floated, and backed out to south. I had hoped to stay on the Lappel for the night, check on the leaking, get a good night's sleep and so forth. It was nearly dark, a southerly wind was fine, since it was somewhat off the land which sheltered us. In any case, I couldn't get back into Queenborough yet for lack of water — there were mud banks in the way. So we settled down to dinner, the dinner which Cecilia had been preparing while we uselessly failed, like King Canute, to stem the rising tide. But it was no serene dinner. Thomas got up first to look at the wind.

He observed it was coming up the river, sat down, and went on chewing.

I tried to do the same. Then I, too, got up and looked outside. It was good mud, so we would hold, but it was distinctly rougher. Just because we are on a weather tide, I consoled myself, and went back indoors.

Then we began to roll a little, and from time to time we could hear the anchor chain snubbing in the hawsepipe as we sailed around, the tide pushing our stern one way, and the wind the other. It was difficult to make out whether the wind was veering or not, but it was a good deal easier to see that this was a rising gale. If it went on rising and if it veered all the way round to north or somewhere like that, we would find ourselves on a weather ebb, and who knew on what patch of mud we would sit. When the wind was south we would have been blown out from our berth into deep enough water to float at low tide. A northerly gale would blow us right up on the mud. We might even hole ourselves on our own anchor.

I decided to leave at midnight. With all the wind, it took us a long time to get the anchor up. We were not tied up in Queenborough until three in the morning.

But once again, the last heroic step was but gateway to the next. No heroism would be required to correct the compass, but correcting it made way for the next endeavor.

Sailors today (the year 2013) may well wonder why I bothered about so small an error. Indeed, one of my less nautical friends asked me why I didn't buy an accurate new compass. All compasses are affected by the magnetic environment of the ship, and you have to remember that when I started sailing, there were virtually no electronic aids to navigation for the smaller vessel apart from radio beacons, which gave a general indication of their direction but not much more. There had been a through-hull electronic depth-sounder once, but it had been removed before I bought *Gray*, possibly because it was a source of rot and leaks. We had a traditional trailing log from which we could work out distance traveled through the water, hence speed, provided it had not become fouled with seaweed. We used a lead line for anchorages.

For deep-sea work, I had a sextant, an amazingly accurate instrument (it is accurate to better than a quarter of one tenth of 1 percent of its full scale deflection — for comparison, think of the thermometer outside your window, marked, say, in Fahrenheit degrees from below freezing up to the 90s, readable only to an accuracy of about 1 percent). But to use a sextant for coasting, you have to have at least two, preferably three, things to look at, and bad visibility abounds in the Channel.

The purpose of a sextant is to measure angles. You look through the short telescope (on the right) at a split mirror (on the left); one half is glass so you look straight ahead (at the horizon) and the other half is a mirror which looks at another mirror (in which you can see a star). It's on a moveable arm (center) which can be swung back and forth over a scale of degrees (bottom) enabling the two images you see to be brought in line. You then read off the angle (altitude) on the scale.

I therefore depended very heavily on accurate dead reckoning, a system used since the start of the voyages of discovery in the late 15th century, in which the distance and direction traveled over the ground is calculated by correcting what you observe on board with estimates of leeway and tide. However good the compass, it always has to be corrected for two errors: for the fact that magnetic north is not true north; and for the magnetism of the ship itself. The former error (called variation) is marked on the chart. The latter error (called deviation) depends upon which way the ship is pointing, angle of heel and latitude. There are errors enough in figuring out leeway and tide, so why increase them with an inaccurate compass?

I had been so taken up with the horrors of the leak, and the fear of the repairs, that I had paid little attention to the children. They wanted to sail, and it was the summer holidays. I quite liked sleepy, charming Queenborough but the children found it a real drag. While it wouldn't be the same as sailing, checking the compass could at any rate be made to involve everyone. We could have organized fun. The tides were right. We all went out, following the dinghy in *Gray*.

There are several different ways of swinging the compass, but I decided to try one which I had often seen recommended in yachting magazines and the like. It consists of putting a good compass onto a dinghy (assumed to have no magnetic field of its own — probably true before the days of engines and fuel tanks), lining up the ship and the dinghy and then comparing the two compass readings, the difference being the deviation.

It was a lovely day with little wind. We tried shouting compass courses from

Gray's compass, 90 feet to the bow and then relaying it some distance to the dinghy out ahead. That gave a lot of employment to a lot of children. Because of the height of the bows, the dinghy had to be way out ahead, so I could see it. That last shout often didn't carry. ("57," "67, you said?," "No, 50, one, two, three, four, five, 50." "My compass doesn't say anything like one, two, three. Is that the back bearing?"). While a calm day for *Gray*, it turned out that it was not so calm for the dinghy whose compass jiggled around. I began to realize that this method was inherently hopeless, not only because of the practical difficulties of communication and accuracy, but for theoretical reasons. And I could see the results I was collecting were inconsistent.

All we needed was a reliable enough compass to cross the Channel. The 12° deviation I had already noted would mean an error of seven to eight miles at the end of a 35-mile voyage—in other words, more or less the distance to Calais, for example. Since I didn't know if that deviation would disappear or double on another heading, I could make some bad mistakes, particularly if there were poor visibility. Hard to remember now (2013) that when everything else closed down, as it often did in the Channel, the compass was the only friend left.

So I decided to correct the compass as we swung on the tide at the Queenborough buoys. By assuming that there are four types of deviation caused by the ship's permanent and induced magnetism (two which vary as the sine and cosine, and two which vary as twice the sine and cosine, of the course) and checking the compass against some distant object of known direction (a star, church steeple, etc.), I knew I could calculate the required set of deviations much more accurately. It worked well: I used this method for the next 15 years.

However, what did my decision to calculate the deviations do for the others on board? They must have seen a day's work of theirs being abandoned in favor of some recondite Dominick arcane punctiliousness, in which they were not invited to participate, and were given no rewarding task meanwhile. It was like having all those relays to work an automatic electric pump—the children might have felt more involved by forming bucket chains to save our ship.

We motored to Calais overnight in a flat calm. The date, 17 July 1974, was later to assume great importance in my life for I never returned to England again to live.

Calais was damaged twice in the Second World War, in 1940 as the Germans invaded and then in 1944 as the Allies pushed the Germans back. I didn't realize until we got there from Queenborough how good a job the Allies had done in flattening the ancient town, the last remnant of the English conquests won in the Hundred Years' War with France. It was lost in 1558, the year that Bloody Mary of England died with Calais engraved on her heart. The little I knew about it comes from the Lisle Letters, from the last English governor of Calais. Our visit that summer made me want to know even less.

We attempted to leave Calais three days after we had arrived — already a long wait for children on vacation. Like other Channel ports, for instance Dieppe, the tidal rise and fall is so great you have to get into an inner tideless basin as soon as you can after arrival. You cannot merely steam into the Channel, sniff around and come back if you don't like what you find outside. You have to leave the basin at high water and wait two hours for the tide to turn down Channel towards Dieppe, a wait which pleasure boats normally spent alongside a steel tug called the *Costaud* (the Hefty, in English). The journey to Dieppe would take us three tides, so an early morning start was desirable.

As dawn broke, and we were outside the basin, the southwest wind started to blow. I knew we could never make it against the wind. Naturally, we had to wait the rest of the ebb and the whole of the following flood, banged around by the tug, and a lot of uncomfortable yachts who were also failing to go down Channel, before we could get back into the basin. There was a swell in the harbor, and the yachts kept getting their mooring lines tangled. Furthermore, they regarded us as the shore, and so our own shorelines were taking all the strain. At one point, we got so displaced that I had to shift everyone off and turn round. In going astern in the harbor to do this maneuver, I started the stern leak all over again. Back in the basin, I dived to repair it. Some lead had come loose.

Day after day the southwest wind blew.

We simply HAD to have a favorable wind.

The children didn't think so.

I would cower in the stern cabin after the weather forecast, dreading to come into the galley amidships to announce that, once again, there was a 24 hour delay: 24 hours because I wanted to make the passage mostly in daylight. Very soon, I began to find excuses for not listening to the weather forecast, forgetting it, being out somewhere, or in some other way boycotting the wretched black instrument.

Cecilia was getting desperate. She had run out of amusements for the children days ago, and Calais wasn't fruitful of them in the first place. She began siding with the children, and I became more and more miserable, felt more of a failure, wished I had never gotten caught up in this boat business...

Wandering about Calais waiting for the wind to change, we came across a couple of Californians and their two children in a fishing smack. It was a powerful little boat, but the four of them looked exhausted after tending their bilge pumps day and night from their own bad stern leak. They had no money and couldn't afford to haul their smack for repairs. They offered to take us out in the bouncy weather outside the harbor, leave just before the top of the tide and back in time before the lock gates shut. I said they were foolish — the leak would only get worse. My children told the skipper not to pay any attention to me: I was a leak freak with port fever. So out we went, bounced around and came back. The smack was now really sinking. I couldn't do much for them, but I had no alternative but to dive yet again to stop their leak for a bit. It was becoming somewhat monotonous.

The next day, there was an ambiguous forecast. We had been there 19 days. I promised that I would set my alarm in the middle of the night to see whether we could go.

When the time came, it was flat calm. I really had no excuse. Sleepily I began to make preparations. I had this sense of doom, that we would never get out, and I was even resentful of Cecilia trying to ease my sleepiness by giving me a cup of coffee. I had no excuse for missing the tide. I gazed down the basin. The lock gates seemed miles away. They looked very narrow. I slowly checked everything for sea. The leak was not too bad. The children were roused.

As we started off for the lock gates, Victoria was peering out of the wheelhouse window to one side of me with Emma on the other. I was at the wheel. I gazed at the lock gates again. Never get through them, I thought with a knee-jerk reaction against previous lock gates and bridges, which crowd me so much that, to get through them, I have to breathe out or stoop down.

But as we got nearer, these lock gates were getting wider and wider apart. Most unusual, I thought. There was absolutely no doubt that we could get through, none whatsoever. Maybe we could find a way of by-passing the *Costaud*, go straight out into the Channel, stall around outside for the tide to change...

I stumbled slightly on an uneven board. Victoria was instantly alert. She caught me prematurely. It wasn't even a proper stumble, let alone a fall. She had been watching me intently.

When we reached the *Costaud*, Cecilia, who had been on deck managing the warps, came bustling up to the wheelhouse. It was clear her two daughters had had some earlier conversation which they were anxious to continue. I overhead Cecilia saying that something had done the trick. The two daughters nodded and giggled, but Emma volunteered it might have been a bit of an overdose as I had nearly fallen over. Maybe try a bit less next time. I began to take notice. What were they talking about, I wanted to know. Ten milligrams of valium Cecilia responded. Some months earlier I had accidentally driven a wood augur through my hand. It has sharp fins which chewed up the flesh between two fingers. No one was on board at the time. Cecilia found me shortly afterwards sitting nursing my hand, but doing nothing about it. She had had a quick look, swabbed it with whisky, and popped an antibiotic into my mouth — only it now turned out it was valium, not an antibiotic.

So that was it, I thought to myself. I wasn't charmed at the realization that they saw me as a coward, but it was not such a bad idea, maybe. An overdose perhaps, but interesting. I don't remember when I next took valium, but it became an occasional lifesaver during the next dozen years afloat. When I learned that I could freeze up with panic, and fail to make decisions necessary for the safety of the ship,

Gray *here has a shorter bowsprit than she acquired later in America (photograph courtesy William Cussans).*

The main cabin also had a small desk and some bookshelves which flanked the entrance to a small private washroom. On the left is the photograph taken from the cabin under the archway into the washroom and on the right you can see the double bed reflected (and, of course, reversed) in the large mirror in the washroom.

I found valium indispensable. I took it prophylactically, before the going got really bad. It worked well.

We got to beloved Dieppe, such an improvement over Calais, but still wanted to make down Channel. A week later we left in the morning, only to return in the evening rolling in the calms, a strong contrary wind forecast. A couple of days later, we tried again with the same result except that we stayed out overnight rolling.

Another four days, and we left again, this time to stay out for a week. The log is peppered with the words "becalmed again" but it was a happy time. William caught some mackerel which we salted and dried in the rigging. We liked the Dieppe fisherman who taunted us to get his skate. We didn't like a bad-tempered Le Havre fisherman who took no notice of us. We swam in the glassy water, the safety line floating out forwards as we made stern-boards in the raging calms. We accidentally burnt a hole in one of the staysails which flopped windless on the cooker chimney.

At the end, when some wind got up, it was slap in our faces, and the leakage jumped right up. I decided I had had enough tip-toeing around in this leaky old boat which started to sink the moment there was a decent bit of wind. I started back to Dieppe with the old southwest wind behind us. Three years before we had found it had a suitable looking floating dock. It only took us a day to get back; it had taken six to get where we were. But it was an exciting sail. The wind began piling the seas up behind us in the setting sun. Emma burnt her hands taking something out of the oven as we rolled. That was one man down on the pump — we did a lot of hand pumping in those days. Another was strapped to the wheel, so we didn't have many left for other things like fiddling with the sails.

Then Dieppe in the distance — the last of three "Dieppe–Dieppe" log entries. We had a brisk wind from behind, the seas were not too bad, we decided to give the Dieppois their money's worth. We set every stitch of sail we could find as we came off the harbor entrance.

11

A daft decision

Coming back to Dieppe for the third time. Coming back for the last time?

The three eldest children, Emma, Thomas and Romily, were now at university. Emma had spent most of her vacation with us, Thomas had come and gone, but both of them had to leave shortly after we returned to Dieppe. Romily had decided to stay with relations in Scotland during the summer. Victoria was in America doing her thing, but came back unexpectedly while we were in Calais, and then disappeared again.

From Cecilia's point of view, Lucy, 14½, and William, 13, were not quite as straightforward. They were both in boarding school, and being the youngest were not regarded as quite such free agents.

During the summer, my attention had been fixed on leaks like a cat on a mouse, but there had been moments of inattention during which I noticed that the international financial scene was not as I might have wished it to have been. The year before, sterling had been allowed to float downward, making it gradually more expensive for us to live abroad. In October the oil embargo led to the quadrupling of oil prices, which resulted the following year in massive industrial disputes in Britain, a three-day work week, and eventually a "social contract" which, as far as I could see, meant that the unions governed England.

Keynesian economics had always held that you could spend your way out of a recession. It might ultimately be inflationary, but at any rate it got things moving. This summer, a new animal appeared. It was called stagflation. The government spending begat inflation, but failed to get things moving. Only banana republics had been known to have it before.

As workers began to develop rights in a continuing flow of income from their jobs, so they also began to develop rights relating to the flow of expenditures called rent. For example, the standard English lease had four parts: a preamble describing the rental unit and fixing the rent and term; covenants by the tenant to, for instance, pay the rent and refrain from trashing the place; covenants by the landlord to provide the rental unit; and the conditions under which the lease could be terminated by either side. By the time I was leaving England the only part enforceable was the landlord's undertaking to provide the rental unit. There was no reason for the tenant to pay the rent. Nor was there any reason for him to leave. Nor did he have much responsibility for looking after his rental unit since that, ironically, was the landlord's responsibility. And, of course, the first person to turn up at the landlord's door asking for shelter in a vacant rental unit had to be given an unenforceable lease.

Then there was the simple question of the money we lived on. It was shrinking, sucked down by the general anti-capitalist environment, not to speak of the sinking pound. Britain still had Exchange Control. This was to affect us later, but at the time it was simply an indication of how much the weak British economy needed protection.

I began to think we might be in a trap. No schooner, and I could go back to England, and protect our property (from tenants), get a (property right in a) job, have my hair trimmed short back and sides. Or, stay in Dieppe, abandon the house, patch up a sinking schooner, and do heaven knows what for money.

So on return to Dieppe, nobody, especially me, was quite sure what to do next. We talked for a bit of going out sailing again, but everyone really knew that this was the end of the school holidays. Everyone also knew that I felt we should not delay hauling *Gray* out of the water, whatever the future thereafter. And Dieppe's floating dock sounded perfect.

In fact, the sudden departure of Geoff Davies in a panic at the thought of being exposed to another sea trip settled the matter. Emma and Thomas had been havering a bit, but Geoff was quite definite: he was leaving. So, all three of them left.

Geoff was a friend of all the children, and had been one of the best guests we had ever had. He had arrived in Calais while everyone was getting more and more fed up with me for not sailing, and had determined he was going to make it fun for everyone, even me. He had arrived with a curly face and two bottles of whisky, in terror that he might be caught smuggling them. The ration was one bottle. He then set to asking me what he could do to help. I wasn't used to children asking to help me, and I think I was quite discourteous to him, if not downright rude. But he persisted, and in the end I gave him a job which was so loathsome I had put off doing it for years, to wit, scrape out all the muck from the bilges so that the limber holes (cutouts at the bottom of the frames) could run free to drain water aft to where the bilge pumps where. He set to and did it without a murmur, and did it so well I blessed him when later we began to leak badly and we needed those limber holes clear.

Admittedly, he had been with us for five weeks by the time he left, but he had evidently been so scared at the prospect of sinking, he was unable to prevent me from guessing why he was leaving. For a brief moment, I saw us through the lens of his normality, saw us the way any parent should have seen the appalling risks we were dragging our children through. Only these children had flipped me into a leak freak with port fever instead of the irresponsible daredevil other children's parents might see.

We ourselves were beginning to feel more normal. In J. M. W. Turner's *Bassin Duquesne* (a painting in the Frick Museum, New York), flanked by the cafés, it was hard not to feel normal. It soon became obvious that our effort to put up all the sails on our final return to Dieppe had paid off. We had been seen, and I sensed there was a way in which we were becoming the property of Dieppe. In pursuit of this public relations effort, we had the Commandant du Port for a drink. He was getting towards the end of his career, and had evidently led a somewhat grand expatriate life in France Outre-Mer.

- The French had a fiction that certain colonial conquests were in fact parts of France which could thus be divided into metropolitan France and overseas France (France Outre-Mer). The Commandant's previous posting had been in Réunion, one of the five overseas departments. As of March 2011, the others were French Guiana, Guadeloupe, Martinique and Mayotte. Algeria used to be one of them.

I forgot about the leak for a few days and began to enjoy Dieppe once again. But, plop, all of a sudden I had to man the pumps for an hour or so to get rid of all the water. We had started leaking again just sitting there quietly at the quayside.

But this time it was not the stern leak. It was coming in from the sides.

I dived immediately, found the leak quite quickly — it was big enough — and stopped it up. It was relatively easy this time. I wondered what ailed the ship so badly she could collapse in a quiet harbor.

When we first arrived in the Bassin Duquesne, the fishing basin, the trawlers, many of them wooden, looked much like each other, tatty, workmanlike, crewed by vertical wasps, yellow slickers up to the waist, black on top.

At some point, we must have lain next to a wooden trawler and exchanged some words with the deckhand, Émile Bocquet. Like Pilot, he had no children, loved them but felt awkward around them. However, with his peers — and I discovered that I counted as one — he had no trace of awkwardness and quite quickly told me how insulted he was that I failed to tu-toyer when I spoke to him. I explained that I had learned French largely from governesses, and this mode of address really hadn't come up. I would try.

Next time he was on his trawler, talking with his skipper about this and that, I set to work to listen to what he said, not so easy as they relapsed into patois and my French was not good. I noticed, however, his skipper was addressed strictly by the more formal "vous." And then, to my astonishment, I noticed that the skipper used the familiar word "tu" back to Émile. In French, this form of address is reserved for the Deity, dogs, children and inferiors when the inferior recognizes his own position and replies with a "vous." None of this Americanizing with "Hey, Hank," to address the CEO. It's pure class distinction in France — the Revolution might not have happened.

The next time I saw Émile, I asked him why he did not use "tu" to his skipper. "No," he said without further explanation. "I would never do that."

They had fished together for 40 years. There were only two of them on the trawler.

Émile was missing when I first went diving. I didn't give it much thought at the time, but the next day his skipper asked me where he was. I said I didn't know.

"I think he must be sick," the skipper said. "Never happened before. Do you know where he lives?"

I did. I gave him the address.

Forty years together? Never been to his house? Always "vous"?

The Bassin Duquesne was a social place. Instead of being stuck out in some outlying industrial area, it formed part of the very heart of Dieppe, or at least one of the hearts, for Dieppe had many. When the trawlers were back from fishing, the fishermen would hang around doing odd jobs, or sometimes more serious work, particularly on the wooden trawlers which needed, as we knew, constant repair. Their children would hang around, too. So very quickly, instead of having one handful of children, we had two handfuls of children mobbing about.

One particular pair of boys, Philippe and Michel, became very familiar. On the whole, I always saw children through some kind of lens, usually Cecilia's maternal lens. I seldom had direct dealings with them. But Cecilia had gone back to England with Lucy and William, leaving me alone. I found myself actually talking to Philippe and Michel, who treated me as though I were an ordinary grownup, and would still hang around the ship when there was only me on board.

Fairly soon after our arrival in Dieppe, Philippe said he wanted to say something to me. I was caulking a deck seam on my knees, so I felt I should get to my feet for the interview. He told me one of the port officers had run a *scrutin* among the trawlers.

It took me a while to work out what the French word scrutin meant. I knew I had heard the word somewhere. Then, I got it: the word used for an election of the Chamber of Deputies, for instance. I remembered it from my Reuters days in Paris.

I was polite, not sure what it had to do with me.

But Philippe then volunteered that the scrutin had been about *Gray*, to find out what the trawlers thought of our presence, whether we were bothering them and so forth. I felt very uneasy, and asked what the response had been. Philippe thought it had been all right, but he only knew what a few of his father's friends had told his father who had passed the information on to Philippe.

So the authorities had polled the trawlers. It was my first lesson in public relations afloat: our ability to stay in any particular port is as long as our charm and no longer. We had no rights; the police were not on our side; Dieppe was asking us for no port dues; we were a net drain on local resources; at any moment we could become surplus to local requirements. Then what would we do?

We must behave ourselves. Keep a low profile. Not make any waves. Wait our turn. Touch our forelock. And hope that we could decide our futures before someone else did it for us.

A couple of days later, the water started pouring in again. Not only was it worse than before, but Cecilia, who had come back briefly with Lucy, was due to take Lucy back to London and stay there herself for a fortnight. Very soon, the trawlers all knew about it, and showed signs of sympathy. Could they do anything? I made gloomy jokes about the blind leading the blind, but no, I had to cope. This reference to the blind sounds pointless in English, but the French "*aveugler une voie d'eau*" (literarily, blind a way of water) means to stop a leak .

So Cecilia and I started the usual business of finding the leak on the inside and then preparing to dive.

By this time, blinding ways of water was becoming a way of life and I had collected some rudimentary equipment which I kept in a glass-bottomed bucket. The bucket itself didn't turn out to be much use in the end, but the equipment became more and more essential — and strange.

The first thing to do was to locate which section of the ship was letting in water. We took up the floor boards (called the ceiling in a boat because they form the ceiling of the frames), and could pretty quickly tell between which frames there was a flow of water down the sides of the ship. Leaks tended to be in the vertically disposed parts of the hull near the waterline, so the next thing to do was to see whether the flow was above or below the listings, the ventilation apertures in the ceiling. At that point, I used a small flashlight bulb, soldered to the end of an electric cable, to illuminate the space between the ceiling and the outer planking, and a dentist's mirror, extended by a piece of stiff wire. I then drilled a hole in the ceiling opposite the leak. Into this hole went a cylindrical magnet mounted in a (non-magnetic) copper tube. Diving on the outside, I used a small compass, the sort of thing you buy for a car, to locate where the magnet was on the inside. To blind the leak, I would usually have to pull out the remains of some rotten stuff in a seam. This would temporarily increase the leak. Tapping by a helper inside would signal this increase, confirming that I had the right spot. More tapping would confirm when I had blinded it.

Sounds very simple, but it was not. And I lived in fear of doing some really catastrophic damage to the outside while trying to repair a small leak.

Women seem to think more collaboratively than men, Cecilia is a woman, so she thought I should collaborate with Émile. It would be useful experience for him because he could then take over the inside job from her when she had to go back to England for the children. So Émile and Cecilia crowded into the crooked spaces inside the ship to find and then gaze at the leak while I went diving. This time, after blinding the leak, I had a better look round the outside. On the Lappel, we had all concentrated on the stern leak, but the last day we had a scrub around of the entire hull above the mud, and I had noticed some loose mastic. I now saw that nearly all the mastic had fallen out of the seams.

I was touched by Émile's concern for us, and tried to thank him.

"*C'est normal*," he said. The French word "normal" usually means anything but normal. It often has a sense of dismissal, like "Don't teach your grandmother to suck eggs." It can also be the equivalent of the word "obvious," but again with a somewhat insulting dismissive sense, like "What did you expect, then?" In my experience it is never used to describe something which really is normal such as a gauge showing the right pressure which would probably be described as "*dans la fourchette prévu*"; normal body temperature is likely to be spoken of as the basal or central temperature.

Misunderstanding him, I said it was not the least bit normal. In England, if they think you are going to sink, they tell you to go sink elsewhere. Not in my backyard, as the Americans would say. The English didn't stretch out their hands to help.

When was I going onto the floating dock, he asked, using the same suppressed premise as though he had asked me why I had not stopped beating my wife.

I allowed that the dock looked fine for us. Had I got a date, he pressed. No, I hadn't. He told me that I had to have a date and that to get a date I had to have a "*priorité*." That meant, I had to be sinking, like the rest of the fishing fleet which fished for coquilles St. Jacques (scallops) during the hard winter months. Since I was obviously sinking, there shouldn't be a problem, so he would take me round to the Capitainerie to get a priorité to present to the Chambre de Commerce which ran the dock.

So we walked off to the Capitainerie du Port. The official behind the desk recognized Émile, but was evidently not on familiar terms. He checked that Émile was the one who fished with Pierre. Yes, said Émile, with Monsieur Pierre. But, it has to do with the *Gray*, which is sinking, Émile said.

"C'est normal," the official answered.

Émile insisted: The *Gray* really was sinking, the boss (indicating me) had had to dive twice — or was it three times — just to keep the ship afloat at the quayside.

On hearing that I was a diver, the official exclaimed that the restaurants were crying out for divers — I would have a great future. In French, deep-sea divers and those who wash dishes are both called plongeurs. The official began to laugh at his own joke. He was not taking me seriously.

Up to that point, Émile had been valiantly paddling my canoe for me, my French being indifferent. But I thought he might never be taken seriously unless I tried to speak up on my own behalf. It was not an effective performance since I knew none of the technical words for things like oakum and paying and sewing on the mud in England.

However, the official listened. He supposed that I should have a priorité but he turned to Émile to mention that his boss, Pierre, wouldn't like it at all. Monsieur Pierre had already been given a date for the floating dock, responded Émile, so he wouldn't be bothered by *Gray* getting a priorité which merely gave him a place in the queue.

When we left with the priorité, Émile explained to me as we skirted the bassin to get to the Chambre de Commerce that while the floating dock was operated by the Chambre de Commerce they couldn't handle the disputes between the trawlers about who should get on first, so they made the Capitainerie do it. They said they were dock operators, technicians, not mediators. Since the Capitainerie, not being technicians, gave everyone a priorité, the Chambre de Commerce was back where it always had been.

I didn't have a great experience of how bureaucracies worked, but I was beginning my lesson on the French model.

As we walked round the head of the bassin past *Gray* on the way to the Chambre de Commerce I asked Émile about the coquilles.

Even if he didn't carry a Communist party card, Émile was the archetype of the French radical, robust, individual, listening to Robespierre in one of the cafés in Paris, except that he was born too late. He launched into a speech about how they worked for their living, but the worst was in the winter when they dredged the whole of the seabed of the Channel for these little shellfish, doing immense damage on the way. But it was dangerous, and regularly every winter there were families who were bereaved, fishermen too badly injured to keep on working.

I didn't attempt to defend myself against the implicit charge of not being a worker.

He explained to me some more details of the gear and the labor of the deck-hands like himself. I could understand well enough. I had seen the wires and the winches. The trawlers had to be staunch, Émile went on. They didn't want to be caught in a winter gale in a leaky ship. That was why they all tried to get onto the floating dock before the season started.

When did it start, I asked. In a fortnight, Émile replied, the first of October.

We had a lot wrong with us, I was sure. But if we blocked the floating dock so the trawlers couldn't get themselves in shape before going off scalloping, I would not be the most admired and desired skipper in Dieppe.

I told Émile I couldn't do it, I simply could not get *Gray* onto the floating dock before the season started. He shrugged. He didn't disagree. I said I might need to have a little help from him, but I could probably keep the ship afloat. He nodded.

Next day, Cecilia and Lucy went back to London.

The following Monday, the Commandant du Port turned up. He was going to tell me to leave. I knew it. Deserted by everyone.

He wanted to know if I would like to move into the Bassin de Paris, another of the docks in Dieppe.

The Bassin de Paris was quite a different affair from the Bassin Duquesne. It was definitely commercial, nothing in it but tankers and freighters. It was long and thin, nearly half a mile long, a long way from anything which might be termed fun–Dieppe. I imagined myself alone, growing seaweed on my body, forgotten, desperate.

Seeing me hesitate, the Commandant told me it would be much quieter there away from the trawlers. Actually, that was a disincentive: I liked the trawlers, as I told the Commandant, and besides they gave me a feeling of support. I said I thought it might be a long wait to get on the floating dock. The Commandant look confused. Hadn't I just gotten a priorité? Why wasn't I the next on the list? I could have been quite straightforward with the Commandant, but for some reason I didn't want to admit that my delay was due to public relations considerations and not to what I actually told him, namely, that the leak had gotten better. He left saying that I should let him know if I changed my mind.

Sure enough, a few days later there was another leak. This time, Émile was not around to help. I could have waited for him the next day or the day after and gone on pumping, but it was a lovely day, and this time I knew exactly where the leak was. A different place, as it was each time. I had never liked diving and I was beginning to hate it. Morale meant a lot to me, so dive in the sun rather than wait for Émile.

I wasn't so successful this time in blinding the leak. On each previous occasion it had been the caulking that had given way. This time, the leak seemed to be coming from behind a frame. It could be a nail sick bolt. I wouldn't be able to do much about that while diving. I still had the previous week's priorité. Maybe I should at least get in the queue. So I went off to the Chambre de Commerce.

- Oak (*chêne* in French) corrodes iron more rapidly than other wood; at that time I didn't know that *Gray's* underwater (*oeuvres vives* in French) was made of beech (*hêtre*), a rarity in ship building, softer than alternatives, but less liable to rot. The topsides (*oeuvres mortes*) were of oak.

The official looked at the date on the form I handed him. It was only good for 24 hours he said, and if we hadn't done them the honor of sinking within that time frame, then the form was no longer valid. One or the other, he pointed out: we couldn't go on threatening to sink and then failing to do so. I explained that I had been diving repeatedly to stay afloat, and couldn't go on like this indefinitely. He was in total agreement with me, he said. That would not do at all. But, he said that every other boat in the harbor had a similar problem. It was very difficult for him, he said, because the stories he heard from the skippers were all heart rending. He and his wife saw their mission in life to cure the sick — indeed his wife was a nurse — and particularly to help her compatriots, for she was English. While they were both dedicated to the cure of the sick — he had even been a trainee priest at an earlier period in his life — they were really not competent to decide who is the more sick. The floating dock was, of course, in constant demand. But I would have to go back to the Capitainerie to discuss with them how sick I was. He said his name was Raoul, and he would do whatever he could for me once I had sorted things out with the Capitainerie.

The man himself looked sick. He might have been a year or so older than me, but he had the yellow tinge to his face which I had seen once on a liver cancer patient. His thin spare figure looked gaunt. I wondered how long he had to live. I also wondered about triage on the battlefield, of which I thought Jeremy Bentham would have approved ("it is the greatest happiness of the greatest number that is the measure of right and wrong"), but possibly not Raoul. Right then I could have done with a triage decision in my favor from Raoul.

So I went back to the other side of the Bassin Duquesne to visit the Commandant. It had started to rain. I stopped off on *Gray* to collect my plastic waterproof, the one I hadn't worn since that horrible journey through the blizzard from Bornholm to Copenhagen. One of the buttons was off, a pocket was torn, there was a rip at the back, but it would have to do. I hadn't figured out how to use an umbrella on board.

The Commandant was at his most welcoming and expansive. He complimented me on sailing with all those children. Such bravery, he said — for which I read the word "foolhardiness." He then proceeded to ask me in detail about the *Gray*, where I had found her, what I had done with her, what my hopes were and so forth. This was an august man, not a petty official, definitely in charge of the conversation, with the urbane presence of an ambassador. Nor was I dressed for such an interview. Apart from the waterproof, I was still in summer work clothes, a little on the chilly side, but not yet in my full mid-season outfit — if I had one. Every time I wriggled my toes, I sensed the water squelching out of my sandals onto the Commandant's carpet, the trickle of rain seeping through the ripped plastic at my back.

After a while, I felt I had to break in to say that I had come for a purpose: to get a priorité. The Commandant looked perplexed — didn't I have one already. He called into his back office to ask if *Gray* had had a priorité, and of course the answer was Yes, I had. I explained the Chambre de Commerce said it was out of date, adding unwisely that I had either to get onto the floating dock or sink within the 24 hours specified in the document.

The Commandant looked shocked. Sink? Oh, we couldn't have that, he beamed. Then he leaned forward confidentially so that the man in the back office couldn't hear, and started to explain that this Dieppe in which he had washed up

after such a great career in France Outre-Mer — it was his last post before retir-
ing — was full of petty officials, whom I should not take too seriously. Everything
was a question of personalities, family relations, who knows whom. When he was
in Réunion, he had hoped for better things than to be washed up here like a beached
whale. Did I know Réunion?"

No, I didn't, I said.

He reminded me about the scend in the avant port of Dieppe, and said that
the one in Réunion was much worse. He had recommended a reconfiguration of
the harbor entrance, but they wouldn't hear of it. Extending his hairy wrist, he
explained that freighters moored up with nylon warps as big as his wrist sometimes
broke them. When they broke, they could do immense damage just with the
whiplash from the kinetic energy stored in them. The port authorities should have
listened to him, he repeated, but they didn't.

> • *Prostar Sailing Directions 2005 South Atlantic Ocean and Indian Ocean*, by the
> National Geospatial-Intelligence Agency, says on page 223: "Rollers, long swell waves
> created by distant storms, affect Réunion. This phenomenon occasionally lasts 4 to 5
> days, frequently causing great damage and suspending all activities, though rarely
> for longer than 24 hours."

Recollecting himself at last, he said he was desolated to realize that nonetheless
he was obliged to get on with the petty details of his job in Dieppe. He stood up
and extended his hand saying that it had been a great pleasure to talk to me, Captain
Jones, one seaman to another so to speak and that he hoped I would not hesitate
to drop by for another gossip. Then he could not resist offering the same poor joke
about the plongeur, assuring me that my kitchen skills could keep the ship afloat
forever.

I went out into the rain. I could live with the leak if it didn't get worse. Yet
the fact that I had nothing better to do in life than to operate the hand pump on
deck every few hours seemed to me to be worse than solitary confinement. It underlined the meaninglessness of my life.

While the absence of Émile had hampered the diving, it also saved me from
an embarrassment with Michel and Philippe, neither of whom he liked. I didn't
know why, but it seemed to me it wasn't my role to ask. Philippe had given me
some fishes that morning, and so I had asked him and Michel to come and share
them with me in the evening, hoping there would be no embarrassment with Émile
turning up unexpectedly.

They had something to say to me. They had talked to their parents, they said,
and it had been agreed Philippe and Michel would ship with us as unpaid crew.
They would get jobs at each port and pay for their keep that way. Would that be all
right? I should meet their parents to confirm, they said.

I hedged. The rain gave me no escape out of doors. While I didn't see how it
could possibly work for long, I could also see it might be the chance of a lifetime

for them. I had noted Philippe painting one of the trawlers with nothing but fishing for scallops to look forward to for the next fifty years.

I switched the conversation to the return next day of Cecilia and Emma, together with my son, Romily, whom they had not met.

That following afternoon, I thought I would go down to the terminal to meet them off the ferry. When I got there, I found no such ferry existed. (Remember, no internet in those days). The next ferry was at nearly midnight. I was lonely. I was looking forward to the company. I didn't feel like taking up the jobs that I had been doing filling in time between leaks. Besides, the only available inside job — it was still raining — was to continue fixing up the pumping system, deep down in the bilges, near that wretched sickness the ship suffered from.

So I had time to think. The rain was not heavy, just pervasive. I still had my summer sandals on. I squelched in water on the sidewalk or in mud near the railroad tracks which ran along one side of the Bassin Duquesne and which had to be crossed to get to *Gray*. Cecilia and I would have to work out some plan at least for the winter, and perhaps further beyond that.

We would probably get on the floating dock after the fishing season had started, but then it would be too late to cross back to England. The weather would not be good; student crew would be harder to obtain. That meant wintering in Dieppe, not what I had intended at the beginning of the summer, but with Cecilia it could be fun. When she joined ship and lived on board before the summer started, I had felt that we were a good team. How much more enjoyable to continue this teamwork in Dieppe, a place for which we both had the most glamorous feelings.

On the longer view, I had grave doubts about our financial ability, and even our will, to maintain two large establishments, one in London and one at sea. The whole boating junket had started as a distraction for the children during school holidays. That was why Cecilia had put her weight behind it. In the last few years, it had become more than that for me. I didn't have, and was no longer looking for, an alternative occupation. Here was the rub: I didn't really know what her long-term feelings were. As I have related, things came to a head between Cecilia and me when the children began to leave home. Subsequently, she had come to live on board. Post hoc, ergo propter hoc? Whether this was cause and effect had not been the subject of any conversation between us.

From time to time when I was alone I thought my doubts about our financial position might just be a difference in attitude to money between me and Cecilia until I remembered an incident a little while earlier. I was sitting on the quarterdeck, my diving gear spread around the ship's waist, once more struggling into those unyielding rubber things which were never big enough for me. A well-dressed elderly man watched me, stepped forward, and with great politeness proffered: "*Monsieur, je suis navré de la situation financière en Angleterre.*" It was said with the solemnity appropriate for condolences for a death, for something completed, historical, public, unalterable. It was the oil crisis, after all.

Cecilia and I didn't talk until lunch the next day following the late-night arrival of the ferry. Cecilia, of course, had a plan. I would get on dry dock as soon as possible and then bring *Gray* back to the Albert Dock for the winter. I countered that I didn't think we could support a three-masted schooner and a large London house. We would have to choose.

What I didn't say until later was nearer the truth: I doubted my ability to be able to repair the ship and bring her back to London as the winter came on, I doubted the likelihood of being able to find an affordable and suitable berth for *Gray* in England, quite apart from the growing doubts about our whole way of life and our ability to finance it. I felt we had to have a new vision of the future, but I was unable to formulate exactly what that should be.

Since I couldn't come up with any viable alternative, while she didn't have any room for maneuver over the children, we essentially came to deadlock during this conversation. Without realizing it, I had been hoping that Cecilia would wave a magic wand. She was good at taking my technical concerns, blowing away the confusion, and coming up with something workable. But I also knew from Port Meirion and Crete that she didn't always do that sort of thing, particularly when her children were concerned. Now I was finding what looked like a separation under which she took my house, while I linked my fortunes to an aging wooden ship, badly in need of repair, basically uninsurable, which could be lost, probably with its crew, at a moment's notice.

The loss of my house came sharply into focus. I had bought it when I was 29. I was now 44. I didn't do much to it until Cecilia brought her family to live there. At that point, to house the merged family, I added a slab of rooms on the top and another down the back, quite apart from a great deal of my spirit. Cecilia and her children only lived there fully for about five or six years before the children began to drift away, but it was a period which had fully justified everything I had put into it.

Just as I was in great doubt how the ship could be made to fit into our lives, and whether I really wanted to lose my house, so she was in no doubt where her own duties lay. She had family responsibilities and she was going to discharge them. It had been her idea to go to sea, her drive that had got the first boat, her support that had enabled me to go through with the purchase of *Gray*. But I don't think she had lost sight of the original purpose of the ship: for the family. I think I had.

Our conversation had taken place on 20 September 1974, just two months after the 17 July 1974 which would later be inscribed in my passport as the date of my emigration from England, the date we sailed out of Queenborough, after the repairs on the Lappel Bank.

12

Le dock flottant

Since the logic of circumstances was forcing us to spend the winter apart, it was redundant to ask whether either of us wanted it that way. It was even more redundant to enquire whether this separation had any implications for the future. So we asked none of these questions of each other and got on with the immediate business in hand: an invitation to dinner from Michel's parents, who would doubtless raise the subject of Michel and Philippe working their passage round the world with us. It could be an awkward dinner.

The quartier where they lived was probably 16th century, or possibly even earlier, and hadn't been changed much. We ducked in succession — Cecilia, Emma, Romily and I — to get under the lintel of the narrow passage which had been penetrated through the houses leading from the damp reflective street into a courtyard within. Doors were covered in graffiti. A winding outside staircase looked as if it had been there for centuries. Pumpkins were the ornaments in the courtyard — it was that time of year. But otherwise it was clean, undecorated, all stone or wood of great antiquity.

We knew Michel's parents were likely to be modest people, but we were very unsure what to expect. Had we had any to change into, deciding which clothes would have been a major problem.

His father stretched out a hand. "*Mois, je suis dans l'affichage,*" he said. "*Et vous, monsieur?*" How did I translate into French my own calling: an idle, lazy, good for nothing layabout? I didn't try, but during the course of dinner I began to be perplexed by what he meant by being dans l'affichage, as though he were in the real estate business or a lawyer. Gradually, it became clearer: he was the local bill poster, brush and pail stuff.

When I had been in Paris, a dozen years earlier, working for Reuters, we rarely met the French. We had been asked to dinner a couple of times in the whole 18 months I was there, and it had clearly been a duty invitation, the other guests the curé and the doctor. I only dimly realized at that time just how bad the French are at informal entertainment of people they don't know. So to make up for their human deficiencies, they will produce a huge spread of food which it would be impolite not to eat in its entirety.

It became obvious at the outset that this meal was going to last a very long time, with many courses. And soon it became obvious that each plate would be copious—and largely inedible. The meat alone was formidable: a squared-off block of muscle which remained in rigor mortis.

Michel was at dinner, of course, but his eight brothers and sisters were upstairs. I wondered how they had been rendered so silent.

Very gradually, after a polite delay, the conversation worked itself round to the ship. Where had we come from? Were we staying in Dieppe? What did we do with the ship? And here, I noted, the questions were becoming less like trite observations on the weather.

They said they hadn't seen their children at home ever since our ship had arrived and were wondering what the attraction was. There was a pointed silence, during which I realized that we had been asked to dinner to be interrogated about drugs—not the last time this was to happen.

We had been through all that drug business when our elder children were Michel's age. The depression of it, the boredom of it... We knew about sex and all this, and we knew about drink and all that, and we had ploughed through all this and all that six times successively, multiplied by this and by that. We had personal experience of drink and sex after all, but when it came to drugs, oh sigh, we had to start learning from the bottom. It all culminated in a teenage party our children insisted on giving — in our house — without us. Cecilia and I went out to dinner by ourselves, and returned grim-faced sharp at 11 P.M., curfew time.

Everything was spotless; the dishes done, the crumbs swept up — and the children sitting quietly in corners drinking milk. There was no liquor to be seen.

From then on, I was all in favor of pot parties.

Explain all this to the bill poster? Impossible. All we could do was laugh with relief and say the children weren't interested in drugs, which was absolutely true — the craze had worn off.

Now that we were going to be residents of Dieppe, the dinner took on more importance. How had we done?

The next day, Cecilia and Emma left. I was alone with Romily.

I suppose Philippe felt he could not be outdone in hospitality by his friend, Michel. Three days later, we were bidden to his parents. His father was the acting captain of one of the cross–Channel ferries. Philippe came round to collect us for dinner, but said it wasn't quite ready. Did we mind delaying for a little moment?

We waited politely. Philippe looked more and more anxious, but made not the slightest attempt to check up whether dinner was ready. Time dragged on, and eventually a lot of time dragged on until, around half past ten, we decided we weren't going to dinner, and would Philippe like to have something with us?

Then, during the meal, it came out that his father's ferry had been delayed. How did he know? He had been with us all the time. It didn't add up.

A day or two went by with Philippe and Michel mobbing around a bit with each other on board, and to some extent with Romily.

I had done this before, but I decided to repeat my lecture to the two French boys, reminding them that we were foreigners, guests in Dieppe, and that we had to behave more correctly than the townspeople, which meant: no mobbing around, and off to their homes at a reasonable hour in the evening.

The next day, much too early in the morning, there was a commotion on the quayside. A woman was yelling for me somewhat angrily. Where was her grandson? she wanted to know. What grandson, I asked. Philippe, she answered. I said I didn't know. I presumed he was at home.

The woman told me to search my own boat.

I went down to the hold where the children slept on the floor (there were no beds in the cabins at that time — only the master's cabin aft, which Cecilia and I occupied). I was furious to find that not only was Philippe there, but that he was late for work, and that was why his grandmother was so upset.

I knew perfectly well the implications: we would be counted a bad lot.

Later on I asked Michel what I should do. "Don't worry," he said. "Philippe is sick. He lies. His grandmother knows. Everyone knows. The invitation to dinner never existed."

Romily left, and I was alone again. I wept privately. I hadn't seen him for the summer. He had preferred to spend it with his relations in Scotland. It had been my life once, I hadn't kept up with it, but it was an entirely different matter to cut myself off from it forever by abandoning my house, and my country, and possibly Romily. Our lives might join up again; but they might not.

The moment he had gone, I hurt my eye with a piece of flying rust from a chain plate I had been chipping. I didn't think much of it until the evening, when I noticed that the street lamps wore haloes. And then I realized that it was not because of the rain on the deckhouse windows. I closed the injured eye and found the good eye could see quite clearly.

I hurried round to Raoul at the Chambre de Commerce first thing the next day. If I went to the hospital, they would want money up front, Raoul said. Did I have any? I had had lobar pneumonia in Paris when I first arrived for Reuters. I was coughing up blood. The ambulance had refused to move without advance payment. So, I believed Raoul.

He asked me some more questions from which he established that the only symptom had been the halo round the street lamp. The eye no longer hurt. I could see quite clearly. He said he would talk to his wife at lunch — I should come back to see him in the afternoon.

When I returned, he told me his wife said the danger was glaucoma which certainly required medical treatment. But to be practical about it, if the halo was gone that evening then there was less urgency, but I should not fail to have an eye examination as soon as I could. She had told him glaucoma was very often symptom free in its early stages, but it could eventually cause blindness, so I should take it seriously.

I felt comforted.

I felt comforted because his wife's advice dispelled the panic, but even more because of the way Raoul seemed to be treating me as his responsibility — to some extent, at any rate.

When I walked back to *Gray*, I found Émile sheltering from the rain in one of the quayside hangars. I hadn't seen him for a few days. I was surprised to find him in his best suit. There was no one on any of the trawlers.

When he had come on board, and we were safely out of the rain in the deck-house, he asked me if I would write some postcards for him. He sat down at the table and handed me the cards and a ballpoint pen. Slowly, he dictated four post-cards, one each to Cecilia, Emma, Lucy and William. As I repeated back to him what I was writing down, I made a mistake with a subjunctive. He corrected me. Was he illiterate? If so, the subjunctive would have come from euphony before it ever got to my classroom, a consideration that had never occurred to me. But the subjunctive was important: Emma, Lucy and William's father was a schoolmaster.

Émile wanted to pay me for the stamps. I refused, but it was a hollow refusal. I had only two stamps and no money to buy any more. It was hard to remember that I was no longer entitled. Émile insisted, we nearly came to blows, but I had to give in, and accepted his *fr*500 note (we were still confused about New Francs — it was really a *fr*5 note), stuck one of my stamps on Lucy's card, and the other on a letter to Cecilia enclosing the remaining cards. I didn't tell her that I had told Émile of my worries over her future with me on the ship. What would she do? Would she be bored? In my letter to her I didn't pass on his opinion: women's hands were much finer than men's and she should be able to do plumbing and electrical work.

At the end of the month, the coquillards finally left on the midnight tide in a full moon towards a rattling thunderstorm hull down over England to the north. The scalloping season started on the First of October. During September, the trawlers had lain against the quayside, flat like overlapping slates on a roof, leaving and returning one by one to go on the floating dock, occasionally going out fishing singly.

- I take this opportunity to be pedantic: The distance to the horizon at sea varies directly with the square root of the height of the eye, on our sort of boat, such distance was about 4 miles. The hull of another vessel farther away than this starts disappearing below the horizon and is said to be "hull down." Distant thunderstorms sometimes appear to be like this when lightning strikes the sea beyond the visible horizon. The world is an oblate spheroid, not round, and at low heights refraction is an important factor, but very roughly the sea horizon (in nautical miles) is about $1.2 \times \sqrt{}$ eye-height (in feet). The nautical mile is 1 minute of latitude (or longitude at the equator), or 6076 feet, as opposed to the land mile of 5,280 feet.

The trawlers were all on the move at once, crawling with their vertical wasps in their oilskins, detaching themselves from the quayside, and jostling and tooting to get out of the lock gates. I had never seen a fishing fleet as a fleet before. The trawler behind us lit up its deck lights. It was steel, and its sharp bow leaned over our fragile mahogany deck. It bobbed down towards *Gray*: its unseen skipper had given his massive engines a kick in reverse. Silence. The bow slid smoothly outward from the quayside and away from us. With another huge kick the trawler joined the rest. "Good luck," I yelled. "Thank you. We'll be back in 48 hours," the skipper yelled back. Then they were gone. I rushed to the end of the mole round the outer harbor to see them streaming out, to see *my* fleet streaming out. Lights were littered all over the ocean. It was now drizzling on the fringes of the thunderstorm. I returned to find stragglers leaving the basin. A few toots outside the lock gates, then silence.

Gray was alone in the rain in the Bassin Duquesne.

And my friends out there? Some would die, some would be maimed during the season. Fishing for scallops in the English Channel in winter is a very, very tough business. I felt effete.

But now was the time for action. The *coquillards* gone, I must get on that floating dock.

I expected it to be empty when I ran to have a look at it early next morning, but it had a *chalutier*, the *Vergoyer*, on it.

I rushed round to Raoul at the Chambre de Commerce, demanding why he had let the *Vergoyer* on ahead of us. He had a priorité he answered. But, so did we, I retorted, forgetting that ours was out of date. The *Vergoyer* had something wrong with the stern gland, Raoul explained, something he couldn't go out fishing with. There would be a constant trickle of vessels needing repairs during the fishing season unless I started to bully the Capitainerie.

He was right, of course. I had a lot to learn about being forceful in this tough world in which I was now living.

I went straight over to the Capitainerie. I told the official we had to get onto the floating dock. That would be impossible, he said. The bâteau porte was ahead of me. What on earth was that, I asked.

He explained that the big graving dock which I had seen around was reserved for the cross–Channel ferries and vessels of that size. Instead of having lock gates at the entrance it had the bâteau porte, which could be floated across the entrance and then flooded to sink it and close off the dock so that it could be pumped dry. He said the usual way would be to have lock gates so constructed that they would jam shut to prevent water coming into the dock. But, if they went wrong, they were difficult to service as they couldn't be got at without a diver, and diving repairs were never very effective. So, they had chosen the bâteau porte option which meant that the bâteau porte could be towed over to the floating dock, scraped and painted, and the floating dock could be floated over to the graving dock and serviced there, a very harmonious system. And, since the general operation of the port was the responsibility of the Capitainerie, they felt able to give themselves a priorité—even bumping such a wonderful vessel as the three masted schooner *Gray*.

One of the ferries needed to be dry-docked fairly urgently, and the bâteau porte was leaking, so it had to be serviced first. There would be no surprises: it would take two weeks, he said. Then I could go on.

Unfortunately, it all made sense. I was lucky to be here at all, I thought. I might have been up the London River with no suitable facilities that I knew of and the Admiralty telling me to go sink someplace else. At any rate, in Dieppe, they seemed to have just the right equipment for *Gray*. But it was depressing waiting in the rain to go on, not being able to concentrate on anything much else.

I had been alone for several days when the fishing fleet went to sea. It rained. We leaked. We moved from the jolly fishing basin to the Bassin de Paris, the huge commercial dock. My only companions were the cranes dripping rust onto their concrete foundations on the quayside. Then another big diving leak, the fifth since we came to Dieppe, and the next day onto the floating dock.

My mother arrived unexpectedly to celebrate her 85th birthday on the day we came out of the water. I fled to her. I was terrified by what the hull might disclose. I preferred to prolong the current uncertainty rather than suffer the certainty (which could be worse) of what even at that time was already known to the ship-wrights. So I settled her into her hotel room, and we talked as though my ship were merely one of many items of mutual interest, such as the difficulty she was experiencing from arthritis in using the typewriter. For her, this was of immense importance, closing down an activity which had been vital to her life for 60 or 70 years, and which had produced among publications, one great book, *National Velvet*, and one great play, *The Chalk Garden*. My mother wrote under her maiden name, Enid Bagnold.

When I eventually got back within sight of the floating dock, I could see the worst had happened. Half a dozen workmen were standing around looking through gaping holes into the inside of my ship. They weren't working: they gestured, talked and pointed. It had to be a specially virulent form of rot, or perhaps all the nails were sick, or perhaps they were wondering how to get the ship to the graveyard.

They fell silent with my approach. Monsieur Bertrand, a tall Norman, the *contre-maître*, took on the attitude of spokesman, the workmen grouped together looking up at him, and he at me, as though we were two heroes about to be locked in combat to decide the fate of nations.

He put his hand inside the hull, then eased it carefully up to his elbow. There was nothing inside, I thought. It had all crumbled away. On the contrary, he explained to me: there was so much wood in this vessel, he could have made two the same size as mine. Then he patted his elbow: his fingers had only just reached the inside of the frame; it was vast.

So that was it: far from what I had feared, I at least had a stout hull on my hands.

While the Chambre de Commerce, operated and maintained the floating dock they had no further responsibility for what went on, other than placing the ship on the central blocks and shoring it upright against the steel sides. It was the end of the day. Monsieur Bertrand and his workmen went away. To the end, I remained a little frightened of him. He was an orator, not cozy at all. To him I was "tu," but he remained "vous" to me. ("*Tu prends ton ciseau.*" "*Oui Monsieur Bertrand.*")

The outline of Raoul, so yellow and gaunt I had not noticed him, disclosed itself from the camouflage of paint daubed on the steel dock walls. He was not particularly interested in me. He was gazing at the hull in a detached sort of way. I went over to him.

The hull had at least half a dozen big holes cut in it, not to speak of other places which had obviously been hacked at preparatory to repair. It was evident that he was not in the best of tempers. First of all, he wanted to know, where had I been when the ship came out of the water. At the Hôtel Aguado seeing my mother, I explained. And why had that been so important? he wanted to know. She was 85, and had arrived unexpectedly, I said. He considered that for a while.

Then he said I had a lot more to learn. I already knew, he said, how the Capitainerie and the Chambre de Commerce worked together, but Monsieur Bertrand and his team of workmen were employed by neither, but by me, and I wasn't there. So what was he to do? It would be unthinkable to have his floating dock standing idle with no work being done, and yet he was the only person around with any kind of responsibility. Other trawlers in the fleet who had dropped out of the fishing season needing to have this or that done to their hulls so they could go out again would put pressure on him to get the *Gray* off their dock if there were no work being done.

So, he had taken it upon himself to authorize Monsieur Bertrand to cut as many holes in the hull as he needed.

"*Une fois les côtelettes en l'air, on ne peut pas vous faire couler*" (once your ribs are showing, you can't go back in the water).

I stood corrected, but deeply grateful.

Like all crises, it slipped from being the objective successfully achieved to being merely the beginning of the passage to the next objective. The next day they began to empty the seams, getting on for half a mile of them. At the beginning I wasn't integrated into the work schedule, and so I had to push forward to see what was coming out. They looked like sand worms ("*capleuses*," they said), brown, many-footed and wriggling. I was horrified. They didn't seem to be concerned, and told me they were good for bait. Nonetheless, to be wheeling my seams away by the bar-row load seemed to me excessive. No one quite knew how they had come there, but it looked very likely that the work I had done on the gridiron in Newhaven had been worse than useless since it merely exposed to the sea some of the caulking which had been partially covered up before, the new black mastic having fallen straight out of damp wood which never had a chance to dry properly as we floated on each tide on the gridiron. When I tried to repair the ship on the Lappel Bank, if it weren't already infested with worms, the caulking could have become infested at that point. Hence, springing a leak repeatedly in different parts of the hull.

We were supplied with four caulkers, two to a side. Periodically, we had a cou-ple of carpenters, that is, *charpentiers/calfats* who had had enough clout to refuse to caulk, since every caulker (*calfat*) thought he was really a carpenter (*charpentier*), a problem of self image which in turn gave me plenty of problems stopping the caulkers doing bad carpentry whenever I subsequently hauled the ship out of the water. But this time I was merely a learner.

Unlike everyone else who used the floating dock, I was living on board with nowhere else to go. I stood around awkwardly on the steel deck of the dock won-dering what my relationship with the workmen might be. It was rather like having your underpants repaired while still wearing them. I couldn't really make out the spoken French — I probably wouldn't have been able to even if they had been speak-ing English, since language amongst close familiars has usually been well elided into a series of portmanteau sounds which stand for whole sentences. "Races?" for instance, might well stand for something like: "Did you go to the races yesterday? And what about the missus and the children? Did you win anything?"

Because of his silence, one of the caulkers on the starboard side seemed more accessible than the rest. At least I wouldn't have to break into an existing conver-sation. Lunch breaks were two hours long, but there was always a mid-morning break, with wine and baguettes. Abasourdi, as I had begun to nickname him from his air of bewilderment, never took his break with the others. He remained in one corner of the dock, out of the way, while the others clustered around the big wooden work chest which contained their tools, exchanged glasses, poured their wine, fed their baguettes into their mouths and gossiped: a never-ending flow of talk.

What made him intriguing was that the original nickname, Abasourdi, seemed less and less appropriate. He was far from bewildered. He was merely silent. He was a good workman and knew exactly what he was doing. In search of clues, I sidled up under the hull of the ship taking refuge from the rain. Crouched up like one of the gargoyles on Notre Dame, he was sitting on an upturned wooden fish box. As I had expected, his caulking mallet never hesitated, the same double tap that everyone else did, but no break (for a gossip or a drink) after the sixth tap, as the others did. He just went on, never dropping his caulking iron, rolling his own oakum. The oth-

My caulking irons to the right (all between 5 and 7 inches long) had different thicknesses and curves and were collected over the years. They tended to be used grudgingly or enthusiastically depending on their personalities rather than on their appropriateness.

ers would do anything to get out of it, deputing one to roll for all, and ultimately triumphantly making me the oakum roller. I hadn't read Tom Sawyer at that time.

I asked Abasourdi if he would teach me to caulk. It was very simple, he said, you merely folded in the *étoupe* (oakum) like so, and wedged it in with the iron followed by a blow from the mallet. He demonstrated, missed, and somehow struck his nose. He said he had done something silly, it was his own fault, demonstrated what he had done, and struck his nose a second time. He dabbed at his nose, said nothing, and went on caulking. After an uncertainty, I moved away in silence. He had a scab on his nose the whole of the time we were under repair.

Towards the end of our stay on the floating dock, he was doing some woodwork repair. I saw him standing in the rain in the middle of the steel deck, looking glummer than ever. What was he doing, I asked. Waiting for the truck, he answered. I had a car, I said, I could give him a ride (our car traveled around on deck with us). What did he want? He had forgotten a small part in the workshop, he explained. He looked at his watch: Could I speed it up — he wanted to finish the repair before lunchtime.

Now's my chance, I thought: he has no escape. What would he be doing when we were sunk again? I asked. He mentioned the *Valençay*, one of the cross–Channel ferries. But she's a steel ship. I objected. With a wooden deck, he answered. Did he like caulking? He hated it. The entire day spent on the knees, difficulty in getting his tubby tummy between them, so sore by the time he returned home in the evening that his wife had to massage his back and his knees before he could even straighten out enough to get into bed to rest.

So that was it: his silence came from being locked into a job he hated, cheated of being a carpenter by some chance of seniority. It was not deafness, teetotality, a solitary disposition — any of the things I had speculated about — it was misery. And it had poured out in the longest speech I had ever heard him make.

And the irony of it was that he was such a good carpenter that Robert, the chief of the carpenters, always detailed Abasourdi for difficult work on *Gray*, for example leveling off and caulking a huge replacement plank after Robert had made the initial fit and caulked the first *mèche* (layer of oakum). More painful for Aba-sourdi must have been that Robert had a young assistant who would eventually take Robert's place and who distanced himself from the caulkers by describing him-self as more of a joiner, really (*plutôt menuisier*).

My mother didn't enjoy her stay in the Hôtel Aguado a great deal. The floating dock was clearly not a place for a woman in her 80s, hip replaced not too well, barefooted as she always was (even in a snow storm in Philadelphia for one of her plays), and tied to her supplies of morphine. The floating dock really did float: there was a watery gap between the steel deck and the shore. Once, she nearly fell in. During the day, she had nothing to do because it was clearly out of the question for me to go and visit her. I dined with her expensively and well every night, dressing up as best I could. At the end of a week my mother departed back to Rottingdean. She came back the next March for a few days. Later, at the age of 88, four years before her death, she would visit us in a horrible berth we had outside Marseille. By that time she had a suitcase full of morphine injections with her which she counted repeatedly. She was a registered addict.

While it was difficult for me to integrate my mother into life on the floating dock, since the two social worlds never met, I was, for the same reason, as much embarrassed as flattered when Robert turned up one Sunday with his son and daughter-in-law who were visiting him from Rouen. By tradition, ships carpenters restrict their work and their concern to the outside of the hull and rarely want to see the inside. That Sunday, Robert said he wanted to show my joinery to his chil-dren. He must have sneaked a look on board earlier without me noticing.

This was the first period in my life when there had been no language other than French in which to communicate. I would judge I used the language like a sophisticated school boy, painfully making sure that I got my tenses right. It was becoming crystal clear that I had to learn French, and learn it better than the French. My first big hole was how to name the parts of a ship, something I didn't know in English — and still don't — so a nautical dictionary would have been useless. I would overhear something technical, stop the workman, and ask him to write it on the dock wall. That evening, I would speak the names on the dock wall into my tape recorder, and start learning them when I shaved in the morning.

A simple system.

"*Eh bien, c'est un serre bauquière, quoi,*" in answer to my question.

"*Voulez-vous indiquer exactement la partie qui...*" to make sure I had the exact limits of the word to come.

"*Volontiers. Tu vois, ce madrier ici, le long du bâteau, c'est le serre bauquière.*"

"*Et comment cela s'écrit?*" I asked.

"*Eh bain, toi, dis-donc, serre bauquière, c'est un 'c' au début, quoi,*" he addressed the nearest workman.

And then the one I had nicknamed Trente-six Années would stop working, come over to the blank steel wall of the dockside, and they would figure out the first three or four letters. When it came to "bauquière" more help was needed. Work stopped completely while they hazarded guesses at how it was spelt. They were only semi-literate.

Trente-six Années was not necessarily the ideal person to ask in any case. He had a fixed routine which he justified on the grounds that he had been with the firm these 36 years past and knew the ropes. He did his two-meter stretch of hull, carefully marked out at the beginning of the day, and no more. While this going-slow sometimes irritated his mate on the port side, the side he worked on, it was also a good safety precaution. Trente-six Années irrigated himself with wine throughout the day, so that by the afternoon, nearing the end of his two-meter stretch, he would start dropping his caulking irons. There was no mistaking the loud clatter of steel on steel as they hit the deck. There was also no mistaking the edge in the voice of the other workmen joking they would have to come to work in hard hats in the future. Once, Trente-six Années actually fell off the stage (a platform hung over the side of the ship) and was only just caught by his mate.

By reason of his seniority, Trente-six Années always felt that any orthographic question should first be referred to him so that he could then be in charge of passing the enquiry down the line. If his mate on the port side, the one nearest the dock wall I was writing on, was unable to help, Abasourdi and his mate on the starboard side would be called in. The only trouble was that Abasourdi was usually reluctant to be interrupted in his work. He lagged in coming round, gloomily dictated the correct spelling and then went back. I took to slipping round to the starboard side to ask him on the quiet.

As far as I was concerned, I loved them: they were saving my ship. And they were teaching me into the bargain. I was mostly too busy to recall my indifferent behavior in Assens. What had happened in those four years? To me? To the ship?

One day, just before the two-hour lunch break, Monsieur Bertrand said he wasn't sure if the men would be back in the afternoon because a two-hour strike had been called.

I was horrified. Had it anything to do with me living on board, I wanted to know. Not at all, Monsieur Bertrand put my mind at rest. But, I had nowhere else to go, nothing else to do but work on my ship. Still agitated, I tried to make Monsieur Bertrand understand. I belonged to no union and had been surprised I was even allowed to be around while his men worked. If I were in England, I had to explain, there would be terrible complications if I so much as touched my ship during a strike. I would be strike breaking, not far from a boss having the office staff take over the work of striking union members, and my ship would be blacked and the strike would escalate. Other ships would be blacklisted. The strike could spread from port to port all the way to Ushant and beyond. Just because one lousy foreigner wouldn't toe the line.

• This was not foolish talk. The power of the unions was bringing Britain to a
standstill, one of the reasons I wasn't reluctant when an accidental tide of events led
me to emigrate. For two months in early 1974, industry was put on a three day week
to conserve energy in the face of a miners' strike; at the end of it, Prime Minister
Ted Heath lost an election fought on the slogan "Who governs Britain?"; it was five
years before Margaret Thatcher started to break the power of the unions.

Monsieur Bertrand gazed at me blankly. The strike, he said, was for two hours.
Had I not noticed that it would therefore coincide with the midday meal, which,
he reminded me, also lasted two hours in Dieppe. So. Bon appétit. He was gone.

The men were back at the usual time to work a normal afternoon.

I'm not entirely sure who took the decision to "sink" us back into Dieppe's
fishing basin, but it certainly wasn't me. The workmen had found the weak spot
near the propeller which had nearly sunk us in London. It was to be covered with
a steel shield to prevent backwash from scouring out the seam which they had
found difficult to caulk because of rot on the inside. Through some lack of communication, the shield was welded up slightly wrong. I was being tyrannical about
this when I was told the ship had to be in the water in two days. I was no longer
the tyrant, they were. Fishermen were grumbling at the length of time we had been
on the dock, and had complained to the Chambre de Commerce, who in turn put
pressure on Monsieur Bertrand.

The uninterrupted rain which went on for the three weeks before we went
onto the floating dock had returned, and with it a biting wind which was directly
in line with the length of the dock. Working was a misery, and if the rain didn't let
up the bottom paint would be washed off. But a requirement to make bottom paint
work as an anti-fouling is that it should not be quite dry when the ship goes back
into the water. It's an expensive paint, so, once on, the penalty for delay becomes
high. I felt miserable that not only should this expensive paint be washed off by
the rain, but also I should still be compelled to sink on time. I cried aloud to the
silent dock one evening that it wasn't fair. And then realized I would have to translate it into French to make the steel understand. My mother had long since gone.
It would be three weeks out of the water. To add to my worries, the ship was showing
signs of drying out, despite the rain. I was living off preserved foods bought in
England such as Sainsbury's Chunky Chicken in Delicious Savoury Sauce. I thought
it revolting, but I had to eat, no time to cook, was far from food shops anyway, and
the dirty plates were piling up in the sink, the ash tray overflowing.

I was miserable, frightened, alone. I knew, even then, that blaming Cecilia for
her absence was merely a construct over my emotion: I needed her.

Two trawler skippers came along to wish me luck going back into the water.
At least, I had presumed they were on the floating dock to wish me well until I realized from the tone of voice that I had better get off or they would make life difficult
for me. They had been waiting too long, they thought, to get their own trawlers

on. I felt they would not be sympathetic if there were a crisis. I was even more alone.

As the rate of sinking slowed, and I felt the ship teetering, I knew we were nearly clear of our supports. I went down to the bilges. Water was rushing like a torrent inside. The fear of the first catastrophic leak in the London Docks gripped me. The decision to sink me had not been mine. I shouted across to the technicians to take the weight again. A Monsieur Marteau, from the Capitainerie du Port, arrived to find out what was the matter. Awkwardly, in his patent-leather shoes, he too teetered as he climbed into the small skiff the shipyard brought for him and crossed to my hull. Somehow a ladder's feet were stuck down in the water and up against the hull. He clambered aboard. The water was still rushing inside the bilges.

He was essentially a clerk, freshly promoted, and probably knew little about ships.

How much water was coming in, he wanted to know. I couldn't tell him. I pointed to the rush of water beneath his feet. At any rate, it seemed like a waterfall to me.

We went back on deck. There wasn't really a choice. He said to me a little wryly: "*Vous êtes entre voie d'eau et voie d'eau.*" The trawler skippers were gesturing angrily from the shore. Their leaks were now more important than mine, politically at any rate. I knew I had to go down. Besides, going up would solve nothing, for it would be impossible to find where the water was coming in.

Later, after hours, on the estacade (jetty), where I lay alone still making water, but no longer in fear of sinking that night, there was a tap on the door. Monsieur Marteau wanted to know how things were. He was on his way home. Like a political prisoner being tortured by the Good guy, Bad guy technique, I had difficulty not embracing him for his solicitude. I promised to dive throughout the night if necessary to keep afloat, I promised him the moon, I promised him I would be his slave forever. It was really quite an embarrassing performance only a little short of tears.

The man who was, after all, responsible for the integrity of my hull, Monsieur Bertrand, was absent for the sinking. He turned up the following morning.

He was desolated to hear that I had not yet sunk. I might have better luck next time, he observed.

I was not really emotionally able to take this kind of heavy-handed joke, particularly as I had woken up to find not a drop of water in the bilges, and, check the pumps as I could, they all seemed not only to be in working order but to have spent a restful night. The lowest bits of planking inside the bilges no longer gleamed with water. They had been dry some time.

So, I got my next lesson: to establish a good blocking plan before getting out of the water.

Monsieur Bertrand reminded me that when we went on to the floating dock three weeks earlier, he had expressed some concern over the fact that the toe of the keel was not only unsupported but was hanging down as though, as he described it, the ship was bleeding at the nose. He said the shorter trawlers usually did not have this kind of problem, so the docking crew wasn't particularly careful to get a block under the toe of the keel, particularly as the blocks were pretty close together in any case. But, the *Gray* was weak, he said, and we carried tons of steel for chain and anchors right over the toe of the keel, something which the trawlers did not. Their gear was more evenly distributed over the length of the ship. In future, I should establish where the toe of the keel was located by striking a mark on the bulwarks afloat. Why afloat? I wanted to know. Because, he explained, ships never float level. They normally float bows up, so as to drain water after to the bilge pumps, and also so that if they go aground on shelving ground there is a better chance of a sliding contact rather than a sudden shock. The blocks on the floating dock were level, unlike, say, a marine railway where they would be inclined. Thus, when we were originally lifted out of the water, some of the bilge water had flowed forward to our bleeding nose rather than aft to the pumps. What I heard when we were set afloat again was the water rushing from the pool in the bows backwards and making more of a noise than it might have done because the limber holes were so filthy it had to jump the frames in places.

He concluded by telling me that before I was taken out of the water again, I should do a lot of diving to establish two things: As he had explained, there should be no doubt when afloat exactly where the toe of the keel lay in order to make sure that it was supported, and if possible I should try to establish the shape of the keel when normally afloat so that blocks could be built up to retain that shape when the ship was out of the water.

I wished he had explained all this beforehand, but he hadn't. I never forgot his advice, which I took on every occasion we dry-docked thereafter.

13

A flying Dutchman?

The *estacade* (jetty), where *Gray* spent the winter, had originally been made of wood. By the time we were laid up against it after the dry-docking in a deserted corner of the Bassin de Paris, most of it was mushroom, moss, and the palimpsests of past greatness, like a mooring bollard or two which held us more by virtue of weight than of attachment to whatever lay beneath. The Dieppe harbor authorities made no charge for this berth, which was totally undisturbed, private and charming. Monsieur Marteau came again in his lunch break to enquire whether I had everything I needed. It was a gesture of concern and friendship, and otherwise nobody bothered me.

What to do next? If *Gray* were to become habitable, the hold conversion had to be completed with proper living quarters, not just the framework for living quarters, the point at which I was by this time. Also, money. We had to leave the sinking ship (Britain) with what we could scrounge before we were sucked under completely.

I kept trying not to think of the future — just one step at a time. The objective in the hold would serve any outcome — living on board or selling the ship. But money worries began to become more and more obstructive. It was Exchange Control which brought it into focus, although not the cause. So at the beginning of December I decided to go back to England, leaving *Gray* alone. Dieppe was so unlike England: There was no shortage of volunteers to act as gardiens. In Dieppe, I felt wanted, I felt the unreserved positive regard that I did not feel in England. Admittedly, gardienage was easy because the *Valençay*, the cross–Channel ferry Abasourdi had been working on, was laid up for the winter on the other side of the estacade. It had its own crew of watchmen, who could watch over us at the same time. But I also had offers from the dock flottant as well as from Philippe and Michel (a token offer as it would have been impossibly far away for them, but the gesture counted).

Soon after I had arrived in London, the father of Geoff Davies asked us to

165

dinner in Dulwich where they lived. It was a surprisingly serious family considering the affectionate ebullience of Geoff. But it was a seriousness which came from an erudition which understood that we were going through something which could alter our lives, which they talked of as the worst crisis since the Depression of the thirties. As we got up to leave at the end of dinner, Mr. Davies summed it up. It was not that there was a financial crisis, but that the will to beat it had gone. "Britain is now like Czechoslovakia under the Communists." That was his native land.

William was changing schools, leaving his primary-grades preparatory school to start secondary education. We all went down to listen to the Walhampton Carol Service.

I had been force-fed the hymnal when I was at Eton during the Second World War. Listening to it daily, when not more frequently, I had absorbed, if not learned, quite large chunks of the Anglican service. The Bible was written in the language of King James, the Prayer Book was relatively modern, a 1927 update I think, but the hymns, oh the hymns, they were something else entirely. What they lacked in antiquity, they amply made up for in 19th-century heroism, fighting good fights with Christian soldiers, redolent of muscular Christianity. Success, ritual, the sun never setting on the Empire, trappings in place while the country tottered... When I left Eton just after the war, that was beginning to change, but Walhampton must have resisted.

By the mid-seventies, when we paid farewell to William's prep school at the lowest point in British history that I could think of, they were singing the same Victorian hymns that I had been brought up on. And there was William, the Head Boy, decked out in the pomp of Victorian authority and security.

I didn't know what to feel. On the one hand it stirred deep nostalgia made worse by the fact that I no longer knew the lines. On the other, how could this anachronism exist? Unless Geoff Davies' father were right? What made it slightly worse was that the school authorities had included a restrained calypso or two, ever so slightly swinging the psalms, as though that was all that was required to get up to date.

That night, Cecilia arranged a big dinner in Newton Road for the children, Geoff Davies and some of our own close friends. One of them, Nigel Ryan, the head of Independent Television News, suddenly launched into his own view of the gravity of the situation for Britain. He had been a foreign correspondent for Reuters when I was working for Reuters in London, so he saw Britain from a slightly more distant point of view. It was not just the economic crisis, but the loss of purpose in Britain which he thought was dangerous. I could see he was turning down the pipe dream that his ITN could be mobilized to give Britain a new focus. Then Peter, his younger brother, turned on me almost furiously for not understanding what was going on, for being isolated in my own world in the ship, for not realizing that at least I should count myself lucky I had a raft under my feet, something others did not. Not one of the adults round the table was confident they would have their jobs next week.

The contrast with Dieppe was enormous. Where we lay was on the fringes of the town, at the edge of a forest of beech. It was well managed, so it didn't have a great deal of dead wood on the floor, but there was enough, and Cecilia and I (she ferried back and forth from London) used to collect it for firewood. While it was always a bit of a struggle to get enough, a well-managed forest in the autumn as I had seen it earlier is a total glory, placing me full in the stage set of every illustrated children's story that had ever been read to me. The canopy of autumn leaves slowly became the winter carpet on which we walked.

For the thicker logs, I used the hand chain saw I had bought at the Army & Navy Stores when a teenager. The teeth were on the inside of the chain (don't picture a power-driven chain saw with the teeth on the outside). It was passed under the log. If one of us put a foot on the log and we worked the chain back and forth, we found the saw could cut remarkably quickly. But there was a snag. Cecilia is much shorter than me, so we were always out of phase. It was an interesting contrast to our cooperation over the ship, since this one small task had to be done as a pair, like horses drawing a carriage, and not in tandem, the way we usually worked together. I couldn't do it alone; nor could we do it one after the other as we did in every other job.

The hold of *Gray* was still largely open plan, The winter's work was to fill it in with partitions. I loved working by hand, because the noises were so much more agreeable than the chatter and scream of electric tools. But there was little opportunity. Also, to my regret, I had to use modern smell-free waterproof glues, instead of maintaining a gallipot of molten horse hooves on a small spirit stove, as I had seen and smelled in the carpentry shops of my childhood.

A lot of our life centered around the wood stove, fed by the beech logs which we had brought back. It was not much of a stove by north American standards, but at that time I found it quite enchanting. It was square and fairly well insulated, so it was possible to rest things on top, things like cold gloved hands, or a cup of coffee, even twigs to get them dried out, as the fire seldom lasted the night.

The wood stove's chimney pierced the deck just in front of the galley. When it was wet and windless and warm enough to have the galley door open, snakes of wood smoke would curl in from outside. It seemed too good a smoke to let it go to waste, so I started my first experiments with smoking bits of piggy. I had a plastic dustbin which I could invert over the chimney and somehow string around inside it some pieces of belly. I wasn't very good at it, and I didn't at that time understand the need to cure the pork in salt before smoking it. Nor did I know anything about temperatures, or why a cool smoke was appropriate when a hot smoke wasn't. That came much later. But the products were worth eating, and I had the excitement of discovering how to manipulate the world around us.

This is where we lived, if we were not asleep or on deck — not much different from a middle class suburban home, except that it had to be tidier and virtually every flat surface had to have a fiddle (a piece of wood standing up at the edge) to prevent things sliding off in a seaway. To take something out of the oven when rolling, Cecilia had to have a catcher when opening the oven door. Round the corner on the right of the picture was the dining table (below).

The table on the right seated six. It had a well in the middle to dump plates in a heavy roll. Extensions could be clipped onto the open side (toward the oval table): a small flap (not shown) could be inserted to seat seven, or the larger extension (on the wall), supported by the oval table, enabled us to seat a dozen. The arm on the bench (bottom right corner) supported its bench. I kept ship's spares (a sort of marine corner shop of "O" rings, springs and other vital odds and ends) under the benches on the far side of the table.

We had by then a primitive record player which was situated below in the hold but wired up to a speaker in the deck house galley, so we could listen to *Aida*, for instance. The smell of wood smoke seemed to enhance the magnificence of the triumphal march. I quashed a question mark in my mind, determined to hear out the last bars.

By the time this protracted march was over, the smell was unmistakably too powerful to be a few lazy curls coming in through the doors. Smoke was pouring up the stairs. We were on fire.

The School of Navigation in the Minories had taught me a lot about fires, but mostly about oil fires. I hadn't thought the precepts particularly appropriate to us, so we had the barest minimum of fire-fighting equipment on board. However, I knew enough to crawl on my belly the 30 feet or so to see where the smoke was coming from. I didn't have time to pay out some rope behind me so that Cecilia could check how I was doing. I was in luck. The cause was my appallingly unsafe habit of drying out twigs on top of the wood stove. They had just broken into flame.

I drew a deep breath from the air near the floor, held it and decided to risk running back to the galley, one deck up, where I had considered a fire blanket more appropriate for a galley than a foam extinguisher. I crawled back with the blanket,

The sitting room in the hold was bounded on the port side by the main cabin whose double entrance doors are shown above. It had a bookcase and a space for a record player. The closed door on the right leads to another cabin.

certain that the flames would be licking everywhere, smothered the twigs with it, prepared to run for my life, and then saw there was no fire any more. Nor had the wooden deck caught fire, nor the wood chips on the floor, nor the new partitions, some slightly scorched but no more. Spending too much time gazing around, I nearly suffocated from the smoke on the way back upstairs.

While I was in Dieppe, Cecilia had had the basement of our London house closed off, and rented it to an American. I could see that Ed Hunsicker was a particularly good acquisition, for the door to the basement was frequently being unbolted for some kind of intercourse to take place. Ed was older than Emma but not so much older that he was out of her generation. So just before Christmas, Emma, a friend of hers, Ed Hunsicker, and I decided we would have an overnight trip back to Dieppe. We would take the ferry, spend the night on *Gray*, and then take the ferry back to London and have Christmas all together. Cecilia couldn't come.

Generally, I don't spend long periods of time with men, and here I was traveling with Ed and enjoying it. And then, Dieppe was like a dream. We walked from the ferry to the market beneath the medieval cathedral and bought ourselves some basic food for the two days. Then we walked to *Gray*, a long way it seemed, and were ready to walk back again to go out to dinner in one of the waterside cafés Turner had covered in color. Just before the ferry left next day, we went to the fashionable shopping area just beyond the market. We separated just a little to window-gaze.

I glanced up to see Ed's back disappearing down the street. "He's drunk," I thought. "This'll wreck the visit." Ed was weaving down the road, staggering from one side to the other. I caught up with him. "Are you drunk?" I asked. "No, not at all," he said, and he was clearly telling the truth. "But every time I get to one side of the road, I see something even more glamorous on the other side, so I've been weaving back and forth unable to make up my mind. And we've just come from the wasteland of the docks. I can't believe it."

That Christmas, we sat down only 16 for our turkey. It had been 24 the year before.

Romily and I left to return to Dieppe on New Year's Day. Four days later he was gone, back to Edinburgh University. Michel turned up. He had come round on Christmas Day to see if I were alone and might have liked to have eaten with his family.

One of the things I had done in London was to find out how we stood on Exchange Control which had been in operation since before the Second World War. Unlike most financial situations, instead of dealing with a broker or a lawyer or some other middle man, the ordinary person dealt directly with the Bank of England — as a form of address "Dear Bank..." made me feel perpetually uncomfortable with the lèse majesté of it. But by the end of 1974, things were beginning to show signs of easing, although controls were not finally abolished until 1979. It turned out that the restrictions then in force would allow me to get money out of the UK to start a business abroad, and so that's what I did. I concocted a somewhat fanciful chartering business which, to my surprise, was perfectly acceptable to the Bank of England.

It was but a precautionary step, since there wasn't much money to export, but it got me thinking about chartering. It got me into the frame of mind of being foreign in the sense of stateless and outside anyone's net and thus able to buy, for example, a shower base in France, without paying tax since we were from a foreign vessel.

I like showers; I had already installed the plumbing to deliver the water; but thus far I stood on some loose planks inside the hold wondering each time I took a shower how I could improve the arrangement. In the luxury of a hot shower, I really didn't much like gazing at the filthy bilge water only a few inches below my feet. Nor did I like hanging my wash cloth on the studding which defined, but did not enclose, the area of the shower.

It needed a base, but all the bases I had seen were attached to sides, top and all the plumbing. The trouble was that I merely wanted the shower base.

I discovered the correct French translation for a shower base and scoured Dieppe's few department stores, each time receiving the same answer: you don't get a base without the sides, top and plumbing. The shop assistants sometimes went a stage further and said what they had to sell me was the then equivalent of "plug and play": why do-it-yourself?

Then one day I saw exactly what I wanted in the glass front of one of the plumbing supply shops. It was clearly intended for another use but, unlike an ordinary shower base, it was as deep as a bathtub. If we could afford the water, we could take a deep baptismal shower in port, and if we used a normal amount of water it wouldn't slosh over in a seaway.

I went inside, gazed at it, and became intrigued by two internal slots molded into the inner sides. Instead of being horizontal, they were at a good rake. My bottom wasn't raked. It was flat. So I asked what the slots were for.

For washing, the shop assistant explained.

My French was improving all the time, but I felt I must have misunderstood. The shop assistant moved off. I still couldn't figure out what or how one could wash at an angle.

I went after him and explained my problem.

The slots were for a piece of wood, he said, adding they didn't supply the wood. He laughed at his own joke.

I couldn't sit on it, I pointed out, since it was at an angle.

"Normally," he said, insulting the abnormal interlocutor I was rapidly becoming—"Normalement, I would not expect my wife to get into the *bac à laver* with the clothes she is washing." Another titter at his own joke. "She stands outside. Let me demonstrate."

He then stood on one side of the *bac à laver*, removed his jacket, folded it inside out, shoulder pad to shoulder pad, flicked out the creases and laid it down on another piece of monumental porcelain, undid the buttons of his cuffs, carefully rolled the cuffs back once, smoothed back the one on his left wrist, then the one on his right, and then gave each wrist a second fold. He was ready. He took an imaginary shirt in his hands, leant down to the place where the inclined board should have been and started rubbing the imaginary shirt against the imaginary board with some imaginary soap, stating the obvious that the *bac à laver* must be installed at the right height for the person who was doing the washing. His wife was rather short, he said, so, on the floor as it was might suit her, but he would have to have it on blocks of wood if by any chance he was the one to do the washing. Not very likely, he added, since his tasks were usually of a less manual grade.

So, I thought, in modern France: washing machine + electricity = wife + *bac à laver*. Q.E.D.

I said I would buy it.

This was the first major piece of household equipment I had bought for the *Gray* apart from the diesel cooker, now our beloved friend. When I had gone along to pay our floating dock bill at the Chantiers de Normandie, we found that all our repairs were tax free. Why? Because we were a foreign vessel.

Could we not buy the *bac à laver* hors taxe, I asked the salesman. Assuredly, he answered. Since we were foreigners, we merely had to go along to the Taxes & Impôts with the requisite documents, and all would be well.

I had gotten into the frame of mind that if we couldn't buy the *bac à laver* without paying tax, we couldn't afford it at all. It had become the nearest and dearest thing to my heart by this time. Frontier life has never appealed to me.

At the Taxes & Impôts things turned out to be not so simple. To get a drawback of tax, the *bac à laver* must, of course, be exported. It couldn't stay in France. But we had a foreign vessel —couldn't it be exported to that? I enquired. In principle, yes (and here again the French phrase means "no"), but that would be within the competence of the Douanes, the customs service.

But I asked, if the shipyard, a French national, not me, the foreigner, installed it in a foreign ship, there would be no tax, would there? It must be routine for them to do this sort of thing, I asked them. They yielded. I had my *bac à laver* tax free. I persuaded the shipyard to cooperate by paying for the *bac à laver* and then billing me.

However, Dieppe is a small place. The Taxes & Impôts evidently lunched with the Douanes. Very promptly, a Madame Pons summoned me to the Customs where she informed me that we were a foreign vessel without permanent papers and would have to leave by 18 January the following year, taking our bac à laver with us, if we wished to avoid heavy taxes on the importation of our ship into France. The period of grace for a foreign vessel was six months, she explained frostily, and that dated from our arrival in Calais on 18 July.

Mme. Pons was not negotiable. I left to contemplate the implications.

Looking at it from the French government's point of view, six months in France as a visitor sounded reasonable. But other governments might have the same requirement. Treating with the Bank of England over Exchange Control had made me think as an outsider. Now this convocation from the Douanes forced me to realize that it wasn't just a question of money, but identity. In effect, the Douanes were saying: "Nice to have met you, but now's the time to go back home." Where was home? On *Gray* might be an acceptable answer. But alone? Or what would Cecilia do? Besides, the phrase "on *Gray*" was not sufficient, for it had to be "on *Gray*, in such and such a country." One nasty thought was that we might be pursued from port to port by successive governments limiting our stay in their country to six months. A sort of Flying Dutchman.

I had always wanted to run a restaurant — one of those hazy pipe dreams, rather than a seriously understood wish. Cecilia was an extraordinarily competent cook and manager. If she came with me, we would have to get some revenue from the ship. Why not pursue in reality the charter fantasy I had sold to the Bank of England?

Then a jerk. Lose my house? Turn my back on my country? Until she had moved on board nine months earlier, Cecilia's life had been becoming more divorced from *Gray*. I commuted to my job every day, and that was that. On the other hand, my recent visit over the Christmas holidays had been very enjoyable. I seemed to be getting over the scowling resentment of Christmas that had led to Port Meirion. I saw the house with a fresh eye, coming back to an old friend, no longer being pursued by a demanding curmudgeon. It was plenty big enough without the basement, now that the children were mostly away. One evening alone, I had very much liked the way Cecilia had set a meal for two in front of the drawing room fire, how she had turned the bleak atmosphere I had created when I originally bought the house into something more stuffed and cozy. If I still needed bleak elegance, I could move into the adjacent parquet-floored dining room, which also had an open fire, but which was largely untouched by Cecilia. Or I could move further through to the 25-foot-long kitchen and dining room we had designed together and where we could comfortably sit 24. In the welcome of my London house, *Gray* had dimmed to a dirty distance.

Moreover, now that Cecilia was getting rent from the basement, the London house might become more financially feasible. I was beginning to dither about the daft decision of September 1974 to choose the *Gray* and abandon my house.

I went back to see Mme. Pons. Could she give us an idea how much duty would be charged? She did not know, the ship would have to be valued, she was not competent herself to do this. Would we have to import the vessel before being allowed to charter it in French waters, I asked. That was so, she answered, but we would also have to comply with safety regulations and that sort of thing. How would I find out, I asked? Go to the Affaires Maritimes, she answered, and see what they have to say.

While the job of the Douanes was to levy duties on goods passing the frontier, the job of the Affaires Maritimes was to police and regulate the French commercial fleets. I presented myself in their offices, and asked some questions which, of course, led to them asking me which particular vessel I had in mind.

The *Gray*, I answered. I said we had been in the Bassin Duquesne since late summer, but that we had been moved to the end of the Bassin de Paris for the remainder of the winter.

Were we not flying the British flag, the official asked. To my nod, he continued that the Affaires Maritimes had no jurisdiction over British vessels.

That seemed to be a little odd to me, since I thought of the Affaires Maritimes as a kind of border police who would indeed be interested in any vessel, French or foreign, which was disregarding their rules. What about chartering, I wondered. There wasn't much chartering around Dieppe, the official countered. Things might be different in the French Mediterranean, he said.

I explained what was on my mind. We had to leave in January or pay import duty into France.

Import was not their responsibility, the official said. It would be for the Douanes. But so long as I did not change the nationality of the ship, the Affaires Maritimes could not help me. Personally, he thought it unlikely I could charter unless I imported the ship.

This looked like becoming a problem for me. If we really wanted to charter in the Mediterranean, the official might be wrong about the details of the bureaucracy involved—it was not his area, as he had explained—but he was certainly right to warn me that bureaucracy would be involved. I thought it unlikely I could nip down the road to some information booth and get all the answers in the afternoon. Without any answers, I might start installing things on *Gray* which would be contrary to regulations which I would only subsequently discover. Could the Affaires Maritimes not have a look at my ship to give me some advice about what to expect at some later date?

The official listened but said that unless I was doing something flagrantly illegal, they could not set foot on my ship without the permission of the British Consul, and that permission would be refused, he thought.

Why would the Consul want to do that, I wondered. The official looked at one of his colleagues and smirked. I realized they didn't think much of the Consul. They didn't know, they said, but I could always ask the Consul myself.

At this point, I began to wonder whether it really was just a matter of another visit to Mme. Pons. She would tell me: no importation without a valuation; the

Affaires Maritimes couldn't inspect, so I might find myself importing the ship, and the Affaires Maritimes refusing it for safety reasons. I needed someone with an overview. Perhaps the Commandant du Port would have some good advice. I went to see him.

As usual, he seemed to have too little to do, and therefore to have the time to be as welcoming as he had always been even in the needy days when I had just arrived with my sinking ship in the rain. Now I was back with a different problem. I explained to him that we had been given a deadline to leave France or pay the import duty, that we were now wondering whether we could afford to do this, and if this would then enable us to go to the Mediterranean and charter off the French coast.

The Commandant's desk was empty. He indeed had nothing to do. He began by making some bland remarks about the sunshine in the Mediterranean, the beautiful girls, wonderful food and so on. But, as he had clearly been thinking of his own past, he quickly switched to trying to get me to talk about Réunion again.

Since the last time we had spoken together, there had been something of a change of dynamics. Earlier I had been prepared to put up with almost any prevarication from the Commandant because I was in a situation of utmost dependency. Things were somewhat different now. I had a sound ship. My French had improved. While I wanted to have his opinion, that was the reason for my visit, not to pass the time of day with him.

I began to explain that it was not merely a question of enjoying ourselves in the south of France but that we had very little money and we had to earn our living. While we would like to go on living in France, we obviously had to be in good standing with the French authorities.

At this point the Commandant began to sway off course again and to assure me that he understood that a man of my obvious probity and honesty would always wish to be in good standing with authorities whether they be French ones or from the other side of the channel.

I wondered how I could possibly persuade him to be a little more businesslike. Did he not have friends in high places. Oh yes, of course, he answered, clearly not wanting to admit that he was friendless. Who had I seen in the Affaires Maritimes, he then asked. I said I was not certain of the name of the official but that it seemed to me that they would not be relevant until after I had imported *Gray* into France, or not, as the case may be. If the terms were too onerous we would have to leave France and try to make a living somewhere else.

He thought for a minute. Yes, he said, he had a friend with whom he played chess. This did not sound very promising to me — another excursion into his fantasy world? But, he continued, they were both from Algeria, what were called at the time *pieds noirs*, Europeans born in Algeria but not ethnic North Africans. I realized that this could be quite a strong bond since the war which finally gave Algeria independence from France involved stiff resistance from the pieds noirs who did not wish to give up their homes and careers in north Africa. It was rather like the Protestant Irish.

He said his chess playing friend was in fact the head of the Douanes.

I suppose I might have expected it but sure enough he began to backtrack and discourse again. Who else had I seen in the Douanes, he wanted to know? I said I had been to see Mme. Pons. In the French bureaucracy he said it is not a very good idea to leapfrog over the head of one official to get to someone higher. You would risk alienating Mme. Pons if you went straight to his friend, he said.

So I thought I was back where I started. The Commandant did not want me to get to his friend at the top after all. There was a pause while he thought about things. Finally, he said it was up to me to decide whether I wished to risk alienating Mme. Pons by getting over her head to his friend who, he said, was called Monsieur Perrin. I said I had no alternative.

So back to the Douanes. They were closed. I was too late. I would have to go next day.

Early next morning I knocked on the door of Monsieur Perrin's office. The moment he called me in the telephone rang. Without glancing at me or motioning me to a seat, he continued with his leisurely conversation. He was as spare as the Commandant du Port was rotund. I didn't like to sit down because I had not been asked to do so, and I was there on a delicate matter in which the last thing was to give offense in any way. I was, however, having difficulty in repressing the growing feeling of irritation at the way I was being received. My ear strayed to their conversation. It sounded as though they were discussing last night's chess game. I assumed, therefore, that he was speaking to the Commandant du Port, but there was no hint, from this end of the conversation, that he had put in a good word for me.

My eyes strayed round the room, and then became fixed on a dingy-looking poster behind Monsieur Perrin's chair. I began to read it in a desultory fashion, and then, all of a sudden, woke up to what it was actually saying. It was something like this:

AVIS
Les déclarants proposent
Les douanes disposent
Matthieu [chapter and verse]

That's really shoving it in your face, I thought.

The telephone conversation seemed to be nearing a close. Monsieur Perrin put the telephone down and sat back in his chair gazing at me without a word.

I looked above his head, grinned, and asked him if he thought the notice was irreligious.

How idiotic could I get? The words were no sooner out of my mouth than I wanted to grab them out of the air and take them right back. Why risk this sort of thing in a touchy situation? I had to be out of my mind.

There was a long pause. He breathed in and tilted his head back so that I was looking up his nostrils. Then he moved his head forward, put both hands flat on the desk as though grasping its edge, thumbs down, very slowly got to his feet and faced me. There was another silence before he said:

Monsieur,
I will have you know
that I follow in the footsteps
of the greatest customs officer of them all.

And then he slowly sat down. I knew his formal French (*Je vous saurez gré de bien vouloir comprendre...*) was much ruder than the English translation above.

His elbows were on the arms of his chair with his fingers touching in front of his face like a church steeple. His gaze shifted from his finger tips to me and then back again. He said nothing. I began to think that he felt he had no further business with me and that I should probably leave. Then he asked me to state my business.

- The notice was an obvious parody of "Man proposes, God disposes" but it was the attribution to the Gospel according to St. Matthew which made me blurt out the inappropriate irreligious comment. However, nearly 40 years have gone by, and in trying to reconstruct the exact attribution which I no longer remember, I could find nothing in Matthew nearer than "Render therefore to Caesar the things which are Caesar's and unto God the things that are God's." It's not a very good fit. Further, the original aphorism ("Man proposes..." etc.) is a translation from Thomas à Kempis (1380–1471) in his book *De Imitatione Christi* (xix, 2)—in Latin, of course.

  Matthew was probably a tax collector. The relevant verse in Matthew 9:9 is: "And as Jesus passed forth from thence, he saw a man, named Matthew, sitting at the receipt of custom: and he saith unto him, Follow me. And he arose, and followed him."

I said I had come about the *Gray* and began to launch into a superficial description of the type which would be appropriate to someone who had no idea what I was talking about. He interrupted. He knew that wreck, or rather, he knew about her as he had of course no firsthand knowledge. Smoothly continuing on, he asked what I would wish to do with such a vessel.

It was a cool day and his office was certainly not heated. I began to feel the sweat trickling down from inside my armpits. I was still standing, since he had not yet offered me a seat.

I said I proposed to import the ship into France. Without any change in expression, he asked why I imagined that the French government would wish to acquire such a dilapidated vessel. I realized this was a rhetorical question which I was not expected to answer and in fact had I not been kept in check by the need for caution I might have carried into action my desire to strike him.

He commented that he did not have the time to pursue speculations about what the French government might feel, however, so we had better get down to business. He supposed that I wished to know how much it would cost me to import my ship. He mentioned a possible value for the ship in the millions of French francs.

There was silence while he selected a newly sharpened pencil and an untouched pad of plain paper and began to write in a neat spidery hand. Then, passing the pad across to me, he reversed it so that it was the right way up for me and underlined the figure at the bottom. He regretted that his handwriting was somewhat small, and at last invited me to sit so that I could make out his figures at closer quarters.

I gazed at the paper in silence.

He leaned back, re-erected the church spire with his fingers, gazed at me, leant forward, put his index finger, so clean you could almost see through it, onto the paper, slid it back towards himself, reversed it, somewhat deliberately counted back two zeroes from the end, divided them off from the rest of the number with a deliberate comma starting with an extra pressure of the pen to make a neat start to the downward stroke, and then prefixed the number with "NF."

Then he slid it back to me with the apology that at his age, he found it difficult to get accustomed to the New Francs.

- 100 old francs were converted into 1 New Franc in 1960, but when I was in France fifteen years later prices for real estate (and I suppose ships) were still referred to in millions or milliards (billions) of the old francs, and then converted to New Francs in the same way that Monsieur Perrin was doing.

I looked at him. The duty had become but a trifle.

He rose and stretched out his hand. I should go to Madame Pons to have his calculations checked and pay the duty. As I went out of his door, he observed that chess was an excellent training for dealing with the French bureaucracy.

When I called Cecilia in London to tell her I had imported the ship, she told me that Ed Hunsicker had stopped paying his rent.

14

Back to England

But that piece of news came out only at the end of the conversation.

It was now March, and I realized I had failed to tell her that I had overrun the January deadline by asking the shipyard to do some more work on *Gray*, but that the deadline still existed until my importation of *Gray*. Instead of being pleased that I had somehow solved an intractable problem, she wanted to know whether this was part of my decision to remain in France. No, I said, it had nothing to do with that. It was only because of the deadline.

Even so, she asked, why should I choose to import *Gray* into France after maintaining stoutly at the end of the summer that we could not afford to keep the house in London and the three-masted schooner somewhere else.

The conversation came to a standstill. Somewhat maliciously, I asked her if Ed Hunsicker was as marvelous as ever. Oh yes, she said, but then she told me that he no longer paid the rent. In fact, he was rather upset about the matter, not, as you might expect, about nonpayment of rent, but about the fact that we had asked him for rent in the first place.

As I write now (2013), this must seem a weird point of view, but that was the situation in England of that time. Ed was an American and his point of view was that we had somehow tricked him by persuading him to sign a lease for the basement which we knew — as he did not — was unenforceable. He felt that this was a moral breach of friendship more than a legal breach of any kind. Had he not been an American our behavior might well be justified but under the circumstances we were taking advantage of an ignorant foreigner.

Cecilia said they still got on very well together on other matters but there was this crossed wire in his head which she could not deal with. I would have to come back.

In fact she said she would be coming over to Dieppe by ferry the next day to help me bring *Gray* back to England. We could try the South Coast which had deeper water than our old grounds on the East Coast and we might be able to find a berth for *Gray*. Fine, I said, adding that I would get in some food.

179

I could not contain my curiosity before hanging up and so I asked her if she had already decided to come to Dieppe before I had called her. No, she answered and we hung up.

I knew perfectly well what this was all about. She still maintained that *Gray* could be kept in England at no great cost so that we could go on basing ourselves in our house in London. I am sure she understood that if I kept *Gray* abroad I would have to live on her and that if I lived on her she would either have to say goodbye to me or to follow. If she got me back to England with *Gray* she might be able to avoid that choice. She had no means of knowing that I simply could not forecast the future, and I was taking one step after the other just to keep the options open.

Emma was with her when she arrived next day. A few days later, Thomas and his friend Adam turned up, and then Victoria and a friend, Mike. Cecilia was not one to be daunted by rounding up a prize crew at a moment's notice. After living alone, I found it was getting quite crowded with seven on board. Cecilia and I had our cabin, but the other cabins were still in various stages of being built. The dining room table held six. However, shortly before we were to leave Dieppe, Victoria took Adam and Mike away with her.

During the winter, my confidence in *Gray* had risen. I knew ships never leaked in the winter in dock, but that didn't stop me reveling in it. Try as I would, I couldn't prevent myself from feeling that we had a good strong ship back on our hands. I had enjoyed being in Dieppe. The French have a reputation for hostility and rudeness. I knew what that could be like from my Paris days in Reuters. But Dieppe was different. Perhaps the whole of France, apart from Paris, was different. Without exception, each Dieppois I had had contact with had been helpful and welcoming, even the officials, for all the elaborate game-playing I had occasionally been obliged to endure. It was all very unlike England.

So I was leaving because we could not live the rest of our lives in Dieppe and we had to move on to the next step whatever that might be. I was not much looking forward to being back in England. A year earlier, I would never have dreamt of leaving England for more than a brief visit abroad. Now I knew I had to go back to England to face changes in my life which I could only see as problems at this stage, not solutions.

One of the problems of course was money. The short-term solution was getting round Exchange Control. But until I left Reuters, I had earned my living the whole of my adult life. Could I make a living through *Gray*? Chartering was a vague thought. I had absolutely no intention of earning my living illegally, import/ export — that kind of stuff.

The experiment in cutting down Newton Road to a manageable size didn't look like a success with Ed Hunsicker not paying his rent. It was not just his failure to pay the rent, but the reasons and the law behind it.

And then there was the over-riding anxiety about Cecilia. Émile had said she could do electrical work: women had finer fingers than men. His suggestion was an inverted parable. For Cecilia to want to leave Newton Road and live with me on the ship, there had to be a role for her considerably more interesting than doing electrical work. Her logical place was in England with her children.

So that led right back to me — did I really want to live on *Gray*? Did I really want to abandon my former life, my house, possibly family, for an uncertain future on *Gray*? But, and this "but" always made me come to a halt, if I sold *Gray* and returned to Newton Road, whether cut down or not, even if there were no financial worries, what would I do in life?

Fortunately, there was not too much time to consider these matters. We had to leave Dieppe, and that meant packing away a winter's living.

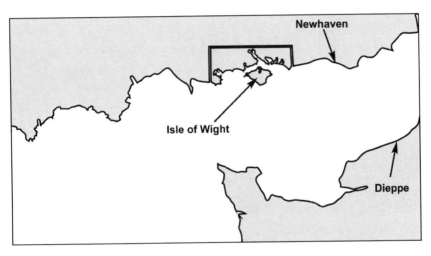

From Dieppe to the Nab Tower, east of the Isle of Wight, is about 90 nautical miles, but we covered a lot more ground making the passage. Below is a detail of the area surrounding the Isle of Wight, showing its relationship to the Nab Tower.

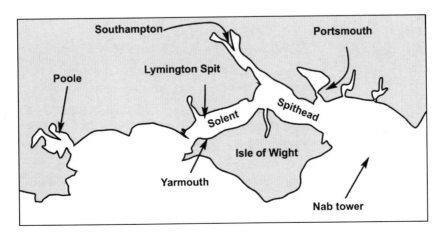

Leaving the Bassin de Paris was a dramatic matter. We didn't just slip out. As it was springs and high water springs occurs around lunch time, the entire Dieppe lunch time traffic was halted while the road bridge was swung out of the way and we slowly slid past. We could be seen approaching from a long way off and by the time we reached the lock gates, a large crowd had gathered to watch the *goélette trois mâts Gray* put out to sea.

We wanted to go northwest to the Isle of Wight, where Cecilia had friends, acquired while she and her first husband were running a school in that part of the country. William's prep school, the one he had just left, was also in the area.

The wind was somewhere north of west and west of north, hard to tell quite where, but generally contrary.

I still didn't yet know too well how close *Gray* would go to the wind. Since we left when the tide was west-going, we could either head east of north, which seemed counter-intuitive as it meant we would be losing our westing, probably even with a fair tide, or we could go along the French coast in the hope that the wind might veer or some such unlikely miracle. You have to remember that the whole strategy in the Channel is shaped by the westerly component of the prevailing wind, sometimes northwest, but mostly southwest, and definitely rarely east in the summer, except, of course, when I did, or didn't, want an east wind (Beachy Head, the Lappel Bank, St. Vaast-la-Hougue). So, going down Channel along the coast wasn't such a bad idea, particularly as the coast trended to the south a bit, getting more southerly as you went along.

As we left Dieppe, it started to snow.

I felt obliged to help the sails by using the engine for the first two or three hours when the wind did indeed seem to veer, and gave us the chance of an offing. In fact, until the early hours of the morning, we were able to head north of west, which seemed to be a stroke of unbelievable luck. Then a squall, rain and flat calm. We rolled uncomfortably, the sails slatting back and forth. There was nothing to do, no way in which we could ease the ship, ease ourselves, get a grip on life instead of life having a grip on us.

Except one way: put on the engine.

A flick of a switch, you might say, and there you are defying the weather.

First of all, there was no switch. I have already described the awful strobe-like effect of an engine turning at 240 countable revolutions each minute. To start it, I descended into the lowest part of the ship by a vertical ladder, over and by the fuel tanks, and a bit of a squeeze. I then took a rusty, greasy bit of bent steel the thickness of my wrist, plunged it into a socket of the three-foot diameter flywheel. Next, I heaved the engine round to just past top dead center, banged open the bottles of compressed air (they stood up to my chin and were equipped with heavy, loose wheels designed to hammer the valve shut or open as desired), suffered the whistling of the leaky valves and joints, slammed open the inlet to the engine, a finger of the other hand on the throttle, and prayed. I could do this three or four more times before losing all the air in the bottles, which were normally recompressed by the engine after it had gotten going. It usually started without hesitation, but not always, so it could imprison me out of sight in the engine room attending to diagnostics just at a moment when, by definition, we needed an engine and I should have been on deck with an alternative strategy.

...It took a couple of hours to recompress the air bottles from the diving compressor if the engine failed to start and the air bottles ran out.

...There was a valve on the side of the cylinders for starting the engine with explosive charges, but I had never found out where to get the explosives from.

...The fear of dreadful consequences if the engine would not start tended to make me turn it on ahead of time, and then to keep it running too long.

...So much for turning the ignition key.

As you follow the coast westward from Dieppe you have to round Cap d'Antifer to reach the bay which has St. Vaast at the other end of the Normandy invasion beaches. We weren't going to weather the cape. I turned round to go back to Dieppe. There was rumbling pressure to start the engine, mainly from Cecilia and Emma, but they, like me, were unsure what *Gray* could do as a sailing vessel and wanted to know. So we trudged back towards Dieppe under sail, when the wind veered again, forcing us into the shore. In a fury, having held out so long against the mutineers, the treacherous wind forced me to start the engine. We had to make the lock gates. Three hours later we were tied up on the *estacade*.

That was a real disappointment. We had left with such confidence yet we had had a lousy sail, rolling around in calms and squalls and rain and snow. And now we were back where we started.

The others didn't seem to mind so much, and anyway it was Thomas's birthday, so we went to a restaurant. Thomas asked in a neutral sort of way why I hadn't put the engine on, motored into the wind to get an offing, and then tried to sail.

I felt beleaguered.

As things had turned out, Thomas was right. But I suppose I had a split personality about sailing. On the one hand, as in Calais, I knew when it would simply be too tedious to bang into the wind under engine, at any rate, too tedious for me. But that was neglecting other people whose wishes also included the excitement of arriving in a new place, however we got there. It was fairly certain to me that no one shared my almost academic curiosity to find out what exactly *Gray* could do under sail. I feared the answer was going to be a disappointment, and yet I wanted to find out in case it were a triumph. It would be far easier to do this when constrained by land, rather than out at sea where errors of sail trimming wouldn't matter.

The conversation drifted off onto something else. A little later, I brought the dinner to an end by saying we had better get some sleep as we were going to try again the next day. Privately, I knew there was no real need to get to sleep early as the lock gates wouldn't open until the middle of the day. But I thought I would give them a hard time for their pressuring over the engine.

They all looked rather pleased, however.

We locked out next day, and this time, instead of hugging the coast, I secretly took Thomas' advice and motored more or less in the right direction against not too much wind, which was in any case dropping all the time. After about three hours, I went down to the engine room to stop the engine without consulting anyone. We put the sails up.

After a while slopping around not doing much, I listened to the *météo*, which was miserable. We were in a squash with a high somewhere to the left of us and a low to the right of us, and a persistent "fairly strong" northwest to north airflow forecast. I wanted to go back so we could try again in more favorable weather. So there was the usual standoff, and I had to give in.

So we took down the sails and motored—for the next six hours. By this time there was a bit of wind, so I stopped the engine while they set the sails.

When we had settled down, we found we could head northwest, exactly the right direction. Damn them all for being right. I went to bed.

For the whole of the next day, we sailed on the starboard tack, but all the time the wind was backing ever so slightly so that by dinner time, we were heading southwest and I decided to go onto the other tack, the port tack, where we found we could head north.

We had decided to aim for Portsmouth on the ground that it would be likely to have enough room for us. It might not be particularly pleasant, but we could move on. To reach it from the south, we would have to pass the Nab Tower, which marked the end of the Isle of Wight and which we would need to leave to port. We needed a fair tide to get up Spithead to Portsmouth. If the wind persisted from roughly the northwest, we would be on a weather tide and it might be rough. I therefore wanted to get as close up to the Nab as possible before turning into what might be some nasty motoring into the wind with the tide behind us. Also, I didn't want to go inside the Nab. This was just caution: the chart showed there should be enough water, but if we lost sight of the Nab in poor visibility, or misjudged the distance, we might be too far inshore.

Emma had picked up the light from the Nab by two in the morning. Meanwhile the weather was closing down with a squall. I thought we could easily find ourselves swept up Channel in the wrong direction, having to pound back in more open water to get to Portsmouth. So I decided to get out to sea again to try to gain a little more up wind. By the time we were back at the Nab 12 hours later and a little further upwind it was just after lunch, and the weather was lousy, squalls, wind backing and veering, and little visibility. We all saw the object loom out of the gloom. "There's the Nab," shouted Emma.

"The alleged Nab, you mean," I growled at her.

But Emma was right. However, we were now going in the wrong direction again, losing all the ground we had made up during the previous 12 hours. I thought we would never get there. Every time we went onto the other tack so that the wind was favorable for a bit, it then started to shift against us. At least we were not being forced to tack about like this in the relatively narrow Spithead. We were now shooting back to sea, and would have to tack yet again. But after this tack, our first bit of luck: we found we could head in the right direction, right up Spithead. With everything in our favor, even a fair tide, we boomed up the channel and into Portsmouth, a thrilling couple of hours, not to be matched for four years until we were fired out of Gibraltar by a quartering gale to begin our crossing of the Atlantic.

It's not that we went four years without a wind — we had a nasty gale crossing the Bay of Biscay — but that the humdrum everyday business of running a ship like this turned out to consist of a lot of motoring, much more than I had ever imagined, and a lot of dragging anchor. Not, of course, to speak of the daily problem of keeping the ship dry.

Portsmouth, a naval base, was no worse than we had expected. Cecilia was in favor of going to Poole, on the other side of the Isle of Wight, with its large sheltered bay. This time of the year, we might be able to find quay space. Later, when the summer got into full swing, we could probably anchor in the bay. But on our way down the Solent, the wind fell light, the tide turned foul, and we decided to pick up a buoy and spend the night off Yarmouth. It was a big buoy, somewhat like the Admiralty buoys near Pin Mill. But there was a difference: the tide was stronger and the position more exposed. Hardly surprisingly, during the night I was shot out of bed by a heavy thud up forward. It was raining, some sleet, blowing a bit. Well, more than a bit when I got on deck. This time from somewhere in the east, that was the irony of it. There was the black hulk of the buoy, several feet in diameter, right under our starboard bow, tapping it from time to time as it was driven up against us by the weather tide. I looked aft. *Gray*'s stern was shifting rapidly to port against the shore lights. The wind came on the starboard quarter and we were blown off the buoy. But not for long. We slanted up the tide back towards the buoy again. This could have been a stable situation, but with a temporary slackening of the wind *Gray* drifted a little aft, the hawsers went slack, and the buoy tapped its way against our hull up to our bows, crossed the stempost and shot out to port. At this point, the hawsers came tight and snubbed *Gray*'s bows to port. All I could see was her stern traveling increasingly fast to starboard against the shore lights. The buoy came up close on the port bow, started tapping us again, doing damage. I realized this could go on for hours until the wind slackened or the tide changed.

While we were hard up against the buoy, our hull was more or less safe from damage, but inherent in the swinging was that every few minutes the buoy would be free, a wave would come and slam the buoy against the hull. I did not think that

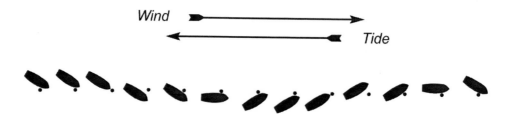

In the 1st, 2nd and 3rd silhouettes above, the buoy (the dot) is sliding down the hull. When it crosses the bow it swings free of the hull (4th), snubs the bow round to port by slamming into the hull (5th). The ship then turns round the buoy (6th and 7th) and the whole procedure starts again on the other side.

our hull was capable of standing much of this. Furthermore, every time the mooring hawsers, which were an inch and a half in diameter (5" in circumference), crossed our stem, they got chafed. Fat though they were, they wouldn't last forever, as I had seen at Gravesend where we had only 3" warps (by circumference).

I went aft. There was no dinghy to be seen. It had been on board for months while we were in Dieppe, but we had launched it in order to secure to the buoy. The procedure earlier that day had been for me to try to keep *Gray*'s forefoot near the buoy, while someone in the dinghy tied up to it with a light line. This was not so easy because the buoy was, of course, out of sight from me under our bows and I couldn't tell if I were running up on it or in some other way endangering the person in the dinghy. However, once the light line was made fast, I could afford to drop back a little while the heavier mooring hawser was passed down, dipped through the huge steel eye on the buoy and then secured back on board. The light line was then removed, the dinghy streamed aft and we could slip the buoy quite easily by letting go one of the ends of the hawser secured on deck. However, if we had lost the dinghy, it would be hard to anchor anywhere since a dinghy was essential for getting ashore.

I peered into the darkness. A ridiculous gaze, I realized, unless the dinghy had only just broken free. Even then, how would I ever reach it? I gazed over the side, nearer to hand, and sure enough, there it was, itself blown back onto us by the wind. Right now, it was simply lying quietly against our side, but every time *Gray* sailed around, so it, too, started to shift to the counter where it banged its way on the rudder all the way round to the other side.

I went below to wake Cecilia and tell her we had to leave the buoy. Why, she wanted to know. Because we're banging into it on the weather tide, I told her. Where would we go? I said there seemed to be no one around and it was a shelving shore. It shouldn't be too difficult to find somewhere to lie at the right sort of depth.

I started the engine.

How do you anchor? Pull a catch somewhere and let it go? This was definitely not the case for us. On the foredeck was the windlass which was operated by manpower. It had two handles which turned a gear which slowly turned two toothed wheels, one on either side, which engaged with the chains which could be fed through a hole in the deck from the chain locker below, over the toothed wheels and into two steel hawsepipes. These hawsepipes were angled downwards by some 20–30 degrees. I never measured the angle but it was definitely too shallow, for the anchors would rarely slide out when the chains were slack. That meant you had to push them overboard with a stick, or your boot, and if the latter, you risked being fed out overboard yourself.

When you let the anchor go, you really want it to be in a particular spot, and with the ship proceeding at a particular speed and in a particular direction. For a start, you don't want to overrun the anchor when it hits the bottom because it will then be the wrong way round and the chain could get entangled with an anchor fluke as it drags the anchor round the right way. This is less of a danger with the stockless anchors, but the fisherman always has a fluke pointing skyward just waiting to be snarled up with the chain. The best point to drop is when you have lost enough way for the ship to be just starting to travel sternwards. Having let go, you might have to check the sternward travel so that the anchor doesn't get snatched out of the ground by the weight of the ship. You can get a good idea of whether the anchor is holding by leaving the steering position and watching how the chain behaves just before you think it might be about to hold. It's very hard to get the right moment to abandon control aft in favor of observation forward at the best of times, but anchoring on a weather tide is even trickier. Of course, there is a further complication if you want to drop two anchors; but usually the second anchor is let go only under stress of weather, and taken up when the weather eases, or the chains get wrapped round each other, and you may even have to go diving to see which way to drive them unwound. It did happen to me once!

So, you really don't want to have a long period negotiating with a reluctant anchor at the critical moment when you ought to be dropping it. When you still have room to maneuver, you get the anchors out of the hawsepipe and leave them either hanging above the water, or what we termed "stock awash," which of course made no sense since the anchors had no stock. But it meant letting enough chain out so that the anchor was just below the water. This produced enough drag to be able to make it easier for me to turn the ship around without bumping the anchor against the underwater parts—given slow speeds and calm conditions.

In our particular case, neither of these conditions applied, and there was the additional risk that if we let one of the stockless anchors out of its hawsepipe it might find a way of getting muddled up with the buoy.

We waited. The buoy popped round the bow on its way out to starboard. When our hawsers were nicely untangled, but not tight, I carefully dropped the lower end in the water praying that it would not flick back and somehow get into a snarl-up either with the other hawsers or in the buoy shackle itself. It didn't, but of course *Gray* then lay broadside onto the waves and began to roll.

Before I left for the wheel some 90 feet away from Cecilia on the foredeck, we decided not to prepare the anchor for letting go in the usual way because of the risk of damaging our hull as we rolled. It was a wide open anchorage, and there would be time for me to come forward and help get the anchor away later. Which is exactly what happened.

I had had to go a little farther inshore to find shallower water. The anchor down, Cecilia went back to bed. I envied her ability not to worry. I went into the deckhouse where it was warm and gazed out of the window at the shore lights. After a while, I found what seemed to be a pair of fast marks abeam. That is, a shore light and a feature directly behind it, sufficiently far back so that the light's parallax would change quickly if we dragged.

Some change of parallax was to be expected as we sailed about at anchor. I had to get used to the normal, by simply gazing and gazing out of the window. But over a period of time, it was gradually clear that we were dragging, not fast, but dragging

All the bunks had wool quilt covers made by Cecilia. The double bunk above has 60 crocheted squares. There were six single bunks and our double bed aft, all with these quilts, a huge manufacturing process. There are two recessed spaces for books, watches, alarm clocks, all the trinkets which accumulate by bedsides. There was also a small book case housing indirect lighting for reading in bed. The edge of the bunk was curved merely because I happened to be lucky enough to find a curved piece of mahogany in the pile. There were drawers underneath.

nonetheless. How long until daybreak? Still another hour or so. I wanted to go back to bed. Once everyone was up, I knew I had no chance of more sleep. Would we drag into danger if I did nothing? It didn't look like it. There was no one else around and no dangers that I could see. When did the tide change? We would lie quieter then, but with the wind and the tide both pulling in the same direction, we might drag a lot. I decided to go back to bed and get up at slack water, just at daylight.

The dinghy banging on our sides was a good alarm clock. I gazed around. We had dragged quite a way. Dismally, I could see there wasn't much future in lying at anchor all summer. We had no choice but to move. So we crossed the Solent a couple of miles to the north and anchored in the river leading up to Lymington where the holding ground seemed to be a good deal better. This was opposite William's old school at Walhampton, which brought me face to face with the inexorable passage of time, since William, the youngest, was now nearly 14, very soon too old to be compelled to take vacations with his mother and me. But we were nowhere near the town harbor, where Cecilia's friends lived, and for two days we were unable to get ashore because the weather was too rough to risk it with an outboard engine which was misfiring. And once we did, it was obvious *Gray* was too big to get nearer the harbor and would be in the way even where we were during the summer when the yachting started.

The children came and went. There was a considerable amount of shore life, the big difference being that when we left for home at the end of the day we went seaward and everyone else left in the opposite direction. By about mid–April, I was alone on the ship, worried about the future, both for *Gray* and for the house. Managing both was certainly not being straightforward. Cecilia was already in London. I decided to follow, leaving the ship totally unattended at anchor outside Lymington.

Cecilia had people to dinner every night of my visit. I expect she wanted both to please me and to show that the house still had some vitality left. We had arranged for Ed to come up from the basement and have a talk with us about his rent. We waited in vain for about half an hour, and then went downstairs to find him kneeling on a chair with its back to a table on which was a strong table lamp illuminating a large tray full of beads. He was sorting them with a pair of tweezers.

He didn't turn round immediately so we waited for a bit before announcing ourselves. He said he was sorting beads to make a necklace. But, his eyes were getting strained, so could we come and help looking. In one corner of the tray he had separated out a few beads which he said he had firmly decided upon, but he needed to add other ones, and our task was to choose some possibilities. After a while, Cecilia asked the obvious: who was the necklace for? For Lucy, of course, he said, adding that he liked the children.

After a while of bead sorting, Cecilia said we had come about the rent. Such a disagreeable subject, he said, he had been hoping to avoid it, but there it was, he supposed we had to speak of it. But, not of the rent, of course. He had been very grieved by our behavior. He loved the basement, he loved the garden, he loved the children and the pitter patter of going up and down to our part of the house, but all the time there was this sore lump inside him that couldn't quite explain away why we had, so he described it, duped him, a poor foreigner who didn't know any better. At the time, of course, but now he had had time to learn about our laws and could see that we had been inexplicably duplicitous with him.

His little speech was delivered without the slightest trace of rancor, more in sorrow, so to speak. We looked at each other and risked a grin, as his back was still turned examining the beads on the table.

What on earth did he mean, Cecilia asked. He had never realized he was signing an illegal document when he originally signed the lease — rent is illegal, he said.

He had a point, we thought, in a ludicrous kind of way, so we both started laughing. He turned round at that to say it wasn't a laughing matter for him. He was quite seriously upset.

I explained that rent itself was not illegal. It was just that if he failed to pay, the law prevented us from evicting him, so he could go on living in our basement rent free. We would not be happy about that, but we certainly had had no intention of tricking him over the rent, and did not suppose he had originally intended not to pay it. If he failed to pay, we wouldn't be able to go and live on our schooner. Cecilia immediately contradicted me: we could keep the schooner and live in our house. Despite the fact that we were disagreeing in front of Ed, I had to point out to Cecilia we weren't finding that option at all practical. It might be possible if we left England, but England was too crowded for a ship the size we had.

Ed asked what we would do with the house if we left for sea. Would we sell it, or would he be allowed to look after it? Not if you don't pay your rent, we said jointly like a comedy turn on stage. Oh, he'd love to look after it, and he didn't want us to sell it, and of course he'd pay his rent now that he knew we hadn't intended to trick him into paying it.

He went over to the desk where the check for rent and arrears had already been made out. He handed it to me, caressingly closing my fingers over it.

What a weirdo.

When I got back to Lymington, *Gray* was where I had left her.

It was clear we couldn't make a base there. Cecilia had been talking to friends in Lymington, who had suggested we try Southampton, where they had a contact. I had romantic visions of the Boat Train, all purple velvet and brass, the Orient Express of the Home Counties, going down from London, crowded with passengers off to visit all parts of the world. I knew Southampton Water was a natural harbor which had been used from time immemorial, and that parts of Southampton town itself would have some old buildings. By the time we got to the Town Quay — we had an introduction to the harbormaster — I had our whole future planned, commuting easily to London, our country house (for which read: country ship) moored at the now disused dock, since passenger steamers had been rendered obsolete by aircraft. Furthermore, as we entered the harbor, we saw another Baltic trader at the quayside. As we passed it, a couple of young men shouted a welcome saying this was the place to be and they'd been there for months.

The harbormaster had opted to have his belt at the level of his navel, distributing the fat evenly above and below, part in his shirt and part in his trousers. Allowing the belt to slip to the hips, so that the tummy hung out from above it, barely restrained by the shirt, was, I knew, a lower-class option. He was wary. Did we need a berth for the night, he asked? He could do that, and even allowed that a couple of nights might be in order. We thanked him and tried to maneuver the conversation round to the other Baltic.

"Oh that," he said. "They're giving me the run around. They say they have engine trouble and can't leave. Do you have engine trouble, too?"

No, no, we reassured him and left feeling that it was not the right moment to start negotiating longterm.

Besides, we had to get food, so we went off shopping. That is, shopping on wet concrete, for it was raining. Food, such as there was, came gift-wrapped from a supermarket. The wind whipped paper bags, ice-cream cartons and cash register tally paper across the pedestrian shopping precinct. What was left of 17th-century Southampton had been carefully preserved, cleaned and labeled. After the market in Dieppe, huddled under the great medieval church, it was a real culture shock.

Back to the quay, where we were greeted by the young men on the other Baltic. Like the place, they asked? Oh, yes. Well, they said, all you have to do is have your engine taken out right away and then they can't get rid of you. That's what they did. The harbormaster can't do a thing about it, they said.

It's always a good thing to get on with one's neighbors, but I found it hard to smile sweetly at them and say how clever they had been. The harbormaster had little to do until the summer got into full swing. As it became clear to him that we strongly disapproved of what the other Baltic had done, he let us stay on for a few weeks. But it had to be a temporary pre-season arrangement, and finally we decided to have another go at Poole. Perhaps Poole would be sufficiently in the West Country for there to be less pressure on berthing space.

The town of Poole is inside a whole system of inland waterways, very sheltered. It was a lovely sunny June day, and I was edging us in to the quay with more care than usual owing to the crush of pleasure boats. Cecilia had got a spring on forward, but we were still free aft when Emma pointed at a mooring bollard. I didn't pay much attention, thinking she was referring to a warp aft. It was in the wrong place, I said absently, knowing that Emma knew perfectly well it was in the wrong place. With some irritation she said of course the bollard was in the wrong place, but she was looking at something on it.

I left the steering position with the engine going slow ahead, gradually closing the quayside, looked and saw what Emma had seen. Simultaneously, we both leaped onto the top of the bollard. Emma landed first, her left foot crushing the wharf-borer. My right foot landed on hers. We both fell onto the quay, picked ourselves up, and examined the crushed corpse. There was no doubt about it — from the black tips to its brown wing casings.

We had fought these creatures for years, and thought we had won.

Emma went to prospect.

She came back later with the news that the worst had happened. We had chosen to visit Poole at the same time as a much prettier Baltic which was the rage of a then current television serial (a BBC series called the *Onedin Line* which ran from 1971 to 1980). We had watched many episodes and hadn't noticed that we only saw her port side. Emma said she had seen the starboard side and it was in a bad state.

We met the skipper later. Emma was right. He didn't know what the insects were. We told him they would eat his ship right up unless he did what I told him to do.

The quayside was crowded with visiting ships and tourists going to visit them. Small barrows of stuffed toys, candy floss, nougat, fake jewellery, and jellied eels were dotted around. I bought some eels, but nothing else appealed to me. Both Cecilia and I were still suffering from living in this distinctly modest island of ours. We were lucky to have found a space on the quayside. The summer was getting going and I could see we would have to leave here once again.

A day or so after our arrival, I came up from the engine room to overhear Cecilia talking to a young man on the quayside.

I heard "opals" and started to listen properly. Then I heard "black opals" and began to take more notice, for I had heard that black opals brought bad luck and had something to do with the evil eye.

Cecilia turned round to introduce me to Gareth Schwartz, who she said was a dealer in black opals. She said he was going to come with us but only as far as Gibraltar. We would be leaving at the end of the month, she said, and she thought £90 would cover our out of pocket costs.

15

Emigration

How to do it

I looked at Gareth, lent across the rail, and shook his hand. I had no idea what to say, so I said nothing. Cecilia got the telephone number of his hotel, and said we would call him.

I had been caught this way before by Cecilia, when she would turn to me for support in front of the adversary. The trouble in these situations was that Cecilia would wait until she was in no position to back out or compromise, and so I was faced with publicly disowning her or backing something I did not believe in.

After he had gone, I faced Cecilia. She got in first. It was impossible to stay in England, she said, as though I had never said so myself. However, France seemed to have a completely different attitude to us, so we had better leave for the Mediterranean — too cold to stay up in the north, she added. Besides, I had imported the ship into France, which should make things easier.

And Newton Road, I wondered, playing Devil's Advocate.

There was Ed, she said. He might be a weirdo, but everyone liked him, and he was responsible. Since we clearly could not continue with both house and ship, she assumed that I would be happy to plump for the ship, and leave the house to look after itself — or rather to look after the children who could use it as their base from school.

I thought I couldn't have said it better myself.

As for the technical side, my side, apart from provisioning, the ship was as ready to go to Gibraltar as to go back to northern France. To our existing crew of Cecilia, myself and Emma, Thomas added his friend Adrian Hero. And we had Gareth Schwartz, albeit in a position which was to prove a little troublesome, neither guest nor crew.

In a fortnight, we had left Poole behind us. There was a Scandinavian high which gave us winds from the north and east persistently down to Spain. Off

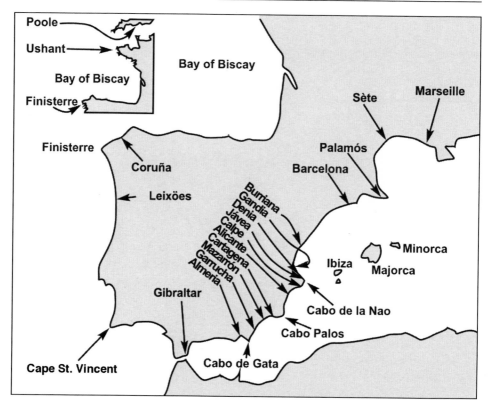

We left Poole on 26 June 1975. Gray never returned to Europe. With many stops on the way, we arrived in Sète, France, on 6 September 1975 to spend the winter.

Ushant, the most northwest island of France, Cecilia provided roast lamb and gravy, roast potatoes, and peas for dinner. In the middle of the Bay of Biscay, the wind strengthened so much that, once again, I realized we might capsize if I tried to turn the ship round. But in the morning we were becalmed, something which would plague us for the next few years in the Mediterranean. We slopped around for a day and then had to motor into Coruña.

We made good time (for us) on this leg—more than 100 miles a day. But the next leg to Leixos dropped to 40 miles a day, picking up to 85 miles a day for the final leg to Gibraltar. With nothing much to do except drift along lazily now that we were out of the tormented Bay of Biscay, I thought we should have some more practice going about, either wearing ship (stern through the wind, also called jibing—British: gibing—in smaller ships) or tacking (bow through the wind) if we could. A straight keeled ship of our size sometimes has difficulty in tacking.

Gareth wanted to take part. I gave him a job near me, and saw to my horror that he was about to be garroted by one of the sheets. The sheet was still slack, but it would jerk tight—round his neck—as the sail filled on the other tack. I yelled at him to let go, scuttled out of the wheelhouse, and pushed him to safety.

He had taken to sunbathing on the port side of the main deck in the morning and then changing to the starboard side after lunch when the sun was on the other side of the sails. He sent for me from his deck chair, and I listened, for a good half hour, on how I had been abrupt and rude to him, whereafter he started to instruct me on the elements of man management and leadership.

I learned a simple lesson which all skippers learn on long voyages: you have to reach your destination without anyone drawing a knife. A ship on an extended passage is one of the few remaining environments which you cannot leave if it doesn't suit you. Prison is another. Until the 20th century, your village would be a common environment where you had to make do with what you've got, but no longer.

Off Portugal, the Atlantic swells were immense. Successive wave crests were at eye level if I stood in the waist, which made them about 10 feet high. But they were so long that we merely rose and fell as they passed under us. For the first time, we began to see whales and dolphins, and then the bowsprit bobstay broke, the bowsprit swiveled upwards, and the headsails were rendered useless.

One option was to do nothing except take down the useless headsails. I didn't like that idea. We could get along well enough in fine weather, but what would happen if it began to blow and we couldn't keep the head of the ship out of the wind?

Apart from the swells, the weather was calm and the dolphins had gotten bored of us. They used to dive across our bows if we were going any speed. Besides, I saw that the bobstay had not in fact broken. The pin of the shackle holding it down had fallen out. It just needed a new shackle. So I decided to try to replace it. I got into a wet suit and Thomas and Adrian let me down on ropes the 12 feet over the bow to the shackle at the waterline.

What appeared from the deck to be a gentle pitching of a few inches or so, turned out to be quite different when actually at the waterline. Every time we pitched, I was completely dunked in the water and slammed against the ship's side. We had taken all the sails off, but there was enough wind to sail us very slowly ahead. Furthermore, there was just not quite enough slack in the bobstay for me to be able to get the pin in the shackle.

Thomas and Adrian knew, as I knew, that it's not a good idea to lose your skipper at sea. So after several failed attempts they hauled me back on board. I had an idea for slackening the bobstay. They were adamant: I could not return. So was I. I prevailed. I remember seeing their faces screwed up in tension as I got my first dunking the second time around. But I got the pin through the shackle, and in a moment or two I was back on deck.

I had my second lecture—about heroics—that night at dinner. They were right and I knew it this time.

We said goodbye to Gareth in Gibraltar, and quickly switched berths in case he might change his mind and want to sail on with us to France.

Emma, Thomas and Adrian left and Lucy and William arrived in Gibraltar to go with us through the schizophrenic Straits of Alboran where we saw whales all over the place, dolphins, pilot fish under our forefoot. But the going was slow and once we found the pilot fish had deserted its post at our forefoot and was now just behind the rudder as we drifted idly backwards. We experienced an electric storm off North Africa which folded its arms together to puff a foul sirocco right on us personally as it spun us round three times in squalls, gathering up its moisture on the way north. In the dark, I thought I saw Cecilia perplexed for the first time.

We stopped in Spain on the way up to Sète, little known as the Venice of France. It was at that time the vacation resort for Jewish Communists, a rather narrow section of society. It is crisscrossed with canals. We lay in one of them, trying to avoid offending our neighbors by refusing to get involved in the local occupation of stealing diesel oil. They got caught eventually, and we found ourselves smelling very sweet. Eventually the children left us alone to spend our winter in Sète. We had sailed some 1,850 miles from Poole in England.

We were still short of cash. We lived, the two of us, very modestly and enjoyed it. We both had *bleu d'ouvriers*, the shapeless, serviceable uniform worn by a self-respecting French proletariat. Once a month, we felt we had enough money to have lunch out on Sunday. We couldn't afford more than the soup. I was allowed extra garlic, since it was provided free. So, of course, was the bread. The wine we had to pay for, but it was well worth the consequent feeling of repletion and fulfillment as we walked back to the ship along the canal banks on a Sunday afternoon.

It took a little while, that is, a few years, to understand the implications of not existing as far as any government's fiscal arrangements were concerned. It wasn't a question of avoiding taxes. I eventually realized that governments didn't much want itinerants and vagrants like ourselves in their tax systems because, once there, they had to be given things like personal tax allowances, and might become a charge on the social security system which looked benevolently on its own poor citizens while wishing to exclude the poor of other countries. France was our first experience of not being harassed by the government. However, we were never protected by the police—that was the flip side. So our stay anywhere was as long as our charm would last, since we had no rights.

The Wrigley's Chewing Gum charter

After spending a happy 1975-76 winter in Sète, we had our first, and only successful, charter, promoting Wrigley's Chewing Gum off the beaches from Toulon

This shows the mob of holiday makers and small boats we had to take special care not to hurt. Standing up in the work boat with the big white outboard is one of our crew whose job was to nudge mothers and babies out of harm's way. Inset top right are the Wrigley's windsurfers gilling around waiting to perform (photograph courtesy William Cussans).

to Menton and return — a total of 32 beaches. The month-long contract stipulated that if we missed a single beach or a single day, we forfeited all our contract money. I signed the contract with my eyes covered.

Why?

You have to remember that mine was not the kind of emigration you might expect. For a start I had never fully intended to get into the big sailing ship business. I was a good technician, and getting better, but somehow the thrill of the sea never filled my mind with happy visions of our hero in oilskins braving a storm saving his ship from disaster, rescuing young maidens, all that sort of thing. The period on the barge had been great fun because it was episodic and, of crowning importance, we thrilled by surviving our mistakes. Then I got myself trained and never made a serious mistake thereafter. I became a sort of truck driver. My career to date had been what biologists call responses to stimuli — prods to see if the specimen still lives. Since leaving Gibraltar, I had begun to realize that the wind was not going to be our ally in the same way as it had been with the barge, which could sail in light winds over placid estuary waters so shallow, they said, they could sail over a heavy dew. *Gray* was not like that. She needed a bagful of wind — at which point

I got frightened something would break. Further north, the winds were often quite accommodating. But I began to learn that in the Mediterranean the winds were either majestic or nonexistent.

Without having formed for myself a clearly mapped out future, I grabbed at the next excitement which was Wrigley's Chewing Gum.

Our employer was called Provecteur, an advertising agency. Wrigley's Chewing Gum had engaged it to mount a big publicity campaign to take market share away from their rival, Hollywood, which we were told had 97 percent of the French market at the time, the remaining 3 percent being Wrigley's. Provecteur had considered television but had worked out that they could get more hits for their money by hiring some vessel like ourselves to distribute individual pastilles of Wrigley's Chewing Gum along the French beaches during the height of the holiday season. The rather small pastille was encased in what was called a blister, stuck to a virtually indestructible bit of plastic advertising which got strewn all over the beaches. It never occurred to us in those days that there was anything ecologically wrong.

The idea was that *Gray* should be equipped with banderolles (banners) between the masts and on our bulwarks advertising Wrigley's Chewing Gum, and should then sail very slowly parallel to the beaches while four windsurfers (the boys) with Wrigley's Chewing Gum on their sails would perform stunts between us and the shore. Four models (the girls) would go from one end of the beach to the other offering holidaymakers a pastille of chewing gum. It was a really wonderful idea, but presented me with significant challenges, quite apart from the fact that, unknown to us, we were breaking the law by sailing within 300 meters of a bathing beach.

Before offering us the contract, we had to demonstrate to Provecteur that we could do the job. That meant demonstrating that we could maintain an almost stationary position hanging in the wind (usually onshore during the calm summer weather) and then break out to sail parallel to the shore and as close as possible. It also meant demonstrating that we could accommodate at least eight extra bodies, provision them for a month, launch and recover them for their various jobs, and provide radio controlled dinghy support for the girls.

I was certainly able to make *Gray* hang with her stern to the wind but it was absolutely necessary to keep the engine going in case the wind failed or in case we had to back off a shallow spot.

We got the contract and started from Toulon on Bastille day 14 July 1976. We immediately ran into poor weather which meant there was no point in distributing chewing gum on deserted beaches. When we got to Cannes, the riot police came aboard, fining me *fr*200 for motoring within 300 meters of the shore and for advertising offshore (publicité en mer). It was just a short hop next day to Antibes, but we had been doing some beaches on the way and therefore approached in the late afternoon. For some reason I now forget, we were fairly far off shore when I noticed a speed boat apparently trying to catch us up. When it came nearer I saw that it

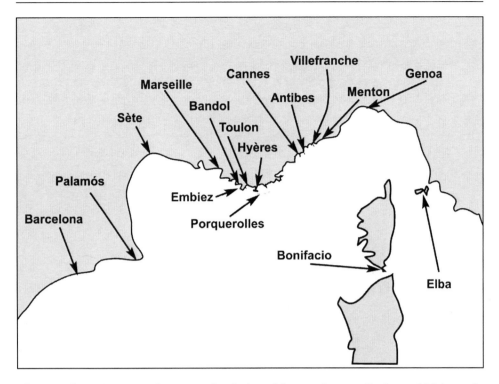

The Côte d'Azur is a somewhat vague description of the area between Toulon and Menton, the extent of our Wrigley's charter. From Sète to Menton by sea is about 200 nautical miles; from Toulon to Bonifacio, the way we went, about the same.

was manned by two policemen. It came alongside on our sheltered seaward side, the wind having changed to offshore for reasons the police did not notice, and told me that I was under arrest. I would have to follow them (in their speedboat?) to Antibes. Because I was standing on the deck I was able to see the gathering thunderstorm over the shore. So I leaned back over to seaward to ask them how they would like to proceed because, I told them, their speedboat could be swamped in a thunderstorm.

> • Mediterranean thunderstorms are notorious. They figure in at least two Verdi operas (*Otello* and *Rigoletto*). I was trained to believe they occur at weather fronts, a more northerly phenomenon, but my experience of the Mediterranean is that they occur in the evening, nothing to do with fronts, and can sit on top of you pouring down heavy rain and tumultuous winds, whose direction is quite unpredictable since they radiate directly from the center of the storm, and you don't know which periphery you occupy. On more than one occasion we have been suddenly laid over, visibility blotted out, scrambling to get sails down before they are torn to shreds. Half an hour later, a placid sunset insults you with its calm.

The policemen began to moderate their high-handed tones, clambered aboard, and I took their speedboat in tow. However, fraternizing with the police did not save me from being immobilized in Antibes for 24 hours while I negotiated with my employers to get the necessary authorization for us to continue. I think it was a question of political favors which they did not want to call in before they had to.

Fairly soon after that we began to have labor problems. The windsurfer boys were beginning to get bored, staying ashore all night, returning exhausted and hung over in the morning, refusing to sail until they had had their breakfast. When I forbade them shore leave, they wanted to bring their friends on board, which I also forbade. Then they started playing sexy games with each other, borrowing Cecilia's makeup, and leaving inflated French letters (condoms) around the boat.

Dominick (photograph courtesy William Cussans).

Eventually I got fed up and fired them. Fortunately my employers were not upset and provided a new set of windsurfers.

The girls were altogether different. They were professional sports models who took the job seriously to the extent that they never missed an opportunity to improve the tan on their bodies. This included the insides of their thighs. I therefore found myself motoring from one beach to another gazing at four spreadeagled sets of genitalia, soaking up the sun on our deck house roof. I felt insulted because I thought I was good looking in those days, not just part of the scenery.

It was the period when it was becoming fashionable for women to expose the bosom, so whenever we had visitors, they would ask politely whether we allowed *seins nus* (bare breasts) aboard or not. Of course, we did, and it became so routine that imparting this information shifted from a discreet whisper by Cecilia to me saying in my captain's speech of welcome that *seins nus* were permitted. The publicity girls, of course, followed the custom. William, 15, was responsible for taking them to the beach and then collecting them after they had finished distributing their

William and one of his charges (photograph courtesy Emma Grainger).

wretched load of chewing gum. He was always in radio contact with me on the (false) assumption that I could easily speed up or slow down to suit the progress of the girls. One day he radioed me in disgust to say he could not find the girls because they had stripped naked and looked like everyone else. William was scowling when he eventually returned with four topless models.

I thought that Provecteur's plan for this publicity was extremely ingenious. But I began to realize my boss did not understand very much about the risks I ran. He tended to carp that I was too far offshore. One day in very calm weather I noticed something on the surface dead ahead, altered course to seaward, and got the usual complaint. As my stern swung inshore I gave a big kick on the propeller and was oh so satisfied to be able to point to my slipstream which had caused waves to break over the submerged rock. In very calm weather, young mothers would propel their small children with water wings towards the lowest part of the vessel so that they could talk to anyone over the side. I would try to shoo them off the propeller: one mother asked what a propeller was. So occasionally I would find myself with no means of propulsion surrounded by kids. No wonder the police took exception to this.

Almost immediately after the charter was finished we started out for Corsica. We could smell its herbal tones several miles offshore. We anchored in a deserted bay facing the northwest. The surrounding hillsides were so densely covered in brush that we had to keep to a path in order to have a picnic lunch.

- In the southern parts of France and in Corsica, this brush was virtually impenetrable and was called the *maquis*, a name adopted by the French resisting the German invaders during World War II. They were called *maquisards*.

The path had been a used car dump over which the brush had grown. In the afternoon a Mistral started and we decided to take refuge in Bonifacio.

- The Mistral is the defining wind of that part of France's Mediterranean coast. It blows from the northwest and is precipitated by a squash between a low pressure area in the Gulf of Genoa, and high pressure over Spain or in the Atlantic. It is also a katabatic wind meaning that once it starts to pour over the mountains (Pyrenees, Alps) a siphoning action can keep it going for days on end until the cold air to the north has all been exhausted. It produces a blue black sea of great beauty in which the white spray is etched vividly on the wave tops. I always thought of it as a great lion—it would reach its shrieking height, then flip its tail just to show you that at this devastating strength it was only playing. The school children get edgy and are sometimes sent home. If you murder your spouse, you can use the Mistral as a defense if it has been blowing long enough.

We were not welcome. It was stuffed with millionaires' white yachts and they did not want to have anything to do with a dirty black schooner. As the Mistral increased — it became a whopper — they began to drag their anchors, and clung onto us to prevent themselves collapsing against the quayside.

• In our part of France, it was unusual to lie alongside a quay: instead, you selected a spot, dropped your anchor a couple of boat's lengths to seaward, turned through a right angle and backed in. You secured your stern with warps to the quayside and were thus suspended between that and your anchor. If the anchor dragged under the weight of wind, your vulnerable stern would get bumped on the quayside and eventually you would have to collapse in a huddle on the quay with other boats. Our own anchor normally lost no opportunity to skim lightly over the bottom, but for some reason it didn't in Bonifacio—and didn't riding out the 1985 Hurricane Gloria in Maine mud after we arrived in America.

When we returned to France I was left alone with two boys to help get me back from Villefranche. There was a depression in the Gulf of Genoa which kicked up a small but uncomfortable following grey-green sea. When we were in the lee of some islands, I noticed what I took to be miniature rogue waves. The wind had of course dropped somewhat but from time to time I would see a mound of water forming behind us, slowly catching up, and then dumping tons of green water on board. As there was no particular stress of weather I spent a considerable time trying to figure out why these lumps formed and got the strong impression that it was the result of two wave trains going round the island on different sides and then interfering with each other. Years later on a trip to India a year after the Indian Ocean tsunami of 2004 I noticed that adjacent shorelines had been devastated or spared without any clear explanation. I wondered whether this was a result of wave trains from different centers of the tsunami a thousand miles away interfering with each other.

Later off Spain, still in the Mediterranean, I had another taste of the freak conditions which could occur. Cecilia and I were alone on board taking the ship to Alicante with a small but disagreeable following wind from the east. I had to do a repair at the hounds. Cecilia was steering. I was enjoying slowly making the repairs as the ship swayed in the sunlight. We would be in Alicante soon. Suddenly, we were on our beam ends, the wind stiffening from the other beam. I got down, furious, and in my fright lashed out at Cecilia for being so dumb as to tip me into the water. Back on course, I returned aloft to go on with the repairs, but this time, distrustful of Cecilia, I kept my eyes about me. From forty feet up, the sea looks more or less flat even when there are some quite big holes at eye level. Then I noticed, slowly coming up astern, a roller that stood out merely because it was visible. I could see Cecilia at the wheel, but there was no possibility of shouting to her. I clung on. The roller gradually began to mound up under our stern, lifting it quite gently, and trying to make it move forwards a little faster than the bow. I could see Cecilia had by this time noticed the change in the steering. She had stepped to one side of the wheel, the better to get a purchase on it, and was heaving it over as fast as she could go, but to no effect. We were on our beam ends again, me hanging out over the water.

This time I had the grace to go down and apologize.

Back in Marseille, I refused to join my fellow large wooden sailing ships on the Jetée du Large. I told the port authorities the ships were too fragile to withstand the swell which affected it. To my surprise, even though this was a radio conversation, they accepted my point and directed me to a nearby port at l'Estaque.

L'Estaque was originally just a little fishing village across the hill from the Vieux Port in Marseille where we had originally moored. It was less than five miles north westward by sea. It had become an artists' colony (rather like Dieppe) and boasted Cézanne, Renoir, Dufy and Braque. But, in our day, l'Estaque was a pawn in a political fight between the local fishermen and Gaston Defferre, mayor of Marseille in 1944 and 1945 and again from 1953 until his death in 1986.

We thought we had been invited by Defferre to decorate the Vieux Port (along with some other wooden sailing ships), but the reality was that our free berth there had not been agreed to by the port authorities. That was why I was offered the Jetée du Large, almost in the open Mediterranean, on return to Marseille. I had been on it briefly and could see how dangerous it was. The quayside had sunk, or the Mediterranean risen, so it was impossible to keep fenders in place. Besides it was prey to the small swell which swims around in the Mediterranean and bumped us against the quay.

Defferre's offer to us was part of his plan to clear the Vieux Port of fishing vessels and to relocate them in l'Estaque. Fishermen had lived on the hill overlooking the Vieux Port from time immemorial and had no intention of leaving. On one occasion they blocked the port entrance by linking their fishing boats together across it, and were only dispersed by water cannon.

Meanwhile, l'Estaque remained empty. So, that's where we were when the big mistral of 1-2 December 1976, reputed to be the worst for fifty years, damaged my colleague boats (*Outlaw, Berthe, San José*) on the Jetée du Large. An ore carrier broke loose in one of the inner docks taking bollards with it despite being pressed against the quay by tugs. It crushed and sank a research vessel with its Christmas stores. Île Pomègues (outermost of the Îles Frioul outside Marseille) reported 56 knots (Force 11).

I was not popular. Why was I there, safe and sound, my colleagues wanted to know; why hadn't I shared my secret with them when I scuttled off to safety, they wanted to know. It was a difficult question to answer as I knew they had never regarded me as swashbuckling enough to be in the same line of business as them. I didn't want to have to apologize for my short hair and teenage children. We might have been OK with a papoose or two, but our children walked upright. I was desperately domesticated. Not cool at all.

Nor were we popular with charterers, who were failing to stand in line awaiting the pleasure of our company. Except for a period of about a month when the port authorities decided to sandblast the cargo hatches of a bulk carrier on the open

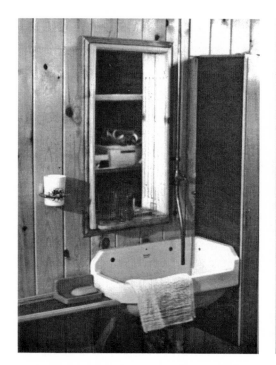

Inevitably space was limited, but I tried to make the washing areas as comfortable as possible by providing shelves wherever there was an opportunity, if necessary by recessing them into the walls.

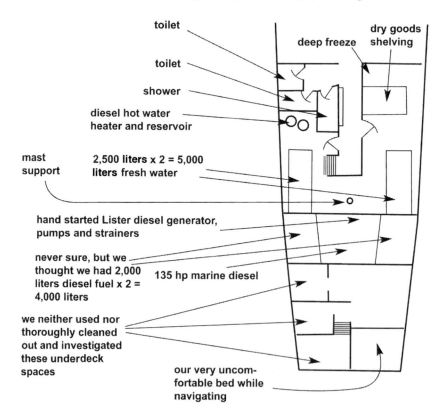

toilet

toilet

shower

diesel hot water
heater and reservoir

deep freeze

dry goods
shelving

mast
support

2,500 liters x 2 = 5,000
liters fresh water

hand started Lister diesel generator,
pumps and strainers

never sure, but we
thought we had 2,000
liters diesel fuel x 2 =
4,000 liters

135 hp marine diesel

we neither used nor
thoroughly cleaned
out and investigated
these underdeck
spaces

our very uncom-
fortable bed while
navigating

space beside us, the port was quiet and safe, and gradually began to fill up with a few other pleasure boats. So there was a pleasant quayside life which usually peaked in the middle of the day with the barbecuing of fresh sardines. One of the sailing wives was going to have her baby underwater. But, the real stuff of life seemed to be eluding us. We made a few day trips out of Marseille and then decided to try our luck in a more touristy place like Bandol, about 25 miles in the direction of Italy, and about halfway to Toulon. We got some sort of document there which enabled us to do day trips, so we took turns on a stool on the quayside next to the man selling candy floss who was doing a much better trade than us. It was all rather dispiriting and so by the end of the year we decided we had had enough of France and would try our luck in Spain.

The trouble was that we seemed to have been doing less and less sailing while sailing itself in the Mediterranean summer was becoming less and less rewarding. We seemed to be motoring everywhere we went. The log shows that we could keep up the snail's pace of something less than 100 miles a day, but more of it was motor sailing than had been the case in the North Sea and English Channel. Leaving Poole in England had given us a reasonably substantial sailing experience to get to Sète. The following year with the Wrigley's Chewing Gum charter and the trip to Corsica we had probably traveled only about a thousand miles but by the time we decided to leave France, that summer's travel had been negligible and we spent a lot of time hanging around for charters that did not materialize. I was reluctantly realizing that *Gray* was not a particularly good sailing vessel. She didn't like light winds; I didn't like strong winds; and we never seemed to get something we both liked, particularly in the Mediterranean.

We leave France

So, in October 1977 we left for the 400 mile sail to Alicante in Spain and then back a few miles to a small port called Calpe where we hauled the boat out of the water. I acquired a hand adze (which I still have) the same as all the carpenters. Unlike the American version, which has a long handle to be held by both hands, the blade of the Spanish version was held by a curved piece of wood which you made yourself to suit the way your

The most effective of my adzes is sharpened on the outside edge (as shown in the above sketch). But some are sold for sharpening on the inside. In all cases you make your own handle to suit the blade.

single hand best struck the wood. That is, I curved the wood from the point of attachment towards the blade so that my hand would form the center of an arc of which the blade was part. If the hand was abaft this point, the blade would not come into contact with the wood; if forward, it would get caught in the wood instead of slicing through it. Some adzes are sharpened on the side nearest your hand and some on the side nearest the wood. I preferred the latter since you could make small adjustments to the bevel to ensure that the cutting edge was part of the circumference of a circle of which your hand was the center. I found that I could produce such a flat smooth surface that the next finishing tool was a cabinet maker's hook scraper. The whole operation of fairing up boards was much faster and easier than using an electric plane.

Calpe is on the south side of Cabo de la Nao, a promontory which has to be doubled if you are sailing up from somewhere like Alicante to the southern coast of France, say, Marseille. In a mistral, you would have a soldier's beam wind to get you under the cape, but you might have a hard time getting much beyond it. If that were to happen you could try to beat into Jávea, about five miles away on the northern side of the cape to shelter until the mistral abated. Jávea is such an extraordinarily sheltered harbor that it's hard to see any wind which could disturb it: the mouth curves round southward away from any mistral to face the land. But, in the Mediterranean you can never be sure. When we finally left Jávea a thunderstorm nearly drove us onto the riprap and then drove us north to Burriana, instead of south, the way we had intended.

We had transferred to Jávea from Calpe after hauling. At that time (February 1978) Jávea didn't have much traffic, and certainly no yachts because of the strange configuration of its breakwater. There are plenty of pontoons for yachts today (2013), but they didn't exist when we were there. The only place to moor would have been the thousand foot long breakwater, the 700 feet of quayside which it protected being reserved for the odd commercial vessel. The breakwater was built on a foundation of riprap so there was no question of coming alongside. However, it did have a strange feature: there were three 45 or 50 foot square concrete blocks built out into the harbor, clear of the riprap, more or less equally spaced along the breakwater. So, I did a deal with the military port captain (there were two: the other was the civilian port captain, both called Don Pepe). If he let us spend the winter on one of these concrete blocks, we would serve as a staging point for yachts who could tie up to our outer side. I pointed out that as we had 90 feet on deck, this more or less doubled the capacity of his port. He came from Cadiz, speaking a Spanish that even the locals had a hard time following. We sat in silence as he turned the leaves of a coffee table sized book of pictures of the great days of sail, sitting in our cabin.

Jávea was our base from February to July when we left, according to one of my logs, "to avoid arrest." I think the log note is a little over dramatic. We had indeed been in trouble with the port authorities for illegal chartering in Spain. I was hauled up before the military port captain in Denia, just along the coast, and told I would be arrested if I did it again. The charter had not been particularly successful, I wasn't broken hearted, and besides we had other things on our mind.

It appeared I could not avoid the logic of crossing the Atlantic.

Sailmaking

When originally thinking about *Gray*'s sail plan, soon after I had bought her, I figured we wanted as few spars as possible. Loose-footed sails had worked well on the barge and if we dispensed with a horse (called a traveler on sailboats), there would be little capable of hurting young children. The one exception was the mizzen which clearly had to have a boom and a gaff as well as a horse.

Throughout *Gray*'s life with us, sail design continued to be a matter of trial and error. Consequently, I can only hazard a guess that we never had more than 3,500 square feet of fore and aft sails, and 900 sq ft of square sails. Using conventional rule of thumb measures, this is at the lowest end of the sail area to displacement ratio. We were limited by the decision to have single pole masts only 65 feet off the deck, but even so, we could have carried more sail higher up, provided I was prepared to have headsticks—which I was not.

The fuel tanks were not large enough to permit us to motor across the Atlantic. In any case, the whole point was to sail.

In our early years, all our sails had been made of flax. It is used for the making of linen (a much lighter weight cloth), linseed oil (for eating among other things) and a large variety of products like ropes (many of ours were made of flax) dye, paper, medicines, hair gels, and soap. The sailmaker Jim Lawrence lived in Brightlingsea, near Maldon. He had made all the barge sails out of flax which weighed 36 to 39 ounces per square yard. He delivered them on the quayside without any dressing so they could stretch for a year. Our job then was to find red and yellow ochre, make a slurry with a little water (and possibly stale beer to give the sails a sheen) and then mix in cod oil. Depending on the proportions of the ochres the result was sometimes like the robes of a Tibetan monk, sometimes too yellow, or sometimes too red. The usual mixture was two of yellow to one of red by weight, but one or the other ochre might be in short supply, so our barge sails varied. Having mixed large quantities of these ingredients, we used brooms to spread it on the sails on the quayside. Turning the sails over to do the other side inevitably meant that our clothes got covered, and just as inevitably all the bed clothes because there was never enough water to scrub really clean. The smell was terrific, a fishy badge of honor advertising the arrival of the real thing.

Jim had made the inboard sails for *Gray* in rapid succession in England. One was actually delivered to us under sail at sea. Without the mizzen sail *Gray* seemed to sail relatively well. But I had built a hole for it and so we ordered it from England after we had left. It took about a year to arrive and because we had moved around in the meantime we had it delivered to somewhere in Spain and had to fetch it by car. It was extremely heavy and had been dressed with Kanvo, a modern preparation made by D. S. Weston & Company, of Glasgow, which stayed put on the sail. As a single item, the sail required two men to lift it, provided of course that they could find something to grab hold of. Then it had to have various finishing touches like brails, sheets, halyards and gaskets. I sat on a milking stool under an umbrella in Jávea in front of my bench which had holes for all the spikes and mallets used for making grommets and so forth. I felt enormously nautical. For the first and last time in my life, when passersby gossiped with me, I laid down my work, and abandoned my usual surliness to strangers interrupting me.

However, one way or another the mizzen sail had also been expensive, maybe the sterling equivalent of between three and four thousand dollars (2013). It was clear we would have to make our own sails in future. So, we bought natural fiber canvas in Alicante. The rolls worked out at only between 10 and 11½ ounces per square yard. The cloth for a sail the size of the mizzen would have cost around £50 in Spain (say, $230 to $300 at today's prices), but would have weighed only a quarter of the flax sail. We made two sails at Jávea — a fisherman (set on a diagonal stay between fore and main mast, but otherwise flying), and a fairly large fore staysail. Within a year, both sails had to be replaced (the fisherman got bigger, and the staysail got smaller), but this led to a new attitude toward our sails: we were quite hazy as to appropriate shapes, so if we had to replace them cheaply and frequently we might learn better shapes. Also, we could set them in places we would not have had enough strength for had they been in flax. All four of Jim Lawrence's sails lasted the life of *Gray*. The three staysails remained basic throughout, but we found that the mizzen, a magnificently made and durable sail, was seldom used because it made us heavy headed.

• Sailing vessels with long straight keels—like *Gray*—tend to have a center of lateral resistance well forward of where you might like. Yachts with deep fin keels can push this center further aft. With us, we needed a lot of headsails to keep us from rounding up into the wind, called being heavy headed. The mizzen, being the last sail aft, made us even more heavy headed. Thames barges, on the other hand, usually only have a small steering sail aft to help tack. Its sheet was attached to the top of the rudder so that it was held to windward when the rudder was put over. Otherwise you can visualize their main sail plan as having been shifted forward by the length of the bowsprit (which is usually about a fifth of the overall length of the barge), leaving an empty space around the steering position aft. We never had heavy headed problems in *Gipping*, although we sometimes had problems tacking as we didn't have the small steering sail aft.

Sewing up new sails in natural fiber went on for about five years, spanning the preparation for crossing the Atlantic until well afterwards. In 1983, four years after arriving in America, we changed to Dacron — and was that a change!

Dacron is like slippery sheet steel, totally unforgiving to creep. Since the cloth will not change shape on the bias, it can only be folded in one plane at a time. Natural fibers can be folded in two planes simultaneously enabling tiny gathers to absorb excess material. The Dacron we bought was described as heavy duty. But, it weighed only 8.3 ounces per square yard (a bit over a fifth of the weight of flax). A heavy duty Brother sewing machine was able to punch a stitch hole through three or even four thicknesses, but when it came to the reinforcing patches at the corners we had to deal with about twice that thickness— by hand.

Going back to the sail making before crossing the Atlantic: We needed square sails—a heavy course set on a yard which was hoisted aloft, about 25 feet long, and a lighter raffee on top, both of them rigged on the center mast of the three we had. I would have liked to have rigged them on the foremast, but I also wanted to be able to bring the yard down on deck fairly easily in case of foul weather. There wasn't enough room to slide the yard down the forestay where it would have arrived right over the stem head.

To help with the heavy headedness, we also made a large fore staysail to go on the end of the bowsprit.

My records are not clear but the large fore staysail could have been 350 square feet.

Cecilia sewing Dacron sails — this must have preceded the bucket up to the yardarm.

The first obvious question is: How much sail did Gray carry? And the answer is: I don't know. That may seem a strange answer given that I designed all the sails, and that we made a lot of the sails on board. The trouble is that there is a whole stack of my neat hand drawings, some of them dated and some not, but none of them confirming that this was the design actually made. Furthermore, we were constantly replacing worn sails with different designs until we started making sails in indestructible Dacron. The four darker sails above, made by Jim Lawrence, remained a constant throughout.

So, I have tried to reconstruct what we must have had from a photograph (above) probably taken towards the end of our time with Gray. The areas are consistent with the records that I still have.

The total fore and aft sail area adds up to 3,420 sq ft. We occasionally set a flying jib at the very end of the bowsprit. It might therefore have brought the total fore and aft area to about 3,500 sq ft.

Yacht designers use a rule of thumb which produces an index derived from the sail area and a root of the displacement. One I have come across is $16 \times$ sail area (sq ft) $\times$ displacement (pounds) $^{(-2/3)}$. On this basis Gray's index is 11; the 19th century Gloucester fishing and racing schooner Bluenose *gets a 26.*

Another photograph of Gray in the Atlantic gives a silhouette for the course and raffee totaling 725 sq ft. The two sails were designed with big bellies showing more than 900 sq ft of material when laid on the ground.

It didn't last long as it was too big and baggy for sailing on the wind, our normal sailing situation since we could only barely make good to windward, so we virtually never had the wind free.

- It was easy to observe how well *Gipping* could make to windward because we were usually in sight of the shore, maybe even in a wide river. Close hauled on a lee tide,

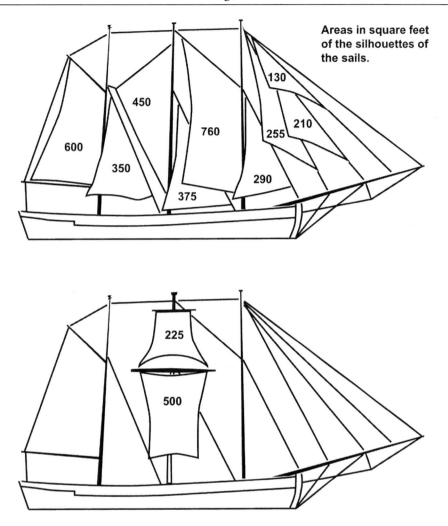

The above sail areas are somewhat conjectural. To derive them, the sails were traced into a CAD program from a photograph. The CAD program then calculated the areas of the silhouettes. These areas were then checked for good sense with any drawings I could find in the knowledge that the drawings all referred to intentions and were never updated for actual cutting. Consequently, because I designed the sails with belly, the sail areas are all less than the area of cloth actually cut. In the case of the square sails, belly was considerable as both of them were cut with convex sides, whereas the silhouettes have concave sides. I would have a hard time reverse engineering the cut sizes, but whatever the result Gray *would still be under-canvassed.*

we could see if we were level pegging the bank. We would sail until a leeboard touched on the mud, turn round the leeboard, and then do the same thing on the other tack. We had alert and excited children working the leeboards to pull them out of danger of being broken. Measuring how well we sailed on *Gray* was much more difficult since we drew so much—three times *Gipping*—we were usually a long way from fast marks. Besides we dare not risk touching shallow ground with our hull as we did in *Gipping* with our leeboards.

The log over the Atlantic is dotted with entries about how to make these three sails (the course, the raffee, and the baggy fore staysail) work best. The course and raffee were fixtures for the crossing. If I rigged the bowsprit sail, our speed picked up but we had to come off the direct course to our destination to avoid blanketing the bowsprit sail with the course. With no bowsprit sail, we could waddle more slowly but in the right direction. I never really solved which was faster over the ground.

• Later, in America, I replaced the earlier wooden bowsprit partly because it was rotten, partly because I hoped to be able to carry more sail further forward, and partly because the Coast Guard were throwing away some tapered steel lamp standards. The new steel bowsprit was nearly as long as a mast, and increased our overall length to 137 feet. The last 10 feet were made from some plumbing pipe I found lying around, which Cecilia had volunteered that I should not use. My son, by then a pipeline engineer, was appalled when he saw it. But it carried a flying sail occasionally.

Like its predecessor, the new bowsprit was hinged inboard so that I could steeve it up to avoid paying dockage on more than the length of our hull. Rigging it was hair-raising, not only because it became more and more unstable the further Cecilia and I eased it outboard, but I was apprehensive a strong young man would stride aboard to give a hand to two obviously incapable oldies like ourselves—and would upset the unstable equilibrium.

Cecilia sewed the cloths together; my job was to make the corners. In natural fiber, this wasn't much of a problem, but when it came to Dacron it was a different story. The sewing machine was quite unable to penetrate the 8 to10 layers of cloth we thought necessary to reinforce the corners. I therefore made aluminum templates, drilled with precisely spaced holes, through which I inserted a specially adapted electric soldering iron to melt stitch holes in the Dacron. The corners became works of art, much tidier than anything I achieved in natural fiber.

To help Cecilia feed the cloth through the sewing machine, I attached a rope to the material she was sewing, led the rope through a block (pulley) at the yardarm, and attached a bucket of water. The weight helped the material through so I didn't have to stand opposite her endlessly pulling — although she, of course, endlessly stitched.

Having sewn the cloths together, we then had to find a spare area to lay them out and cut the edges—a football field, gymnasium, dock loading area. Instead of being straight from corner to corner, the sail edges were, of course, curved, usually part of an ellipse, less usually a circle, although I did experiment unsatisfactorily with a sine wave. The marks to cut the curve were calculated as offsets to the straight lines connecting the corners. This was usually a heavily pre-planned operation because not only were large enough spaces seldom available for long, but the wind might get up, and shift a carefully smoothed out sail.

At home, sewing a cotton dress or something like that, you have to make a hem to turn in the cut edge of the material. Cotton lends itself very well to this because you can get it to expand or contract enough to accommodate slight differences in length. But this doesn't work if the hem — called a tabling in sailmaking — is wide, and particularly if the material is Dacron. Therefore, you cut your sail four to six inches too wide, cut off the excess material, and move it laterally inwards to form a doubling round the edges with (and this is the important part) the same bias as the underlying sail. The tricky part is to make sure this excess material (the tabling) really follows the edges of the cut out sail when being sewn and doesn't start bunching or swerving off to one side.

This was such a hard job with Dacron that we had to use double-sided adhesive tape down the center line of the tabling, followed by a line of stitching down the center line before we could turn the edges under for sewing. All the stitches were proud of the Dacron, exposing them to chafe, thus entailing more stitching than in natural fiber to keep this horrible material together.

But, once made to a certain shape — and it had better be the right shape — here was a nearly indestructible sail, which only slowly suffered from exposure to sunlight. Dacron sails were light enough to stow inside for the winter; beloved, kindly flax was impossibly bulky.

16

Traveling again

The Balearics

We left Jávea because of the indefinable sense of fear (in this case, of arrest) which still persisted in post–Franco Spain. The Generalissimo who had ruled Spain for nearly 40 years had been dead three years by the time we arrived in Spain. But, I suspect not much had changed. In our case, the Guardia Civil was present everywhere, and tended to be unfriendly because, like the French riot police, it was deliberately recruited from outside the areas in which it served. When we visited Barcelona, for instance, a Guardia Civil was stationed at the end of our quay with the sole purpose of watching us. No interference, nothing like that, just watching — maybe sitting down, smoking, but armed with his rifle. Similarly, the ports had two captains, a military officer and a civilian, in our case Don Pepe I and Don Pepe II respectively. The boss of Don Pepe I was the military commander of Denia. He was the one who had threatened me with arrest if I chartered illegally.

One day, when we had decided to leave, I was walking back over the sunbaked loading area for the commercial quayside after a fruitless quest to find Jaime the Water, so called because he drove the tanker which supplied the town with fresh water. He could never be found during working hours presumably because he was off providing a refill. The only chance of finding him to order water was to go to his house during the three hour lunch period (1 P.M. to 4 P.M.) where his wife would angrily denounce (and give the address of) whomever he was sleeping with. Jaime, who had the lowest job in town, came to glory once a year when he mounted a white stallion to head the procession opening the annual bull running festival.

I needed to do two things before leaving: fill up with water, and load the car.

In the middle of the deserted, dusty loading area, Don Pepe II was sitting on a brick, a fairly small brick. As I approached he got down off his brick (he was a very small man, so he descended) to shake my hand. He agreed he looked dejected without explaining why. I explained we needed to load the car. Cars were forbidden on the quayside, he pointed out, neglecting the fact that they had evidently not been forbidden when we arrived and unloaded. But, my Spanish couldn't run to disentangling that. I was about to go on my way, when he announced, without explanation, that the Guardia Civil changed duty during the lunch period. He reminded me that one of the jobs of the Guardia was keep an eye on me. I was well aware of this because we had tried and failed to make friends with the Guardia as they patrolled our part of the quayside. Don Pepe II went on: the headquarters were in town. He had observed from his office that the morning Guardia walked up to the headquarters around this time of day, and that it was not until some time later that his replacement would walk back. Don Pepe II thought the period with no Guardia might be as long as half an hour; then he fell silent.

Then he wished me "*que aproveche*," which expresses the hope that I would enjoy my forthcoming meal.

I went back to *Gray*. Cecilia and I tried to figure it out. We could leave without water, but we could not leave without our car, which was normally kept outside the port gates.

Accordingly, the next day, Cecilia got into the car around 2 P.M., drove through the unattended gates, did a circle inside past Don Pepe's office window, drove the car back out again, and turned it round to face the port gates, remaining in it herself with the engine running.

I suppose she thought she could wait there inconspicuously to see if anything would happen. But she looked like a gangster's moll, arm out of the window keeping cool, dark glasses, the only being to move in the heat, waiting for her boyfriend to come back from robbing the bank. The new Guardia would certainly pick her up on suspicion, never mind the car.

We had done a little spying ourselves, and realized that Don Pepe was not the kind of man to take advantage of the long lunch period, and that he tended to remain in his office overlooking the loading area, across which the going off duty and the coming on duty Guardias would have to pass. After a while he came out, contemplated Cecilia, nodded, and went back into his office. She then drove straight past him on to the quayside next to *Gray* where I had already swung out the derrick. By the time the afternoon Guardia trudged past us, we were sitting having our lunch with the car on deck next to us wrapped up in an old tarpaulin.

We spent the next two months sailing round the Balearic Islands. One of them is Ibiza, which had a reputation for being somewhat hippie. We finally had to content ourselves with backing into a quayside just by the abattoir which had discharged so much coagulated blood into the water that we really lay couched in soft mud, rather than in water. Being a good decent family, we felt uncomfortable among all the hippies and particularly so after a drunk on the next door boat had fallen into the water, clambered on the quayside covered in coagulated blood, decided that we had pushed him in, and returned to avenge himself on his aggressor, which he took to be Cecilia. Her nose bled profusely and somehow that sobered him up. In this context when we met a nice curly headed young man who was interested in having an ordinary conversation with us, we were quite attracted to his suggestion that he come with us across the Atlantic. It was agreed that we would meet him in Gibraltar and that he could bring a friend. But of course we made the same mistake that we had made when crossing from England to Gibraltar and asked him to pay no more than the cost of his food and any other out of pockets directly attributable to his presence.

We had intended to haul the boat out of the water in Calpe, which is just south of Cabo de la Nao, itself just south of Jávea, the easiest mainland port for us to return to from Ibiza. But when we got to Jávea, we found that the port was full, that is, that one or two craft occupied the concrete blocks on which we had berthed. So, I anchored outside the harbor sheltered by the breakwater which curved beyond us and back towards the shore. The next morning was, as usual, calm and Cecilia and I went ashore to make telephone calls to the children in London and to Calpe. As usual, Cecilia did all the talking so I was left with nothing to do.

I don't remember noticing any change in the weather, but something made me extremely nervous. I pulled Cecilia off the telephone and began running back to our dinghy. We took off without any consideration for our wake at our top speed

Just by the door of the deckhouse was a fairly steep companionway ladder leading down to what used to be the cargo hold. My principal job was to convert the 45 foot long hold into living space, for which I bought a 20 foot mahogany trunk, a stack of knotty pine tongued & grooved boards, and some 2 × 4s. This sitting room was the last to be converted because it served as the workshop to build the rest of the interior.

of 25 knots. By the time we reached *Gray*, we could see she was already dragging her anchor and that Thomas was trying to capture sails which we had left loose the night before. Back on board, the thunderstorm blotted everything out except the riprap behind us.

On a vessel like ours, getting an anchor up in a wind can be quite tricky. The anchor itself is at the end of a heavy chain, and it is the chain that is important to weighing the anchor down in the mud. The moment you start winding the windlass in order to lift the anchor, you also lift the chain off the seabed so that the anchor may cease to hold even though there is a considerable amount of chain left to come in.

A way to mitigate this problem is for the helmsman to drive the boat up very gently onto the anchor, thus slackening the chain and making it easier to wind in. However the ship's bow, no longer held pointing into the wind by the anchor chain, starts to sail around. With bad luck, the helmsman, who is 90 feet away and can see nothing under the forefoot, drives the ship over the chain. The ship then pays off and snubs the anchor right out of the mud. With the anchor chain growing athwart ships, it jams in the hawsepipe, while the helmsman is under the misapprehension that the anchor is up, and that he can get under way. A little later, the anchor snags in something on the bottom and the ship becomes unmaneuverable.

We were too near the riprap to give more scope to the anchor in the hope that it would hold. My only recourse was to drive up on the anchor, slackening it enough for Thomas and Cecilia to wind it in. But there was an additional difficulty: none of the shore was any longer visible, so I only had the compass to determine which way I was pointing. Behind me I had the riprap, but to port, not visible, was the end of the breakwater which curved out to seaward, into the wind — we were thus in the corner of an "L."

When finally I could see from the compass that the ship's head was paying off to port I did not know whether this was because I had overrun the anchor or whether the anchor was up. I was by this time parallel to the riprap. My only chance of getting off it was to assume we were clear of the ground (for which I had no evidence), adjust the throttle to maximum engine revolutions and drive hard ahead to get steerage way. To turn *away* from the riprap, I had to turn the stern *toward* it. But I had no means of knowing if my propeller or rudder would foul an underwater obstruction near the riprap. I had to turn hard to seaward to make the tightest turn possible. Then, the breakwater loomed through the murk, racing by from starboard to port, no seaward end in sight, no room for retreat. Then the end: we were almost on it. I straightened up rapidly to prevent my stern hitting it, and staggered out straight to seaward, straight into the thunderstorm, praying for enough offing to round the breakwater to starboard and run for it.

Once at sea, it became apparent that there would be no possibility of doubling Cabo de la Nao on the way south to Calpe. So, we turned and fled north to Burriana where we knew there were hauling facilities.

Leaving the Mediterranean

Getting to Gibraltar after we had hauled in Burriana should have been quite straightforward. But a Levanter developed.

The wind blows from the east (the Levant is an old word for the Middle East), from the rising sun, and my own experience was that there were two types, both disagreeable and both giving rise to a nasty looking grey-green sea, so the meteorological distinction between the two was in practice unimportant. I didn't like them. The one we had experienced off the southern coast of France was generated by a low pressure area in the Gulf of Genoa. It had given rise to small rogue waves on the lee side of an island. Further towards Gibraltar there's another type of east wind, generated by high pressure over the Bay of Biscay and low pressure over the Atlas Mountains of Morocco. It is more persistent and can be strong. This was our Levanter on leaving Burriana

We were in a hurry to get to Gibraltar on time to meet our children and the charterer we had encountered in Ibiza. Cecilia and Thomas and I were on board *Gray*. We left Burriana after hauling in the usual way, day sailing down the coast, but by the time we left Cartagena, the Levanter had started to blow. You might

I built everything rectilinear and horizontal on a floor which sloped downwards towards the after end (left of picture). We came down from the deck house on the far left; then past a mahogany bookcase; to give depth, all doorways were framed by angled boards (in the middle); on the left of the washbasin (just visible) is the shower; another cabin is on the extreme right. All uprights are fluted.

think it was a good thing it was behind us. We had planned a stopover in Garrucha, a port now embayed at the root of the Cabo de Gata.

I had been somewhat idle in advance planning. Someone told us to look out for a series of windmills before reaching the port. As we went along the coast towards it, every bluff had a windmill, so that wasn't going to be much good as a landfall signal. I was beginning to get a little anxious because we seemed to be going towards a turn in the coast which was covered in breaking water. A little while later, I realized it was Garrucha. It was virtually underwater and there was no question of trying to get inside.

We had to claw off.

When Cecilia rounded up into the wind, Thomas and I got the full force of the gale. We had to get up more sail very fast, or we would be on the rocks. It's rather like a weightlifting snatch — two of you coordinate your pull, heaving simultaneously. Thomas and I stood ready to do this on opposite sides of a halyard. Thomas looked at me expectantly; I looked past his head at the breaking waves behind him.

I did nothing.

Thomas applied his weight to the fall of the halyard. I was not pulling in unison. Thomas straightened up — was I ready?

Nothing.

Dominick, pull. He kicked my shin. At last I pulled. We pulled together. The ship settled down to sail us off.

On the lee side of the Cabo de Gata, the wind came down in volleys. With only the engine and no sails by now (the wind was heading us somewhat), a curious thing began to happen. Naturally enough we were being blown *away from* the shelter of the headland (which rises to about 1,000 feet) even though the ship's head was being turned by the heavy wind *towards* the cape. We were crabbing along and the rudder was becoming ineffective. When we got into Almeria, the port of refuge, it was in a shambles with boats and ships all over the place. A research vessel off the Cabo de Gata had recorded 45 knots (Force 9, strong gale, same as off Newhaven) about the time we had been rounding it.

Atlantic crossing

Our curly headed Swiss charterer from Ibiza turned up in Gibraltar with two friends, not one. True to my stereotype as a leak freak, I spent my 10 days in Gibraltar almost entirely in the bilges making sure the pumps worked. Just before leaving, the Swiss fellow showed me with great pride the aluminum suitcase he had bought stuffed with guns and survival equipment. In true romantic style, he offered the captain — that is to say, me — the custody of this arsenal. I was daft enough not to accept.

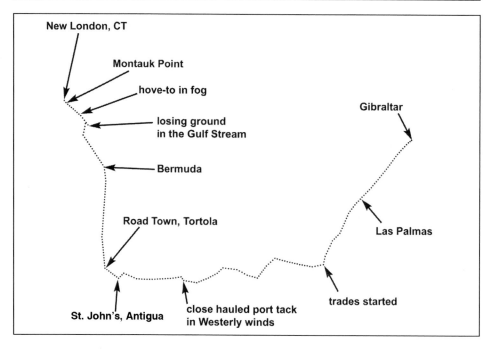

The dotted line is based on sextant sights of celestial bodies plotted with Great Circle coordinates from 41° 21′ N, 72° 06′ W, the root of the pier sticking out into the Thames river from the H. H. Richardson railroad station in New London, Connecticut, which we gazed at for eight years. When you say Thames, think Thane of Cawdor, not Tems as in England. We were berthed opposite the shipyard making nuclear submarines. Somebody had to count them, after all.

We — that is, Emma, Thomas, Victoria and her friend, Ray Smith, Cecilia, me, a small station wagon in which Gibraltar Customs had sealed our booze, and Diego, a black mongrel — were shot out of Gibraltar by another quartering Levanter. It died fairly quickly although it was very exciting to be doing more than 8 knots for a while, quite a change from the Mediterranean.

The usual strategy for crossing the Atlantic from Europe to America is to use the trade winds. The easiest way to visualize these winds, which occur both north and south of the equator, always blowing northeast or southeast, is to imagine two Polish sausages girdling the earth, with a width from 5° to 30° latitude. In each sausage the winds corkscrew around the world producing the northeast and southeast trade winds on the surface and then rising before colliding on the equator to return at high altitude to their starting latitude, only further round the globe. To be sure, there are exceptions to this idea — over land masses, and in the Indian Ocean — but for our Atlantic purposes 30° north occurs around Las Palmas, Canary Islands, at which we aimed initially.

We timed our departure from Gibraltar to coincide with the end of the hurricane season in the North Atlantic (November 30), to make a stopover at the Canary Islands and then to start edging further south until we found the trades—

in our case, about 20° north, further south than expected. To be on the safe side, we did not want to go further south than 10° north, otherwise we might find ourselves in the doldrums, an area which shifts north and south of the equator depending upon the season and in which the weather is erratic and, much more important for sailors, spawns hurricanes.

- The technical name for the doldrums is the Intertropical Convergence Zone (ITCZ). With the heat of the sun the air mass at the equator rises because it is getting less dense and therefore floats upwards. You might have expected that this would suck in straight north or south winds, but it does not, because of the rotation of the earth. There is a phenomenon called the Coriolis effect about which much has been written with an extensive mathematical basis. But put crudely, you can look at it like this: In the northern hemisphere, if you look south at a particle of air, it is always being left behind by the earth. It appears to be traveling to your right because the earth under it is rotating to the left a little faster than you are. That is, a particle of air to your south is drawn to the equator (by the rising air in the doldrums which gives it a northerly component), while the Coriolis effect gives it an easterly component. That's why the trade winds blow from the northeast (north of the equator).

Always retaining their easterly component, they rise in the doldrums and circulate back north to fall again in about latitude 30/35°, regions which are called, for obscure etymological reasons, the horse latitudes. The Sahara Desert and the Great Australian Desert lie in the horse latitudes.

Thus, there is a corkscrewing sausage of wind essentially girdling the earth, but interrupted by land masses, and by the monsoons, which provide exceptions.

The Indian monsoon is one of the more interesting interruptions since it gives rise to the only part of the earth with substantial mixing of the air masses north and south of the equator. In the south Indian Ocean, the trades blow in the same way as just described, in a corkscrew blowing southeast at the surface as you would expect. But the Tibetan plateau and the Himalayas create the equivalent of a giant sea breeze in which the wind blows from the sea towards the more rapidly heating land in the summer. So the southern trades, instead of rising and returning south, are hooked across the equator towards India and form the southwest monsoon, the wet wind which irrigates the whole of India. This could be of considerable importance if there were a massive pollution of one of the hemispheres. The terrifying Nevil Shute novel *On the Beach*, is based on this idea, although he doesn't go into how the radiation would creep south.

The three charterers were not fitting in. The final straw occurred when one of them used our bread supply (we made our own bread) to bribe a local to bring him back drunk in the early hours of the morning. He took the view that he owned the bread since the arrangement with us was that we would charge them only what it cost us to feed them. I disagreed and suggested that he would have a more satisfactory life by returning home. He accepted the suggestion.

That left us with the original curly head and what turned out to be his somewhat retarded sidekick. The children objected to their fairly open demonstration of homosexual activity, and I objected to finding halyards and sheets half severed by what I assumed to be the sidekick's penknife. Throughout our passage which must have been one of the slowest on record (28 days from the Canary Islands to Antigua), I was under pressure from my family to do something about it. Since no one could leave the ship, once we had sailed from the Canary Islands, I was unable to figure out what to do. Besides, they were armed to the teeth because of my stupid failure to take possession of the aluminum suitcase. They wanted to have target practice, for instance. Instead of forbidding it, I temporized and said we might think about it tomorrow, but when tomorrow came, they had forgotten about it. They behaved somewhat like children.

The real fire eaters were my family. I ducked out of facing them by finding that my navigation problems were really quite formidable, and that we needed to know within a square inch where we where several thousand miles away from anywhere. By the time these calculations had been completed (and more calculations, if required, of the date at which we would likely sink, unless we reached land) there was lunch. Having drunk a drop too much, it was time for the skipper's nap, and of course the pumps needed looking at. Pretty soon it was time to settle the ship down for the night, have dinner, and early to bed to take star sights in the morning. Mostly by foul means, I managed to stave off having to be everyone's ideal of a sea captain.

One of the advantages of being alone on the ocean far from land is that we could have meals together, provided I could fix *Gray* to steer on her sails for a while. Sometimes I could, and sometimes I couldn't, but the odd thing was that dinner was frequently interrupted by what we called the "dinner roll." The wind would drop just as it does close to land when the sea breeze finishes with the sun going down and we would start to roll. I have never understood how this could be.

Most of the time however we had to have someone at the wheel. We had a choice. We could set the course and the raffee which enabled us to go more or less directly to our destination with the wind behind us. But, as explained earlier, with only those two sails, our speed was not great and, worse than that, we tended to roll uncomfortably. Or, we could set one or two sails forward of the course but, to avoid blanketing them, we had to be on a broad reach. We picked up speed and rolled less but it meant that it might take more time to get to our destination by following a zigzag course. However, we had a much better chance of leaving the wheel on a broad reach than we had going directly downwind, unless I tried setting sails aft of the square sails. This steadied us up a bit more, but made us heavy headed, the steering more difficult, and the head yet further off the direction we wanted to follow.

Life was slow. After one of my endless dissertations in the log about which combination of sails to use, I noted, "...we should gybe (i.e., change the side on which the wind blows) in about a week's time." I had noticed a bit of caulking hanging out of a seam on the weather side, and wondered what would happen when we jibed (gybed). I didn't say anything about noticing part of our ship disappearing because I didn't think I could do anything about it. When we were about 700 miles from our destination, Antigua, we started to have southwest winds—in the northeast trades—a bit depressing. So, the final approach to Antigua was made motor sailing—in a northwest wind.

The Caribbean

Our destination had been Antigua because it was one of the shortest trans–Atlantic voyages and because the island was English-speaking and connected therefore with English-speaking chartering companies like Camper and Nicholson who indeed provided us with a charter party fairly quickly. The charter did not last long and was reasonably satisfactory, but thereafter we had no work. And because St. John's was a commercial port and English Harbour, on the other side of the island, a busy chartering port, we decided to wait for a charter in a next-door bay.

A typical chartering scene.

For some reason this attracted the attention of the Antiguan authorities who thought that we were running drugs or doing something else reprehensible. I was invited for a drink (as the only guest) to the house of an American ex-patriate where I was interrogated by a British official. At a later stage, the Antiguan authorities became so hostile that I feared they might provoke some kind of physical incident. As a result, I only went ashore with a bodyguard ("Come on, the Heavies, we're going ashore," I would call). I never discovered what was back of this unpleasant campaign, since the charges were never very clearly laid out either by the English or by the Antiguans. But what is certain is that we had absolutely no connection with drug running or any other improper activity. I can only surmise that our Swiss passengers, whom we got rid of as quickly as possible, were already known to the authorities.

In the middle of March, towards the end of the season, we had begun to realize that our hopes for a successful chartering season were not going to be realized, so we left for the British Virgin Islands where our reception was totally different. The customs authorities were welcoming and helpful, clearly related to everyone in town, and so we got referred from one helpful person to another. This was fortunate because we had found that one of our sails had rotted in the rainy summer weather through lack of use. So we had to make another one.

We stayed there more than three months, long after the last charter boat had left, but we picked up an introduction to someone in New London, Connecticut, who might give us a free berth. Then we started the voyage to America, passing by Bermuda and through the Gulf Stream, which was running so hard that we actually lost ground on a couple of days. I decided that we should cross it as quickly as possible by altering course to be at right angles to it, and to determine when we were out of the Gulf Stream by taking the temperature of the seawater. This was fairly easy because one of the faucets in the galley was fed by seawater so that we could do the dishes without using up precious freshwater. Incidentally, there were two other faucets in the galley: one for hot fresh water supplied from the cooking stove, and another for wine pumped up from our 100-liter store in the hold.

I went to bed one night leaving instructions with the helmsman to change course for Block Island if there were a significant drop in the seawater temperature. The next morning I read in the log that it had been 78°F at midnight and had dropped to 72°F during the next two hours. The helmsman had duly made the course change by the time I got up. That year (1979) was very bad for fog, and we

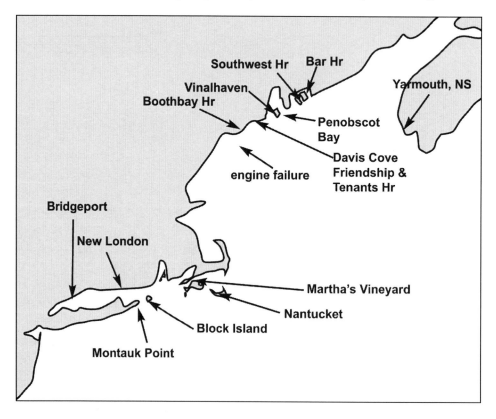

had to stay hove-to in thick fog for 24 hours off Montauk Point. I danced on the deck shouting "Lovely drippy fog" as droplets plopped from our rigging. The last time I had seen fog was in the English Channel — there was nothing like it in the Mediterranean.

Eventually, I got bored sitting outside Montauk and decided to feel my way in to anchor in some shallow ground I saw was behind it. Obviously the best time to do this would be at slack water. As we passed fairly close to the fog horn on Montauk, I realized I had made a dreadful mistake. There were all the sounds of a heavy tide running, little ripple sounds, and the fog horn taking an age to pass from abeam to our quarter. Later, once anchored for the night, I decided to investigate further. Deep sea navigational tables are kept in Greenwich Mean Time; tide tables in local time. In Europe these two times were much the same, but in America they were about four hours different in summer. Four hours is nearly half a tide, so making the mistake of reading the tide tables as though they were in GMT, we had in fact crept inside Montauk at full ebb.

The fog was still as thick in the morning, but it turned out a lookout standing 40 foot up at the yard arm could see over the fog banks. So, that's how we proceeded to New London with the lookout shouting to tell me what he could see. And finally, the pleasure of admiring a pitched roof for the first time since leaving the North Sea. New London Ledge light was built in 1909, incorporating colonial revival and French second empire designs. It was automated in 1987.

Our arrival in America on 17 July 1979 was five years to the day after I had become Not Resident and Not Ordinarily Resident in the UK (a decision which I was told about on 24 March 1977 — nearly two years after it had happened).

17

Life in America

Skidding to a stop

We had come to New London at the invitation of a man whose name we had been given in the Caribbean. But, when we arrived, it did not appear that he had any authority to give us a free berth: it was a political maneuver, reminiscent of Gaston Defferre in Marseille, to attract official attention to one of the most rundown areas of New London near the railroad station, itself a beauty which had been designed by H. H. Richardson, but now surrounded by the results of the flight from inner cities. A virtually unused jetty ran out from the other side of the tracks away from the railroad station. It was to be our base for the next eight years. We were visited by a customs official who cleared us inward. Seeing that we had young children on board, he warned us in a hushed whisper that we should keep our children away from the nearest street, Bank Street. Obviously, the children overheard. Promptly, Lucy, 19, came back from exploring the street with the news that she had found just what I needed: a three-foot double ended dildo.

The pier on which we lay was the dividing line between two totally different worlds. We were on the south side of the pier, rather more exposed to any bad weather coming up the river than the few boats that had found their homes on the north side. Of course, we began to make friends. There was the man who had just done time for stealing diesel, so we had a subject in common right there. Another boat was owned by one of the syndicate who ran the local prostitutes. Except for the psychiatrist who eventually bought *Gray*, they were ordinary people, easy to get on with.

But if I looked across the 20 feet of water to the ferry dock further south downstream, I could gaze at the white gloved butlers taking delivery of the roll-on rolloff lawns to be installed in the gardens of the fancy people who lived on Fishers Island.

I only went to Fishers Island on one occasion — as the helmsman of the ferry.

Dominick Jones and Cecilia Cussans in their early 50s on board Gray *in New London, Connecticut (photograph courtesy Emma Grainger).*

I wasn't allowed ashore. But I knew the ferry staff quite well and used to borrow their screw cutting lathe which happened to be identical with one that my grandfather had left me. It was still in England.

Obviously, all sorts of people were interested in gazing at us, particularly as we remained on the pier, doing repairs, until the summer was pretty much over, when we would usually start sailing again. It was the best time of the year, less humidity and heat, steady winds, fewer pleasure boats and generally better weather. One of our visitors turned up in what seemed to be a knitted wool body stocking. It may have been made in two pieces, but it gave the appearance of being a single piece, which he had knitted himself in rather gaudy colors. It started at the toes and finished at the neck. His head was covered in a woolen night cap with a long tassel. He said he had no money and talked himself into sailing with us. He turned out to be one of the brothers of Katharine Hepburn, who had starred in one of my mother's plays. She lived just along the coast from us at Fenwick, Old Saybrook. Inevitably an exchange of hospitalities took place. Ms. Hepburn agreed to come to lunch with us on condition that she had her back to the pier so that she would not be recognized. It turned out to be quite a large luncheon because we only realized at a late stage that she normally visited with her entourage, not alone. On arrival she switched where she was sitting in order to face the pier, so lunch ceased to be a private get together with my mother's friend and turned into a celebrity event.

Lunch over, I walked her to her rental car where she found she had lost the key. She fell into a tantrum and ordered me to break the window. Fortunately one of my criminal friends from the other side of the pier had tagged along. He opened the locked car within minutes without doing any damage.

However, before all that social life developed our immediate problem on arrival in America was whether or not to go back to the Caribbean for the winter chartering season. I thought the ship was not in very good shape. Since leaving Burriana in October 1978, apart from side trips, we had brought *Gray* nearly 6,000 miles in a year. But the main problem seemed to me that *Gray*, or we, were not particularly successful at chartering.

We had had one offbeat charter in France, one illegal charter in Spain, one (normal) charter in the Caribbean, another on arrival in America and that was it. This was a long way from defraying the costs of the ship let alone providing us with a living so I refused to return to the Caribbean without advance supporting revenue. It would have made more sense both to me and to Cecilia if one of us had had a proposal for what to do next rather than my negative attitude.

In addition, we were somewhat hemmed in to New London by the huge amount of fog that year. We had no radar and I wondered how we could possibly navigate in, for instance, Long Island sound, in safety. So, to a large extent, we spent the rest of the year sitting on the pier waiting for things to happen. They did. We found ourselves the latest social catch to be invited to the Stonington dinner party, the main activity in nearby Stonington, Connecticut.

The next year, 1980, we decided to haul the ship out of the water in Bridgeport, Connecticut.

Hogging

Between bringing *Gray* to England in 1970 and selling her in America in 1987, I hauled her out of the water for maintenance and repairs eight times. I found this an enormous ordeal. As time went on and I began to learn more and more about the structure of the ship and her corresponding weaknesses, I would prepare ahead for longer periods of time. But this did not avoid the frantic rush when fresh out of the water to inspect the ship's hull more or less personally so that I could realistically allocate the work. In the beginning, for example in Dieppe, I knew very little and was therefore fairly passive. But by the time I got to America where the hauling charges were much higher than in Europe, I began to have a better idea of what to do than the shipwrights employed by the yard.

Not only did I get to know where the weak spots where, but I developed some rudimentary tools for probing them. For example, I found that a sharpened hacksaw blade was very effective in seeing whether the caulking was still tightly wedged in the seams. Eventually I made several tools consisting of a piece of wood with the sharpened hacksaw blade forced into one end and a sharpened nail into the other so that my crew could help me probe for faults. Not to be overly dramatic, I knew that a weakness overlooked could send us to our deaths.

I learned the first big lesson as a result of the experience in Dieppe, the first efficiently managed repair out of the water in my time — sitting on the gridiron in Newhaven three years before does not really count because I was by myself, knew nothing, and probably did more harm than good. I learned that a wooden cargo ship with a 75 foot straight keel does not keep a straight keel for long. Depending on what cargo she carries, if any, the middle of the keel may tend to rise with reference to the two ends and to create what is called a hog. In our case, the hog was usually between seven and nine inches. It does not reflect any particular weakness of the ship, but it is inherent in the way wooden cargo ships used to be built. They never had any diagonal planking so they would flex in much the same way that a wooden gate — say a farm gate which is usually much longer than it is high — tends to sag if the diagonal bracing goes.

Instead of a diagonal, a wooden cargo ship does have a curve upwards towards the bow and stern. This curve is called the sheer and is often regarded as a matter of beauty, the structural aspects being overlooked.

> • To consider the effect of this, take sections starting at the bow and proceeding every foot or so towards the stern. The first section, right at the bow, will clearly have more weight than buoyancy because the fine forefoot has only a small volume in the water to support all sorts of heavy equipment like anchors and chains. As you take sections going further aft you will notice that the immersed area becomes larger—that is, the buoyancy increases. But what happens to the weight? If you are light ship (as we always were), the weight amidships may be quite small, so there is excess buoyancy which holds up the two heavy sagging ends of the ship.
>
> Therefore, if you load the center part of the boat with cargo, the bow and stern will gain net buoyancy while the middle loses it. Thus, there is a tendency for the sheer to increase. This has the effect of forcing the boards forming the hull together in the same way that a trellis you might buy from the hardware store closes up when you want to squish it together to take home.
>
> Moving from the bow (where weight exceeds buoyancy) to the middle (where buoyancy exceeds weight) you pass a section where buoyancy and weight are equal. In passing from the middle to the stern, the same thing happens in reverse. At these two points, where weight equals buoyancy, instead of bending, the planks tend to sheer thus giving rise to a greater degree of trouble than elsewhere in the topsides.

So much for the theory. In practice people like myself bought these ships with no intention of loading them with cargo. Consequently they tend to hog and much more importantly the seams tend to become loose.

As I spent a considerable amount of time caulking the topsides (they always seemed to need caulking), I began to wonder whether we could do something about it. One of the obvious things to do would be to ballast the ship, that is, weight down the middle so as to push up the ends. But that had two fairly serious drawbacks. To begin with, there was no space in the hold not already devoted to living. But the other more serious problem was that weight low down would increase stability. You might have thought this would be a good thing, but increasing stability gives rise to more rapid rolling, and the speed with which we rolled was already a problem.

So, in August 1982, I decided to put 20 tons of steel ballast on the deck (above the center of gravity). The ballast was held in place by large wooden boxes, and terminated where I thought the forward sheer point ought to be. My hope was that I would thus shift the trouble spots on the top sides forward from where they were. The deck ballast dramatically slowed the rolling, but I had no means of knowing with any certainty what it did to the topsides, since I continued to have to caulk them.

Having been told in Dieppe that I should have a docking plan, I began to develop one when we hauled near Marseille two years later in November 1976.

It was apparent that if I did not block for hog two unfortunate things would happen. The interior doors which had closed perfectly well when built afloat ceased to close when the keel lent itself to the blocks supporting *Gray* in the dry dock. Not only could the doors be torn off their hinges, but it was a very vivid demonstration of the appalling strain on the ship.

In a floating dock, or a graving dock, the ship is kept upright with horizontal shores. But we were mostly on railways where the shores, sometimes called poppets in America, are more or less vertical. Since you want the weight of the ship to be taken on the keel, you do not want the hull to settle down on these shores as the keel lends itself to a straight railway.

So, the right blocking was very important. What I needed was an underwater profile afloat. In theory this was very simple.

I stretched a string underwater from stem to stern, and then measured the offsets between the string and the underside of the keel. But when it came down to practicalities, the details were somewhat cumbersome. To begin with, the hull was always foul with mussels and other shellfish. What was not covered with shellfish was a garden of seaweed. So, a lot of preliminary clearing had to be done — upside down to clear the underside of the keel. I usually tried to do this measurement in the calm waters of a polluted dock. This meant diving in a full face mask, which is somewhat more cumbersome to work in than the usual arrangement of a mask over the eyes and nose and a separate air intake in the mouth.

I used fairly thin nylon cord which of course was somewhat translucent and difficult to see. It had to be stretched as tightly as possible so that it would be as straight as possible. I also had to set up some sort of 75 foot long tape measure from stem to stern.

Then there was the question of taking notes. I had a sort of slate and pencil designed for underwater use, but it did not work very well and I would sometimes come up from a long dive to find that one of the figures was obviously wrong. They had to be right — all the figures — because overblocking would be far more damaging to the ship than underblocking. So, back I would have to go wishing by this time that I was more like my colleagues in the business who did not care about blocking for hog, and would boast of their straight keels oblivious of the curmudgeon (me) muttering under his breath about opening their now jammed doors.

Anyway, rightly or wrongly, that's what I did, later adding an athwartships profile to give the yard an idea of how big the shores would have to be. This was less important because the shipwrights would feel their way in to the sides of the vessel just after the stern had touched the after block which they could see when the waterline at the stern started to lift out of the water. Like many vessels we drew more water aft than forward, but the incline of the railway was always steeper than the incline of our keel so that we would take the ground forward while still afloat aft.

A mast by the board

A couple of years after our more or less routine haul on the Bridgeport railway we lost a mast. Replacing it meant that we didn't go sailing at all in 1984.

But we made a lot of sails and we had a masting party. New to America, I did not realize that there might be a parallel with the time honored barnraising party in which everyone lends a hand together and everyone celebrates together afterwards. While Cecilia ran our masting party on deck I was in the bucket of a crane high above them not taking any part. One particularly outspoken guest complained of being cheated of the cooperative spirit she had expected.

When we lost the mast I began to be aware, though somewhat dimly, that the days of *Gray* were numbered. We were sailing off Martha's Vineyard in a rare favorable wind. It was a lovely day. I had to turn slightly to windward, smartened up the sails, returned to the wheelhouse to dance to the Tom Lehrer songs we still kept from the children's childhood. As I came to "dropping bombs through the clean desert air" the mizzen mast went by the board, taking with it a large section of deck. The mast stuck out 40 feet on our starboard side still attached by some top hamper. Years earlier, you will remember, I had made the mast cups too good a fit. Had there been any sea running, we would have sunk forthwith. It was a Sunday afternoon, there was a lot of tide running, and motor boats were beginning to gather round to see what was wrong. Worried that they might collide with us, I radioed the Coast Guard on the emergency channel to report what had happened hoping that the little boats would also listen and keep clear. They got the message, but the Coast Guard wanted me to fill up a fairly lengthy form — by radio — giving the color of my hull, the age of my grandmother and so forth. In those days, the Coast Guard was zealously helpful, perfectly happy to use powerful cutters to get careless yachtsmen out of danger, no matter the damage. The last thing I wanted, therefore, was Coast Guard help.

We got into the shelter of a cove, disentangled and salvaged everything, but I had a big repair job in front of me on return to New London.

The mast had broken around the hounds because it had become infected with beetle as a result of lying at anchor in the Caribbean facing the prevailing wind, the sun always on the same side of the mast where the beetle holes were.

Hurricane Gloria

In 1985 we sailed for Southwest Harbor in Maine with the intention of hauling there. It was a lovely summer, I spent six weeks messing around like a kid in seaweed, shells and rocks near to the marine railway, but there was no way in which they would accept a ship of my size. On the way back we had two friends aboard when the engine began to misfire. One of the friends seemed to take a delight in behaving as though he had never seen the sea or a rope, or felt the wind on his face. I liked him a lot for other reasons but was quite astonished when he peered into the engine room where I was fussing around with the engine and speculated that we had a cracked cylinder head, and that he could tell me how to mend it.

So I took off the head, and there was the crack. Following his advice I drilled a hole at each end to stop the crack spreading, gouged a channel in the crack, put stainless steel plugs into the holes, and braised everything together.

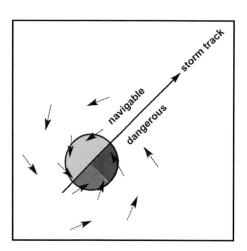

Then we listened to the weather forecast. Hurricane Gloria looked as though it were going to hit us, but not for a few days. Hurricanes are part of American summer vacations but Gloria was looking big, and turned out to be the biggest to hit America for 25 years. We were in Tenants Harbor, Maine, which is wide open to the east. If Gloria went off shore, we would be in quite

The above is a schematic of a hurricane which has re-curved, that is, its track has swung clockwise from NW to NE which brings it parallel to the northeastern seaboard. To starboard of its track, the winds are higher and veering; to port they back. Wherever you are, the wind will start from somewhere in the east. You watch it carefully to see if it starts veering or backing, so you can guess which side of your hurricane hole is going to be the safest.

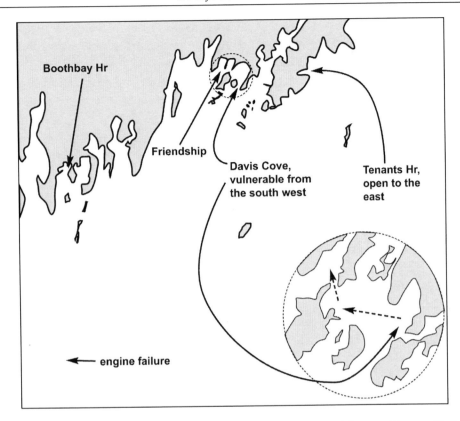

This part of the Maine coast has deep fissures open mostly to the south by west. Tenants Harbor is therefore an exception since it is open to the east. The charm of Davis Cove was the island blocking its entrance. Our first position was under the shelter of the land to the east. The weather forecast made it look as though Gloria might pass offshore, in which case we would have continued to be sheltered by the land; but the wind veered, threatening to put us on a lee shore unless we moved. So we followed the dotted arrow, out of immediate shelter, to be protected later from the worst by the island. Gloria passed about 70 miles inshore of us. The next day we followed the second dotted arrow into Friendship to pick up our friends, and set out again, whereupon the engine finally failed. We anchored in Boothbay Harbor under sail alone.

the wrong place. However round the corner was what looked like an almost perfect hurricane hole.

Our two friends wished us a happy hurricane, promising to return when it was over.

The hole was at the back of Friendship and was called Davis Cove, open only in a narrow sector to the southwest and therefore only dangerous if the storm passed inshore of us—when we arrived the storm was forecast to pass offshore.

The winds in a hurricane in the northern hemisphere revolve anticlockwise round the eye of the storm. The storm itself normally only travels at about 10 to 15 knots but it is enough to make the winds on the starboard side considerably more dangerous than those on the port side, the same sort of logic as a weather tide. Up in Maine the hurricane would be expected to follow the coast line. If the hurricane passed offshore we would expect to have southeasterly winds backing and increasing from which Davis Cove would be completely protected, unlike Tenants Harbor. However if the hurricane passed inshore, we would be in the dangerous semicircle with veering winds which at some point might come funneling in through the only vulnerable open passage to the sea.

Gloria was still at least a day away. We anchored right under the lee of some high ground to the east of the cove, which would make perfect protection in the initial stages of the storm whichever way it passed. The next day it was still uncertain which side of us the storm was to pass. Around lunch time I thought we should get the anchor up and gill around. Both of us knew that once it started blowing we would have no chance of raising anchor if we were in the wrong spot. So, we gilled around for five hours listening to the forecasts and making our own predictions on the basis of what the wind was doing.

Around dusk, the wind began to veer. We were in the dangerous semicircle. I did not want to hang around so I started off downwind to shelter on the other side of the hole. But when I tried to get up into the wind, it was too strong for me to complete the turn. Imagine the terror of increasing engine revolutions towards the lee shore knowing that if this were not enough to get us into the wind, we would be driven ashore. *Gray* slowly shuddered into the wind. Cecilia let go the anchor. We started aft, laying out the chain in front of us, trying to check our stern-boards with the engine and finally braking the chain hoping it would hold and not yank the anchor out of the mud. Good Maine mud held us for the last of the storm. Very soon the wind had veered enough for us to be under the lee of the land. Around midnight, there was a break in the clouds and the moon and Jupiter shone through.

We got drunk.

The next day we threaded our way through a narrow channel to Friendship where our friends joined us to continue our passage south to New London. About 25 miles out, the engine quit, and so we had no alternative but to sail into the somewhat narrow confines of Boothbay Harbor. We coasted into the harbor, took down the sails, foreshot a little, let go the anchor, the moon rose, and Cecilia already had a meal prepared.

Cecilia went back to London for three months. I had a new cylinder head flown out from Denmark, repaired the engine in a couple of weeks and then returned to New London with a couple I had picked up on the dockside.

The keel shoe

The next year 1986 we came back to Bridgeport to do two things.
The underside of the keel was becoming more and more uneven. I wanted to

Do you see the tiny figure working on the side of the ship? That's a human, probably Cecilia, who has to repair what you see and the other side as well.

protect it from further damage with a steel shoe. At the same time I wanted to rig a small extra rudder which I thought would enable us to fit self-steering.

A wooden cargo boat the size of *Gray* would not have a keel all in one piece. Similarly, the stem and the sternpost have to be joined to the keel. These are massive pieces of wood whose width athwartships was something over a foot. They are scarfed together which means that the join between the two pieces of wood is diagonal, probably with a dog leg in the middle of the joint. Bolts are then driven through the two pieces to hold them together. Since it is almost impossible to mate these two large surfaces together so that they are watertight, a fairly large hole — say 2 inches — is drilled across the joint into which a softwood cylinder is then driven. Think of an oversized wooden dowel. When the ship is immersed in water, this cylinder, called a stopwater, becomes saturated and swells to prevent leakage. We therefore had stopwaters in the keel and where the stem and where the sternpost were joined to the keel.

I had noticed that the forward scarf looked as though it might be working loose. I inserted extra bolts to keep it together but I was afraid that the forefoot could be strained each time we hauled the boat out of the water, since the forefoot is the first to be supported by the marine railway. I also wanted to fair the keel so that the blocks on the railway would not by some mischance come under a damaged part of the keel.

I bought three 25 foot lengths of steel channel, welded them together parallel to the keel and had blocks of oak mortised into the keel every three or four feet to be the new load bearing structures. The idea was to float *Gray* off the railway, move her sideways directly over the steel channel and then haul her back ashore so that I could bolt the steel in place.

Right from the start there were snags—in fact, even before the start.

It was a lovely sunny Sunday afternoon. We were due to haul out the following morning. We had made all our preparations and had nothing else to do but to wander about the seamier side of Bridgeport with our dog. Outside a grocery store, another rather bigger dog came charging out with obviously questionable intentions with regard to our own dog. Somehow I grabbed the attacker by the loose skin on either side of his neck while our own dog jumped smartly up into Cecilia's arms. Since the frenzy of what I held did not abate, I was somewhat relieved to see a burly man rushing to relieve me of my burden. Or, so I thought, until he knocked me down and began to kick me on the ground. He claimed later that he thought I was trying to strangle his watch dog—given the criminal look of the neighborhood, I could see his point. I had a brief stay in hospital that evening while a dislocated little finger was put back in place and the jagged cut on my forehead was stitched up.

The next morning, as *Gray* was being pulled out of the water, I remembered that we had forgotten to lay in supplies of anything to put on top of the caulking— what we call paying. Over the years my preferences changed, and the current flavor of the month was to use a mixture of tallow and cement. I had no tallow. This was the last straw, and I stumped around the dry dock complaining loudly. One of the last yacht owners to leave for the night came over to me and said he manufactured soap. Was it really beef tallow that I wanted? It was, I said. He promised to leave us some. I did not give his offer much thought, still hurting from the beating I had had the day before.

The next morning, un-knotting my stiff joints, I looked over the side of the ship and saw a large cardboard box sitting in the yard. When I opened it, there was clearly a great deal of fat inside. I found a small oil drum, built a fire, and started to cut up the fat to make it easier to render. Something dark was buried in the fat. I carefully pulled it apart and found a complete ox kidney. It turned out that there was plenty of fat for the ship, and we ate kidneys for the rest of the time we were on dry dock.

Towards the end, when the blocks of oak were in place, my 75 foot steel channel had been welded together and the sides of the keel shaped to try to make a good fit, I realized I was now way out ahead and completely responsible for avoiding serious uninsured damage either to my ship or to the yard, not to speak of achieving a successful outcome. In short, I was getting anxious.

I slimmed down the docking crew to those whom I knew had the necessary understanding of what was to happen. Neither the owner of the yard, nor I, felt comfortable with this changed situation. But we were both too deep in the project to turn back.

The wind was offshore, so the tide was short. We waited. With 20 minutes to go before high water, there was a little burst of tide. I was swimming around in the water waiting and I had told the crew never to move the cradle unless I was visible on the surface of the water. I think they were as nervous as me. We tried to maneuver the ship, but it was too slow a process for me to keep coming to the surface while they did so. The tide would turn. So I told the crew to count ten after I had gone under and start moving the cradle if I didn't come up, assuming that I was satisfied with the position. I remembered I had left a wrecking bar on the cradle and swam to fetch it. As the cradle started uphill, the ship slid back out of the channel, stretching the mooring warps as I had expected. It then catapulted back to nestle correctly in the channel. That is, almost correctly. I took the wrecking bar and pried the ship right in to its home, and then started laughing at the ludicrousness of shoe-horning a 200 ton lump of wood into a few inches of steel. In my mirth, I dislodged my mouthpiece, put my hand to my face to put it back in my mouth, and encountered, not my mouth, but the full face mask I had forgotten I was wearing. The air supply is inside this face mask, which began to fill with dirty water as I struggled to maneuver the air supply back into my mouth by wiggling the face mask. No one noticed me gasping on the surface because by this time they were more interested in hauling *Gray* up the railway.

When we were originally hauled out of the water a week or so earlier, I had noticed the ship was slightly listed to port. It was putting a strain on the hull because more weight was carried by the shores on the port side than I would have liked. The yard owner said they always shored vessels with a small list to port because the railway had a twist to starboard as it got to the top so that vessels would end up exactly vertical. I checked the railway and told her it was level all the way up. Anyway when *Gray* was out of the water there she was again with a port shore digging a hole in our hull. By the time someone had brought a ladder so that I could get off *Gray*, the docking crew was opening beer on the port side away from their offices. It was a Friday and the crew had been on edge for the success of the operation which they knew to be tricky. I went round to the starboard side, knocked out one of several shores, the ship jerked upright, and for a sickening moment I thought I was going to drop her on the offices. And on me.

The foreman of the docking crew had been egging me on to do this. He suddenly became quite sober. No one in the party on the other side had noticed a thing when we joined it.

The other project during this dry docking was to fit a small auxiliary rudder which we did next.

The auxiliary rudder

The idea had come to me during the Atlantic crossing. I noticed that even when we were sailing downwind at our most unstable, the helmsman had to move the wheel by only a few spokes either way to correct the course. This was an old-fashioned wheel which had 12 spokes. You stood behind it. It operated a gear which dragged a chain over several pulley wheels to pull a tiller from one side to the other. The design of the rudder mechanism had just about everything wrong with it. The pulley wheels were bolted to the deck and never looked secure. The chain itself vibrated with the engine revolutions. The rudder was truly massive and was held at its forward edge by a gigantic axle. There was therefore no attempt to balance the rudder so that part of it would be in front of the axle and help to turn it round. I never had a chance to weigh the rudder but it was made of half-inch steel and must have been comparable to the sort of plate put down while making repairs to the highway on land.

The pilothouse (Dominick steering). The small horizontal brass wheel in the left foreground is the throttle, the compass is behind it and higher up is an oil pressure gauge. Apart from the steering wheel one spoke of which is visible, the pilothouse was sparsely furnished. Eventually, I installed a small stainless steel wheel to port of the main steering wheel.

On arriving in America, I tried to figure out how much deflection of the rudder was required to keep the ship on course during the Atlantic crossing. It looked as though it was only about 3° on either side of neutral. I discovered that a flat plate turned at an angle to a fluid flow would stall around 15°. The resulting equation was obvious: a small rudder turned 15° and one-fifth of the size of the large rudder might have the same turning force as a large rudder turned 3°. In those days, we did not have the extensive literature available on the subject on the Internet, but I noticed that treating this as a linear relationship over a small angle might not be much different from treating it as a trigonometrical relationship.

I must have made drawings and calculations for this small rudder, but they have been lost in the last 25 years. So I cannot be sure what actually happened except that the small rudder, made of stainless steel, was so light that I could carry it by hand. I also made it a balanced rudder — in fact, too balanced — so that it took no effort to turn, rather like an overly responsive power steering in a car. I had a

The New London Day reported that Gray sank at a dockside in Groton (the other side of the river from our old New London berth) early on 21 May 1994. The owner was Michael Friedman of Mystic. This picture was taken by William Cussans two years later (photograph courtesy William Cussans).

section removed from the main rudder and inserted the small rudder, or trim tab, in its place.

When I had finally got it all fixed up with hydraulic rams connected to a small steering wheel behind which you could sit in comfort, the change in the steering performance was sensational. I found I had three alternatives. I could use the trim tab to steer the main rudder, only I had to remember that turning the trim tab's wheel to port would turn the main rudder and the ship to starboard. I could lash the main rudder so that it could not turn and use the trim tab to steer the ship. For maneuvers in port, I found that I could make a tighter turn with both rudders turned in the same direction.

Since there was virtually no resistance to turning the trim tab I coupled it up with a small yacht autopilot. While sailing, clearly an autopilot keeping to a magnetic compass direction would have to be watched, but *Gray* did not sail well enough or frequently enough for this to be an issue. However, I was alone on board for my last voyage under sail (in ideal conditions) from Newport to New London. I knew then that my invention was worthless, as I had no future.

I was still operating in the old world, now dead, but that year I also bought our second LORAN navigational system so that if the original LORAN bought three years previously broke down I could just change LORANs. I cannot say I shed many tears over the realization that my sextant is now a collectible. After all, I had navigated across the Atlantic on another piece of solid-state equipment, a hand held calculator. But if I went back to sea now I think I would still stick to the rule I developed then that all essential electronic equipment should have 100 percent spares. For instance, from arrival in America, I had two identical HP 45 reverse Polish notation calculators.

In the end, *Gray* did in fact sink, in a rain storm at her berth opposite New London in May 1994, six years after I sold her. Apparently, her topsides were dry and open and when she started to fill up from the rain and the slop, it just got exponentially worse. This was the nightmare that had dogged me ever since I saw the lighter sink in the London Docks for this reason almost exactly 20 years earlier.

Had I known that our permanently wet aft was only a leaky old stopwater which could never let in more than a limited amount of water, would I have struggled so hard to keep a quite different part of the ship, the topsides, tight? Would I have avoided the title "leak freak" if I had found the stopwater 13 years earlier in Dieppe? Or, would I have been less vigilant about the topsides, about what proved to be the final death of *Gray*?

Despite all that, I sailed her more than 12,000 miles deep sea.

Afterword

I went ashore for good in August 1987. My friend Fred Lawrence helped me pack my possessions into his pickup and we drove to Boston, leaving behind a world I had outgrown. I was unemployable (no skills worth any money, too old) so I arranged to retrain by taking an MBA (Master of Business Administration) at Babson College, just outside Boston. Tired of living on the wrong side of the tracks, I secured a studio in a brick house in the Back Bay — the Upper Back Bay as I called it to enhance my status. Almost all of what Fred and I hauled to Boston, tools mostly, went into a locker at U-Haul. I put a rubber mattress in one corner of my studio and for six months slept and wept on it struggling to keep up at Babson. The only other furniture in the room was a steel desk, left behind by the previous occupant. It was in the opposite corner of the room, 25 feet away from the mattress.

I spent seven years in that room.

Europeans are led to believe that Americans, among their many other faults, are completely uncritical. My experience is that they will spit you out just as quickly as any European, but the big difference is that they will let you get a foot in the door. Somehow, I managed to get some friends. I built a huge bed which doubled as a sofa to divide the 400 square feet room in half. It was made of bookshelves lined with mirrors. I will die in this bed, I thought, as I watched a million Dominicks reflected in the two mirrors, head and foot, which I had carefully designed to be not quite parallel to each other. On the window side I built an oval table to seat twelve. It matched the bay window. And, I cooked. It was the cheapest way of acquiring friends.

Then Molly Adams turned up. She took a shine to me, and eventually introduced me to the nurses as her son when she was clattering down the hill to death at a very old age. Molly was a theatre person. Pushed by her, I took over as president of the Poets' Theatre which I ran from 1997 to 2003. Molly had a drinks party every Sunday fortnight. I was invited every Sunday fortnight. Although I felt very close

241

to Molly, even flattered to be called her son, when alone with her we found it hard to talk. I was at her deathbed in June 1999.

I wasn't a very suitable president because I didn't know how to raise money — in America, the nonprofessional theatre expects to raise a third of its needs from sponsors and donors and the remainder from ticket sales. Too much revenue from ticket sales and it loses its artistic identity. I could not make the theatre pay.

I had taken to going to singles events. One was a dinner in a French restaurant in Boston where we spoke French throughout. Afterwards, she said she couldn't figure out why a man on a singles date should have eaten so much garlic for lunch. Twenty years later, we still live together, Rosalind Michahelles and I, but first we had to find a house to live in.

We looked at various two family houses, exempted from rent control, but they were too expensive unless we joined forces and lived in one side, renting out the other. Bigger houses were cheaper because they were rent controlled. I noticed, thanks to my training at Babson, that you could borrow money from the bank at 7 percent, use it to make a capital improvement in your tenant's apartment, for which you could ask an increased rent which the rules calculated as though you had lent out the money at 13 percent. The trick was to find a house with lots of possible capital improvements. We bought a four family house in Cambridge, Massachusetts, in 1993. Two years later, rent control was abolished.

When I met him for the first time at brunch one Sunday, I knew who he was. He said I should have a fundraiser for my theatre. He could get me Tommy Lee Jones and Stockard Channing. As neither Rosalind nor I had ever heard of Tommy Lee Jones, except that he was obviously an actor, I called William in London. He's a stock broker and reeled off the films he had starred in as though he were reeling off a list of stocks to buy. We should watch *The Fugitive*, he said.

I watched the video very carefully, what he looked like, his style of acting, how he handled the role, mannerisms and so forth. When the credits scrolled up at the end of the video, it turned out we had both been watching Harrison Ford. I re-ran the video.

That was the result of my first meeting with Daniel Selznick, the son of David O Selznick, the maker of *Gone with the Wind*, and of Irene Mayer, the daughter of Louis B. Mayer, founder of MGM. His mother, and mine, Enid Bagnold, had collaborated in writing *The Chalk Garden*, a successful play which Irene produced in London's West End and on Broadway some ten years after the end of World War II. That was way back in the fifties — 1955 was the year in which both Samuel Beckett and my mother premiered in London — the bookends of two different eras.

My meeting with Daniel took place 44 years later. Shortly afterwards, he called me from New York: "Bob Brustein says you can have the 540-seat American Repertory Theatre main stage. We need a script." Brustein ran the ART at that time.

We trundled through bad idea after bad idea trying to find something local and poetic. One of Daniel's suggestions, a play by Robert Lowell, a local poet, turned out to have an all male cast of 28. I remember because I had to order the script specially.

I will fight Daniel about who thought of it first, but we had both read reviews of a recently published collection of letters between Chekhov and his future wife, Olga Knipper. Ideal for two stars. We decided I should adapt them for the stage.

But — select a drama of less than 10,000 words from letters totaling fifteen times that amount ... and all the collateral research? I felt diminished by the task. I did nothing. Daniel called from New York to say he had secured Stockard. I said the script was coming along fine. A month or so later, he said he had Tommy Lee Jones. I should organize the Benefit before three months were up, as Tommy was off to Turkey for a film.

I thought I had better start getting a Benefit Committee together. I had no script.

I completed the play (*...love, Chekhov*) just before the avalanche of bookings started. As a matter of policy the ART did not offer outsiders box office services, the main stage, yes, but no more than that, except that one of the ART actors Alvin Epstein agreed to narrate. I thought I could merely take the calls for tickets at home, ask for the checks and make a note of it. General admission, that is, you find your own seat in the theatre, first come first served.

When Daniel realized what a success the fundraiser was going to be he came down on me heavily: I had to book reserved seats. With grudging bad grace, I agreed that Daniel was right and spent a hectic night programming a booking system into my computer from scratch. Second payoff from going to Babson. The demand was so great, I sold the house seats — that is, the emergency seats you keep in reserve just in case you've made a mistake. But, I wanted the money. Almost the last to turn up was Stockard's comp. My mind went blank. I had put his ticket in a safe place. But, where? There were no house seats. Rosalind gave him hers. We grossed $34,000 from the Benefit in February 1999, enough to put the Poets' Theatre back into business.

Along with swearing that I would never live on the wrong side of the tracks again, I also swore that I would never have anything to do with a large wooden structure. The house Rosalind and I bought was wood, and weighed about the same as *Gray*, as we discovered when Harvard weighed a similar house which it was moving from one place to another as part of a reconstruction program.

But, I got the biggest workshop I have ever had in my life along with the house. So, I shipped my grandfather's screw-cutting lathe out from England. In its primitive form, a lathe is essentially a toolmaker's tool. It consists of a horizontal axle equipped with a means for holding objects at one end (a chuck), sitting on a bed exactly parallel to the axle. The bed supports tools of various kinds which you use to cut whatever object you are spinning in the chuck. Mine was four feet long, and could turn anything up to a nine inch diameter. The bed stripped of its paraphernalia was a struggle for two men to lift.

Why my grandfather, Colonel Arthur Bagnold, Royal Engineers, had bought an American lathe I don't know. But it must have been in the 1930s, or possibly earlier. It was installed in his house just outside London before being transferred to my own London house on his death. When it returned to me in America, it was missing a small part. I found the manufacturer in South Bend, Indiana, got a parts list, found it had not changed in more than 60 years, and bought the missing part.

My uncle, Ralph Bagnold, my mother's brother, was also a Royal Engineer. A taciturn man, he spent his furloughs between the world wars exploring the then impassable Libyan sands, traversing 6,000 miles of dunes from Cairo to northern Chad in 1932. He revolutionized the scope of desert travel. In the North Africa campaign, he organized the Long Range Desert Group (eventually the Special Air Service) to strike at German forces from their undefended desert flank. After the war, he married my nursemaid, Plankie (Dorothy Alice Plank).

When a trainee officer in 1950, I stood in his workshop waiting for Plankie to cook dinner. Conversation was awkward. I fiddled with a small centrifuge filled with brown liquid and small white balls, some sunk, some floating. Nothing irritated my uncle more than fiddling, so I stopped and asked him what it was. Couldn't I see for myself, he asked. No, I ventured. Mud, was the brief answer followed by a pause, and then the obvious: particles suspended in a fluid of the same density unlike sand. He became an oil company adviser on dredging. In 1977, aged more than 80, he was invited by NASA to be keynote speaker at a meeting on the desert landscapes of Earth and Mars. His 1941 work "The Physics of Blown Sand" was used by NASA in studying sand dunes on Mars.

So, my background had this mixture of science and art, but I have never been political even though my 12th great-grandmother was the last of the Plantagenets, executed by Henry VIII in 1541 (see Antonia Fraser, *The Wives of Henry VIII*, for a grizzly description of the hacking to death of Margaret Pole, Countess of Salisbury, by an incompetent executioner in the Tower of London), and my great niece is married to Britain's prime minister, David Cameron.

Glossary

Animal terms   Many parts of an English sailing ship are called by the names of animals. The traveler, which allows the clew of the sail to change sides on tacking, is called a **horse**, a hook is **moused** (to prevent it from slipping out), you **cat** an anchor, the **hounds** are up the mast supporting the crow's nest, a **bullseye** serves the purpose of a block with a lot more friction (also known as a widowmaker), a **mule** is a floating fender, adjectival **monkeys** have all sorts of uses. I have always assumed this was because crew were press-ganged from farms to serve in the Royal Navy during the Napoleonic Wars.

Backing and filling, jilling or gilling around   To jill around is a somewhat vague expression which means trying to keep your ship still, e.g., waiting for the start of a race, or waiting for the lock gates to open. One way of doing this is to back and fill, that is, back some or all of your sails against the wind to take the way off, and then fill them to get a little steerage way.

Bar (pressure)   The pressure of one atmosphere (about 14½ lbs/sq in), i.e., the weight of the column of atmosphere above a square inch of my head.

Beam ends   To be on your beam ends is to lay over helplessly in the trough of, and parallel to, a wave train, with your lee deck well immersed in water, usually as a result of broaching.

Beat   Make good to windward. See **Lee shore**.

Bending on a sail   Sails are stretched between solid bits of the ship (e.g., mast or spars) by various bits of cordage. The act of attaching the sail in this way is called bending.

Bilge, chine, tumblehome, freeboard   If you take a section of a ship around the middle, you will see a deck connected to a hull in roughly the silhouette of a drinking glass looked at from the side.

- If the sides meet the bottom at a sharp angle, the angle is called the **chine** (*Gipping* had a chine); if the sides are gently rounded at this point, it is called the **turn of the bilge** (*Gray* was like this);
- not to be confused with the other meaning of **bilge** when it means the bottom of the ship where the bilge water collects. In Dieppe, among the wooden fishing boats, we learned that if the bilges stank, we were not leaking: "*Ça pu bien les sentines*"—*sentines* is the French word for the bilges and *puer bien* is to smell to high heaven.
- Sometimes, the top of the U-shape becomes narrower than the part nearer the waterline in which case the hull has **tumblehome** (wooden warships had tumblehome). Both our ships had the opposite, called **flare**.
- The distance from the waterline to the deck or to the top of the bulwarks is called the **freeboard**. On *Gray*, the lowest freeboard to the deck was probably about 3 feet, but to the top of the rail or bulwark, double that, a consideration if trying to haul a sodden person back into the ship.

Bitumen   A somewhat vague term for a sticky, black and very viscous substance which has been used for millennia to waterproof things like ships and mummies. It is also called asphalt (when used on roads), and tar (when slightly less viscous). It is a byproduct of decomposing organic materials, like oil sludges. See also **paying** and **oakum**.

Block   Think of it behaving as a pulley with some differences. Our blocks were made of wood, although the inner strong part was made of steel. The wood formed cheeks round the steel part to prevent a rope from jumping off the pulley and jamming around the axle or merely on the metal side if unprotected by the cheeks. Clothesline pulleys from the hardware store often have this problem.

Boatswain's chair   A horizontal plank of wood suspended at its four corners with a loop of rope. You attached the top of the loop (probably level with your nose) to a halyard or a **gantline** to hoist yourself up the mast. You made fast by drawing a large bight (loop) of the fall (slack bit of rope under you) over your head, down your back, under the feet and up again to draw itself tight around nose level. Making this chair knot ensured that you alone controlled your destiny. In my case (2 inch circumference natural fiber rope), it slithered quite easily so ascending and descending wasn't a problem. American foresters use much the same system to climb trees.

Botters and barges   The North Sea trade generated self propelled sailing barges for use on their sheltered waters and for the short trips from Holland to England. On the English side, they were called Thames barges and were flat bottomed, and on the other side they were called Dutch botters. A slightly stouter craft plied the Baltic, but the idea was the same: trade needed small ships to go from one little hole to another little hole to take on and discharge small quantities of cargo.

Brails   Small ropes from the leech (after side) of a sail to the mast to spill the wind out of it. On the Thames barge, there was the main brail which went to the throat, but there were other brails as well.

Broaching   See **Rogue waves**.

Bulwark, rail   The frames of the hull were prolonged upwards to form the bulwarks round the deck. They were capped with a stout rail. To fill in the area between deck, rail and bulwarks, there were somewhat flimsy planks. The point of the rail was to keep humans on board while letting water come and go as it liked.

Buoy hopping   Going from buoy to buoy (nowadays from way point to way point) without much regard for anything else.

Buoys   You either attach yourself to, or keep out of the way of, buoys that are floating objects anchored in one spot:
- A row of mooring buoys is usually called a **tier** when talking about commercial vessels, or a **trot** when talking about yachts, the main difference being that larger commercial vessels often use two buoys to moor fore and aft on a tier in a river to prevent them swinging around and obstructing traffic, while yachts, being smaller, can swing to a single buoy in a trot.
- Navigation buoys mark dangers or sides of channels, their colors and shapes being distinctive — and confusing. Entering a channel in America, the red buoy will be on your starboard hand, whereas in Britain it will be on your port hand. Just to make things really simple, the French employ the cardinal system of buoyage so that a buoy's relationship to a dangerous rock depends on its compass direction.

By the board   Overboard.

Capstan   See **Windlass, capstan.**

Careen   To lay a vessel over on its side after drying out on, say, mud or sand, in order to repair the hull below the waterline. The vessel may just obligingly fall over (as did *Gray*), but otherwise has to be hauled over by heaving down on its masts.

Cash   The pound sterling was divided into 20 shillings, and each shilling contained 12 pence. The guinea (£1 1s) had disappeared by my time except in a few exotic places like one's lawyer or one's tailor. A two shilling piece was called a florin; a 2s/6d piece was called a half crown (no crowns in my day) and six pence was sometimes called a tanner. Naturally, there was a shilling coin, but threepenny bits had pretty much disappeared, as had the halfpenny. Most currencies in Europe had the same £ s d system right back from Charlemagne's time (9th century); Britain was one of the last countries to decimalize — in 1971.

Cat   To cat the anchor is to secure the lower ends from waving around and causing damage in a seaway.

Caulking   See **Oakum.**

Celestial triangle   The spherical triangle formed by the geographical position of the heavenly body observed, one of the poles, and your own geographical position. You are normally solving the triangle for the latter, the two former being given.

Chine   See **Bilge....**

Claw off   See **Lee shore.**

Clinometer   A simple instrument to measure an angle from the vertical or the horizontal.

Coachroof   Yachts usually have a central structure poking through the deck which gives headroom to the cabins below. This structure is called a coachroof. In our case the structure itself had enough headroom to form the **deckhouse**.

Compass   A freely suspended magnetic needle which never points North, and has to be corrected for variation, deviation, heeling error, change of latitude, the ship's hard iron and its soft iron. In practice, opportunities to check the compass come along pretty readily (against a heavenly body, a bit of land, etc.), so it's an ongoing relationship, provided you know the underlying maths.

Dead reckoning (DR)   Cumulating your course and speed since the last known position and correcting it for tidal currents and drift or leeway. Even with modern charts, tidal predictions and good experience of the leeway your own ship makes, dead reckoning is very approximate, although often the only thing you have.

Deckhouse   A complete room built on the deck. In our case, it housed the galley and dining area. It had a door into the waist on deck, and an internal companionway leading down to the deck below.

Dolphin   Three or more piles driven into the sea or river bed and lashed together at the top so that a ship can lie against them. They are frequently used in ferry docks to guide the ferries into their final positions. I have not been able to figure out the etymological relationship with the playful and friendly animals of the same name.

Double   To double a cape is to sail round the cape. The word is commonplace in French where it merely means to pass, e.g., *doubler une voiture.*

Drift   Except in very calm conditions under power, ships proceed crabwise through the water, the angle with the ship's head being the leeway angle. The crabwise progress results from the force of the wind. See **Dead reckoning.**

Dry dock   A term used variously for both the **graving dock** and **floating dock**.

Fender   A squashy object placed between a quayside and your ship to prevent damage.

Fetch   Describes the open water to windward which allows the waves to build up.

Filling   See **Backing and filling....**

Fisherman   A quadrilateral sail set flying high up between two masts to catch light winds (also called a gollywobbler); the old fashioned anchor with arms near the top set at right angles to the flukes to ensure they bite into the mud.

Fist, make a good   To do something well (somewhat archaic English).

Fix   Working two or more sights so that their position lines cross. See also **Working a sight.**

Floating dock   A hollow U-shaped structure, open at both ends, which can be largely submerged to permit a ship to float inside, and then pumped dry to lift the ship out of the water.

Flying sail   For the most part, sails are hanked (attached with special clips) to the sturdier standing rigging, but a lighter sail might be set flying without being hanked. This was the case with our outer bowsprit jib which had no standing rigging and no net to enable one to climb out to the end.

Freeboard   See **Bilge....**

Freehold leasehold   Under English law, a freehold is the ownership for an indefinite period of *real immobile property*. If the property reverts to someone else at the end of a period, it is leasehold. All very like the American practice although the terms may be different.

Gantline   A rope rigged as a single whip (i.e., no fancy extra pulleys) to a block (pulley) at the top of the mast for the purpose of hoisting goods on or off board. Usually the easiest is to use an existing rope such as a halyard as a gantline (pronounced gantlin), the word thus defining its purpose rather than its construction.

Gilling   See **Backing and filling....**

Gold Albert   A watch chain with a T-piece in the center designed to be anchored through a button hole in a waistcoat (a vest in American), and terminating both ends in hooks, one for a gold fob watch, and the other (in my case) in a gold toothpick. Both have been stolen.

Graving dock   A small inlet with enough depth of water to take a ship and whose mouth can be closed off so that the ship can be grounded out for repairs inside. Usually, the gates keeping out the sea are designed to jam together when shut, but they are hard to service; the alternative (in Dieppe) was to have a floating gate (the *bateau porte*) which could be serviced in someone else's dry or floating dock.

Gridiron   A stationary platform that dries out around half tide, the exact point being a compromise: the lower, the deeper the draft of a vessel able to get on, the higher, the longer it remains dried out, but the vessels able to use it have to be smaller.

Hanked   See **Flying sail.**

Hard   A hard is a stabilized road surface sloping gently down over a length of a few minutes' walk from above the high water mark to below the low water mark. It permits loading and unloading at any state of the tide.

Haversine tables   Special navigational adaptations of the basic trigonometrical tables in which values vary between zero and unity, thus eliminating any negative values. But for this, you would expect to solve the celestial triangle (to find your position) from basic trigonometry, but some of the angles give rise to negative results, a source of error.

Hawsepipe   A steel tube to allow anchor chain to be fed from the deck to the outside of the bows of the vessel.

Heave to   If you heave one or two of the foresails aback so that they are fastened to the windward side of the ship, you take the way off, and with luck lie comfortably, slowly seeking the wind and falling off, going nowhere in particular. It can be nearly as restful as going aground for a meal. But it doesn't work well in heavy weather.

Hog   The amount of upward curve of the middle of a straight keel usually caused by removing cargo or ballast amidships. The reverse (which is rare) is called sag.

Horse   See **Animal terms.**

Hounds   On our ship the hounds were about two-thirds the way up the mast and were equipped with trestle trees supported by cheeks to take the load of the shrouds (wires) holding up the mast. Above the hounds, our masts were unsupported so you had to use the boatswain's chair to go further up.

Hull down   You can see the waterline of a ship near at hand, but as it gets farther away, the curve of the earth begins to hide the waterline. At this point, and yet farther away, it is said to be hull down.

Irons   See **Points of sailing.**

Jilling   See **backing and filling....**

Junked up   This could be a local term, but it means one vessel being moored onto another vessel which is moored to a quay or a buoy. The junking up situation arises where there are several ships of the same sort of size and not enough quay space for everyone to have a bit.

Knee   A solid block of wood which is normally used to reinforce the joint between two other wooden members joined at right angles to each other. The supports for a windlass would normally be cast iron, but in the case of *Gipping*, they were of wood and referred to as knees, by extension, because of their shape.

Knot   A speed of one nautical mile (6076 feet) per hour. The nautical mile is about 15 percent longer than a land mile. It is useful in celestial navigation since it relates to a minute of arc at the Earth's surface. Since knots are imprecisely known to landsmen and celestial navigation is obsolete, there is a tendency to talk of miles (meaning land miles) per hour for speed. I have generally referred to nautical miles since that is the bygone world I am writing about.

Leakage   It's a marvel that wooden boats ever floated since they are made of bits of wood awkwardly joined together and for the most part with no bracing, unlike a modern plastic hull that is seamless. As skipper, a large part of my time was concerned with watching the leakage of seawater into the ship, and ensuring the pumps could cope. *Gipping*'s basic leakage may have been around 35 U.S. gallons per hour; when rolling in a seaway, *Gray* might take on 50 U.S. gallons per hour, mostly from immersing the dried out topsides (our normal pumping capacity was about double that, so the margin was slim); under way ordinarily, I could put up with 2–3 gallons an hour; I went around with that nice full feeling after a good meal if the leak was below 4 pints/hr. Leaks often clogged up in harbor, giving a false sense of security.

Lee shore   The shore onto which the wind is blowing and trying to wreck you. If you beat your way off it, you are said to have clawed yourself off.

Lee tide   See **Tidal streams....**

Leeboards If you are trying to sail, the wind comes from one side and you rely on good lateral resistance to sail forwards rather like squeezing toothpaste out of a tube, otherwise you simply slide sideways. If the hull is deep enough and the keel straight enough (as in *Gray*), you don't need anything further. But if you are flat bottomed, like *Gipping*, which could sail over a heavy dew, you just skid sideways. So, there are two alternatives: you stick a flat plate down through the middle of the ship (called a centerboard) or you put boards on the sides of the ship (leeboards). In the latter case you need two boards because the one that does the work is on the lee side, while the board to windward is not braced against the hull and it would simply break off if you didn't wind it up out of the way.

Lighter A small barge used for ferrying small quantities of goods around in a dock. They were traditionally steered with long oars called "sweeps" using tidal currents as motive power, somewhat in the same way that modern American harbor dredgers maneuver with their spuds. (And see next entry.)

Lighters, light ship, light vessel Lots of room for confusion here.
  • A lighter (see above) is essentially an open box into which cargo is stowed. It has no motive power of its own, and is either pulled (tugged) or pushed. A tug can pull (tow) a lighter in heavier weather, but is less maneuverable; to push the lighter it attaches itself more rigidly, is more maneuverable, but cannot operate safely in waves.
  • Tugs usually look ship shape, but in sheltered waters they can sometimes consist simply of a small floating box with a powerful engine, when they can be called pushmen.
  • When any vessel is traveling around with no cargo, she sits very high out of the water, can't see a thing in front of her, rolls like a cork, and is called "light ship."
  • But this is not to be confused with an anchored vessel displaying a light for navigational purposes which can variously be called a light ship or a light vessel.

Limber holes Notches cut into the underside of frames for drainage. Ours were large enough for one's flat palm to be slid in, but they were constantly getting blocked with debris from old cargoes which had slipped through the lining of the hold.

Lister The makers of a workhorse hand-cranked diesel engine. They are usually used to power generators—as in our case. They have a reputation for reliability.

Listings The interior of the hull was lined with planks as stout as on the outside (to withstand being knocked around by cargo). The top three or four planks were even stouter. A gap of about three inches was left between these top stout planks and the rest of the lining. In trade, this gap was normally covered with short lengths of inferior wood which could be removed for inspection purposes. These lengths of wood were called the listings. To ensure some ventilation, we never replaced the listings, but when we rolled badly the filthy bilge water shot through this gap.

Lop The state of the sea when the waves are short and lumpy.

Lumpy See **Seaway**.

Marks   We were concerned mostly with the apparent relationship between two marks to see whether we were dragging anchor. These two marks might be, say, a church and a pier head — in any case, two clearly visible objects attached to the land. If their relative positions change, we were dragging anchor. Fast marks changed relative position rapidly, and were consequently widely separated one behind the other.

Maroons   These were special rockets used by the (British) Royal National Lifeboat Institution, a charity founded in 1824, to summon lifeboat crews in an emergency, and to tell the locals to lend a hand, keep out of the way, whatever might be required. They were discontinued in favor of pagers in 2006 after more than a century in use. The rockets were launched from the land to seaward, and designed to explode with a special deep crump at around a thousand feet. The fear now is that the spent casing could be blown back onshore in a gale.

Mediterranean winds   To my mind winds have such strong personalities that they must feel insulted to be named by a mere point of the compass. A few of the more interesting winds we encountered were the Mistral (turns the sea blue-black — from central France — plead it as a defense in crimes of passion), the Levanter (the one from Genoa — turns the sea grey-green), the foul-mouthed Sirocco blowing sand from Africa across the schizophrenic Straits of Alboran. The Eastern Mediterranean has its own winds such as the Meltemi which drove the hippies to shelter in our apartment in Crete. For an extensive description of Mediterranean meteorology see *Geography, Technology and War: Studies in the Maritime History of the Mediterranean, 649–1571*, by John H. Pryor, Cambridge University Press, pages 12 et seq.

Mole   Pier, jetty or breakwater but of more massive construction, built to protect a harbor mouth. But I think a lot depends on local usage. For instance, the Jetée du Large at Marseille was no mean little jetty — it was massive, equipped with vaults (in one of which my Lambretta scooter found its last resting place).

Monkey   See **Animal terms.**

Mooring warps   A warp is a heavy rope suitable for mooring, but the word can also be used as a verb when it means to maneuver a ship from one berth to another using only its warps.

Mule   See **Animal terms.**

Oakum   Fibrous material pounded into seams to make them watertight. The act of pounding is called caulking, and the person who does it is called a caulker. The soft mastic which is placed over the caulking is called paying. Note that in American usage the soft mastic paying is called caulking.

Offing   The farther from the shore the greater the offing; it is normally used in the context of getting an offing from a danger.

Oil sludges   See **Paying** and **Oakum.**

Pall of a windlass   The mechanical advantage of the windlasses we had was furnished by a set of reduction gears. There was a heavy piece of metal loosely hinged at one end to the main frame of the windlass, and allowed to flop over the straight gears at the other end, thus preventing them from freewheeling in reverse. On a smaller scale this would be called a ratchet. The heavy clanking of the pall over the gear wheels could easily be heard 90 feet away at the steering position, giving an idea how fast the anchor was coming up.

Parbuckle A mechanical advantage of 2 obtained by making ropes fast inboard, passing them down under a cylindrical object, and heaving on the free ends. It works quite well rolling a barrel onto a stationary cart — but getting the ropes round a drowning man beside a heaving ship might present problems reminiscent of keelhauling.

Paying See **Oakum.**

Pitchpoling See **Rogue waves.**

Points of sailing The tack defines the side of the ship from which the wind comes, e.g., on the port tack, the wind comes from the port side. Tacking a ship is to change the side from which the wind blows. This normally means going through having the wind dead ahead to having it on the other side, but sometimes it is hard to do this because the ship gets head to wind and then stops, when it is said to be in irons. If that happens, you may have to go the other way round, with your stern through the wind, and this is called wearing ship — or jibing if you do it accidentally.

Port and starboard Think of a ship as being a person with a left and a right, only it's called port and starboard. So, it is perfectly acceptable to use the words left and right on a ship provided you are referring to a human being, not the ship. "Fine on the port bow," e.g., would mean that if you were on deck and looking at the bow, something would be just to the left of the bow. Overall it is less confusing to use port and starboard so that someone looking aft at the time knows where to look without first finding out which way you're facing.

Proud Elevated above the surrounding surface — the way stitches will not bed into Dacron in the same way they will into cotton or linen; or, of a plank which is slightly higher than its neighbor, warning that it might have **started** (q.v.).

Quarterdeck Traditional sailing ships had superstructures on their decks. At the stern, the highest would be the poop (we did not have one). Next forward would be the quarterdeck, and right in the bows would be the forecastle (pronounced folksul). The area with no raised structures between the forecastle and the quarterdeck would be the waist. Since we had no forecastle, and our surrogate for it was much further aft, our waist was only a small piece of deck, about six feet fore and aft between the deckhouse and the quarterdeck step, a stepup of just more than a foot. We frequently shipped green seas in the waist, obliging me to jump between deckhouse and quarterdeck as I didn't like getting wet.

Racking, working Distorting a ship so that the planks slide relative to each other.

Riprap The mound of hardcore laid on the sea floor upon which a jetty or pier may be built. It often prevents a vessel from lying alongside.

Rode A collective noun for the chain, cable, or rope which connects the anchor to the ship. The ratio of the length of rode to the water depth is known as the scope.

Vessels sheltering among the sandbanks after leaving London River used ropes, so the scope was huge; less scope is needed for a heavy chain.

Rogue waves   A following sea can do nasty things, like sticking a racing propeller out of the water, **broaching** (lifting your stern to turn through a right angle — rather like skidding a car), or in an extreme case, **pitchpoling** (lifting the stern right over the bow). And a rogue wave (a large wave for a given sea state) can either lift your stern and make you broach, or simply walk on board and inundate your stern — we had both with quite small rogue waves.

Rove (unrove)   See **Shackle**....

Scarf joint   A method of joining two pieces of wood end to end by giving each a roughly 10 percent taper, and then bolting them together. It can be a weak joint in tension, so the tapers are usually notched in some way to present compression areas. Since a keel is usually much longer than the available timber, there will be scarfs in its length in addition to scarfs to take the stem and rudder post at its ends, all of which have to be waterproofed with **stopwaters**.

Scend, ressac (French), draw   My little world used these words to describe the horizontal movement of water associated with very little vertical movement. In a harbor, we might refer to the scend or ressac generated by some meteorological condition, but much the same movement would be called the draw if it were generated by a passing vessel. The dictionaries I can find do not corroborate this terminology.

Scrambling net   A rope net with large meshes hung over the side of a ship for men to climb up or down.

Sculling   Sitting to propel a small rowing boat by maneuvering an oar with one hand through a notch in the transom in a flat figure eight (∞); doing the same thing standing up with two hands, the second hand replacing the notch; sitting in a racing shell on a river with two oars going backwards (the only sport in which this is done).

Seaway, in a   In the open sea, in a rough sea, or as the British might say: "a bit lumpy out there."

Set of a tide   Tides set **towards** a point of the compass; winds blow **from** a point of the compass. Thus a northerly tide and a northerly wind are going in opposite directions.

Sewing, sew   Apart from the ordinary meaning of stitching some cloth together, the verb has a nautical meaning for drying out on the mud as the tide goes down. If the waterline has thus dropped a foot, the vessel is said to have sewed — rhymes with "food" — a foot. It is derived from the idea of "sewer" which drains water away from somewhere.

Sextant   One of the most accurate handheld mechanical instruments there is — it measures angles.

Shackle, turnbuckle, rigging screw, thimble, chain plates, standing and running rigging, shrouds   A wire is bent round a thimble and spliced in place. A shackle is the

U-shaped piece of metal equipped with a pin which is screwed across the top of the U so that the shackle can connect the wire eye and thimble with the rigging screw or turn-buckle. This latter consists of a metal tube internally screwed at both ends, but in opposite directions, so that it can shorten or lengthen itself. The chain plate is a massive strap of steel bolted to the side of the ship and through into the frame which acts as an anchorage for this entire assembly. In our case, wires from this assembly formed the shrouds which supported the mast, and would collectively be called the standing rigging. It stayed aloft year round, whereas the running rigging which manipulated the sails and other things could be **rove** and unrove for winter storage, repair etc.

Sheer   In naval architecture, sheer is defined as the height of the bow or the stern above the lowest mid-section on deck. In our parlance, it was slightly modified to mean the graceful curve (or absence thereof, as in *Gray*) from forward to aft. In wooden cargo vessels, the amount of sheer had structural significance when laden or light ship.

Shelving coast   A coast can be either shelving or **steep to**, by which we referred to the underwater parts and not to the coastline itself. Thus a shelving coast has very little slope and can contain underwater dangers, such as wrecks and sandbanks which might be hard to see. A steep to coast on the other hand is less likely to have underwater obstructions but will have more waves if it is a lee shore.

Smack   A fishing smack (French, *chalutier*) is a small fore and aft rigged sailing fishing boat with traditional lines and sails. In our time, most of them had been converted to power alone.

Soldier's wind   A nice easy beam wind which can get you there and get you back again — even a soldier could sail with it.

Springs   Used together with breast ropes to attach a ship to dockside. While the breast ropes are short and at right angles to the dock in order to keep the ship close to it, the springs are long and run parallel to the length of the vessel to minimize fore and aft movement.

Sprit   In our world of Thames barges the sprit (pronounced "spreet") was a heavy spar which crossed the quadrilateral mainsail diagonally. The lower forward end pivoted where the mast joined the deck; the other end supported the upper free corner of the sail and was controlled by vangs (pronounced "wangs"), or long pieces of rope made fast on either side of the deck. Since the sail remained aloft for the season, it was short-ened by gathering it up in brails, or rope strops, against the mast.

Spud   A vertical steel pole traversing the entire hull so that it can be driven into the mud to keep a dredger in place. I have seen an American dredger with three spuds maneuvering rapidly on tidal flow only in a harbor with no disturbance to traffic such as would have resulted from wires stretched across a harbor mouth.

Stand on   Continue without changing your course or speed.

Start, spring, sprung   This collection of verbs is used to describe a plank which has come loose from the frame; in our parlance the plank might have started (if it were only a little proud of its neighbor), or sprung (if it was really loose from the frame).

Steep to   See **Shelving coast.**

Steeve up   In our restricted meaning we related the phrase to a bowsprit that is pulled up from the horizontal. There is a more general meaning which has to do with cargo handling.

Stern-boards   A stern-board is a decoration on the transom of a ship, but we used it in a verbal sense — e.g., "making stern-boards," which meant traveling backwards in the water, usually as a result of weighing anchor or failing to tack through the wind.

Stockless anchor   The stock of an anchor is the upper cross bar which is at right angles to the flukes which (one hopes) get rolled over to catch in the mud or sand. However, the stocks are difficult to stow, so anchors came to be designed to dig into the mud without the help of stocks.

Stopwater   A soft wood dowel driven across the mating surfaces of an underwater scarf for the purpose of swelling in water to provide a watertight barrier.

Suet, *suif* (French), *sebo* (Spanish), tallow   A good lubricant, solid at normal temperatures, excellent for roasting potatoes, makes good candles. It is harvested by wrenching the hard pellicles of fat from the kidney of an ox.

Sweat, steal, tail, belay   To sweat is to take the slack out of a piece of rope, such as a halyard (lifts sail up the mast) or a sheet (stretches out the clew or after corner of a sail). To do this, there has to be some friction in the system under which the piece of rope passes round something solid (like a cleat) on its way from the load. If you pull on the taut section between the cleat and the load, then release it, you can steal a bit round the cleat and thus tighten the rope. The tail of the rope is the part on the other side of the cleat from the load. It terminates in the bitter end. To make the rope fast on the cleat is called belaying. In our case, each mast had a horizontal mahogany plank bolted to the bottom of the shrouds (wires holding up the mast) through which I had drilled maybe half a dozen vertical holes that fitted the belaying pins which served the same purpose as cleats. Our own pins came from an order from the South African police for truncheons which for some reason had been rejected. In modern ships sweating and stealing can be much more difficult because there is often so little friction in the system.

Tack, luff, throat, head, peak, leech, clew, foot   The lowest point of attachment of a quadrilateral sail to the mast is called the tack. Proceeding in order round the sail, the side against the mast is the luff, it terminates in the throat, the highest point of attachment to the mast; the next side is the head, terminating in the peak which is kept stretched out by a spar (gaff from the throat, or sprit from the tack); the trailing edge is the leech which terminates in the clew which is controlled by a sheet (a rope). The final side is the foot. If there is no spar (boom), it is called loosefooted as all but one of ours were on *Gray* to avoid accidents if the spars broke loose. From the sailing point of view a loosefooted sail is not an efficient arrangement.

Tidal streams, weather tide, lee tide A weather tide is a tide running into the wind. A lee tide is headed in the same direction as the wind. Winds are designated by the direction they come from; tides by the direction they are going to (or setting); thus, a southerly wind and a southerly tide are going in opposite directions and therefore make a weather tide.

Tide and wind directions See **Tidal streams....**

Tier See **Buoys.**

Tingle Patches of lead or copper to cover damage to the planking. This sort of repair is really only suitable for a work around below the waterline since above it the tingle collects moisture, and thus rot, behind it.

Track The track is what you plot on your chart, that is, a succession of actual geographic positions made good — the phrase "made good" being used to distinguish your progress from what it looks like through the water — which, of course, may be moving. See also **Dead reckoning.**

Transom The planking of a wooden ship runs fore and aft. At the bow, it usually terminates by being notched into the stem, the extension of the keel, which curves upward to join the deck and form a fine point of entry into the water. However, at the stern, there is a choice: some vessels terminate in a sternpost similar to the stem, but others terminate in a flat section of planking (called a transom) at right angles to the line of the keel.

Triatic stay A piece of wire rigging between the tops of the masts. In effect, some of the weight of the mizzen sail aft would be borne by the topmasts and transmitted forward to the forestay and thus to the stemhead.

Trot See **Buoys.**

Tumblehome See **Bilge....**

Waist See **Quarterdeck.**

Warp, warping For the seaman, the noun is generally applied to the stouter ropes used for mooring; it can also be employed as a verb to mean moving a ship around in harbor by means of its warps.

Weather tide See **Tidal streams....**

Williamson Turn A maneuver used by a power vessel, particularly in heavy weather, to swing the ship through 180 degrees, bringing her back onto the same path but in the opposite direction. Named for John Williamson, USNR, who used it in World War II.

Windage Resistance to the force of the wind.

Windlass, capstan A windlass and a capstan do much the same thing: they are both fitted with a mechanical advantage to lift heavy weights, like anchors. The difference is that a windlass has a horizontal axis, whereas the capstan has a vertical axis, thus allowing the rope or chain to be lifted off. A winch is a smaller version of a capstan and can be mounted horizontally or vertically.

Working a sight   Combining the altitude of a heavenly body above the horizon with the time of the observation to calculate how much error there is in your position resulting from dead reckoning (DR). Note that working a single sight gives you only a position line (at right angles to the azimuth, or direction, of the heavenly body) which you then plot at the distance calculated from your DR position. See **Fix**.

Index

And see the Glossary